A Surgeon's World

A Surgeon's World

William A. Nolen, M.D.

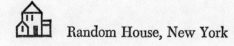 Random House, New York

To Harold Wilmot, M.D.
a fine doctor,
a good man

Preface

The doctors in this book are composites, with characteristics adapted from all the doctors I've met over the last twenty years. None of them is modeled after any one living person. Excepting, of course, the author.

Just as I've disguised the doctors in this book, so have I disguised the patients, the cases and the locales. By fragmenting and recombining my medical experiences in Minnesota, New York, Massachusetts and South Dakota with those of doctors in these and other states, I've tried to produce an accurate, representative picture of what the medical scene in the United States is like in the 1970's. It's a picture that I think is more important than the portrayal of the unique medical experience of any one doctor. And by writing about medical-surgical practices in this fashion I have tried to avoid casting aspersions on any specific person, hospital, clinic or medical school. The purpose of the book is not to single out individuals for criticism or praise, but to show how, with all its flaws and virtues, our medical system works.

W.A.N.

Contents

III

I

1

How I Came to Be a Doctor

I'm a surgeon. Almost every day, for the last seventeen years, I've picked up a scalpel, cut into two or three patients, and rearranged their insides or their outsides. I earn my living trying to save lives or improve health. Most of the time I'm successful. Sometimes I'm not.

What attracted me to this life? I'll try to make it brief. I've rarely been fascinated by authors who begin a book by telling the reader where their great-grandparents were born.

I do, however, have to begin with my parents because they, more than anyone or anything else, pushed me toward the profession of medicine. My father, particularly. He was a lawyer and when I was a kid he often said to me, "Billy, if you're smart when you grow up you'll be a doctor. Those bastards have it made."

He knew what he was talking about. In his law practice, in Holyoke, Massachusetts, he had many clients who were doctors, and he spent much of his time trying to keep them from going to jail for income-tax evasion—a disease to which members of the medical profession seem unusually prone. Since he had access to their financial records my father knew that all doctors made a damn good living and that some of them made, if you'll excuse the phrase, a real killing. He had to knock himself out for weeks, practicing law, to earn what a surgeon could pick up in three or four hours on a busy morning in the operating room. To him it seemed as if doctors had a good thing going for them.

He was also aware of the fact that you didn't have to be a genius to acquire an M.D. People often said then—back in the early forties when I was in high school—"If you want to be a doctor you've got to study very hard and be smart besides." People—particularly parents who want their children to be doctors—are saying the same thing today.

It's an exaggeration. I agree that an individual with a borderline I.Q. might have difficulty getting through medical school, but you certainly don't have to be a genius to become an M.D. I was a B student all through South Hadley High School, Holy Cross College, and Tufts medical school. I never made the ProMerit Society, Phi Beta Kappa or Alpha Sigma Nu. Still, I think I'm quite a good doctor, and to be perfectly honest, I think I'm an excellent surgeon. Modesty has never been one of my most notable characteristics.

But honestly, it wasn't the money that drew me to the medical profession. My father earned a good living as a lawyer and judge, and we kids—there were five of us—always had plenty to eat, enough clothes to wear and adequate spending money. Kids who have enough but not too much money when they're growing up rarely think about money. Money doesn't motivate them when it comes to choosing their life's work. It's the poor kid who doesn't always have enough to eat—or the wealthy child whose parents are obsessed with the notion of wealth—who makes the acquisition of money his goal in life.

It was something other than my father's comments on doctors' incomes that directed me toward medicine. It was his general attitude toward doctors. Cynical as he was about them, he still held them in a certain awe. They knew things that he didn't know—things that had to do with life and death—and he had a grudging respect for men who dealt with these problems routinely. My father never talked explicitly about these matters but I could tell, watching the way he behaved when any of us was ill, how he felt.

When I was a senior in high school, on the day of our first varsity basketball game, I woke up with a stiff neck and had difficulty swallowing. My mother made me stay home from school, but I insisted on getting dressed, and at noon I walked down to Mary's Kitchen, the soda shop where my gang went to eat their lunch. I wanted the other fellows on the team to know I wasn't really sick, since I was scheduled to start as center that night against Rosary High School in Holyoke.

But by three o'clock my neck was stiffer and I was running a temperature. My mother called Dr. Doonan, our family doctor, and he took me to the hospital, where, after several unsuccessful attempts, he managed to do a spinal tap. The fluid showed that I had polio.

I was fifteen at the time, and like most kids, I wasn't frightened by the news. I hated to miss the game, but I figured I'd be better in a week or so and back in the line-up.

My father, on the other hand, was terrified—as I would be now if one of my kids had polio. He spent most of the next three days sitting by my bedside, stuffing sulfa mixed with applesauce into me. Sulfa was new then, and since Dr. Doonan didn't know anything else that worked on polio—no one did—he decided to try that. He came to see me every morning and evening—I was treated at home—and we waited anxiously for each visit. All Dr. Doonan had to do was walk into the room and my mother and father and I would breathe sighs of relief: as long as the doctor was there nothing bad could happen. Doctors made people well; even my father believed in their power—I was impressed. The sulfa made me sicker than hell, but despite it I got better.

My mother was very explicit with her suggestions that I ought to consider medicine. "These doctors," she'd say, "they don't work nearly as hard as your father, and look at the money they make. If you graduate from medical school I'm going to give you a pile of shoe boxes to keep your money in. That's all you'll need." My mother is a very practical woman.

She wasn't easily impressed by the mystique of the medical profession. With Mary, Betty, Jimmy, Judy and me to raise, she was constantly dealing with one minor illness or another. My mother had—and has—a lot of common sense, and she was well aware that aspirin, rest and time would cure most of what

ailed us. She called Dr. Doonan when major problems occurred, but she didn't waste money calling him in to treat every
rash, sore throat or sprain.

Even now, she herself stays away from doctors as much as
she can. "You doctors have got a racket," she tells me whenever we see each other. "If I get sick call the priest first, then
the undertaker, then—if I'm still breathing—the doctor." At
seventy-two, she still works regularly in the library in Ware,
Massachusetts, bowls in the winter, plays golf all summer and
spends a lot of time worrying about the Red Sox. She must be
doing something right.

My parents ranked first in influencing my choice of medicine as a profession, but our family doctor ran a close second.
He was a G.P. who delivered us, took care of my grandfather's
heart trouble, treated our colds and flu. He was one of the last
of the Leonardo da Vinci school of medicine; he took all of
medicine as his domain and he mastered most of it pretty
well.

Now that I'm a surgeon I look back in awe on some of the
things he did. I can still remember the day he took out my tonsils. My Aunt Molly, my Uncle Bill's wife, was a nurse. She
retired when she married and hadn't worked as a nurse for
years, but that didn't bother Dr. Doonan. One morning he had
her come over and drip ether onto a mask while he took the
tonsils out of, successively, my sisters Mary and Betty and
me. In the parlor of our home! I'm sure the light must have
been bad—he probably just used a table lamp—because along
with my tonsils he whacked off my uvula, that tail-like piece of
fleshy tissue that hangs down from the back of the palate. No
great harm was done, we all survived the procedure, but I'd
never have the nerve to do that kind of surgery today.

Dr. Doonan was around a lot. Even with my mother's policy
of treating minor things herself, with five of us children, plus
my grandfather, who lived with us, Dr. Doonan had to make a
lot of house calls. Those were the 1940's, remember, when
most doctors spent a good part of the day making house calls.
When he'd come he never acted rushed; he'd joke a little while
he examined us, and after he'd written out a prescription he'd

have a cup of coffee with my mother before he left. Even at that age, about ten or eleven, I was conscious of the relief I'd feel after his visit, even before I'd taken the medicine he had prescribed. The idea of being able to make sick people well just by visiting them appealed to me.

The third factor that influenced me in the direction of medicine was my reading. In the 1940's Paul de Kruif was writing "science" articles for the *Reader's Digest*, and I read the *Digest* religiously during study hall in high school. My kids read it now. He portrayed doctors, particularly doctors engaged in research, as men who lead exciting, rewarding, glamorous lives.

I also read A. J. Cronin's *The Citadel* and *Shannon's Way*, Sinclair Lewis's *Arrowsmith*, Sidney Kingsley's *Men in White*. Unreal, perhaps, but the sort of books that are likely to make a boy of fifteen think about becoming a doctor. That was the effect they had on me.

After graduating from high school and spending a year at Deerfield Academy to, as my father put it, "learn to study," I entered Holy Cross College in Worcester, Massachusetts. My father thought I ought to have a Catholic education.

I didn't enjoy my four years at Holy Cross. Like all the other premedical students, I worried constantly about grades. We knew that there were usually forty or fifty thousand applicants for eight thousand places, and that we'd have to maintain at least a B average if we were going to be accepted by medical school. The fear of being rejected by medical school after college graduation haunted me during all four years— just as it haunts all premeds in the 1970's.

Even if I hadn't been worried about getting into medical school, I wouldn't have enjoyed Holy Cross.

One of the reasons, I think, was the overemphasis on sports —varsity football, basketball and baseball, that is (there was virtually no intramural program). I had always played on teams and, damn it, I wanted to play on the Holy Cross football team.

So I went out for it, worked very hard, and never made the traveling squad. I always felt I was good enough to be on the

team—even now I insist that was true—but because I wasn't on
scholarship the coaches gave me no chance. (If you think this
sounds like the bitter reminiscence of a frustrated jock, you're
absolutely correct.)

Holy Cross was segregated along athlete/non-athlete lines.
My freshman year, 1945, was one in which the Holy Cross football team got into the Orange Bowl and achieved big-power
status in basketball; Joe Mullaney, Bob Cousy and George Kaf-
tan, all of whom later joined the Boston Celtics, played at Holy
Cross while I was there. The jocks were the big men on campus,
worshiped by faculty as well as students, and I suppose I was
jealous.

There was a sameness about all the students. Ninety-nine-
plus percent of us were, of course, Catholics. We had seats assigned to us in church and were expected to attend daily
morning mass. Attendance was taken, and if you missed twice
in a week you couldn't go out on Saturday night, when fresh-
men were ordinarily allowed to visit downtown Worcester as
long as they were back at eleven. From the fact that we were
all Catholic it follows, roughly, that we were all of generally
similar racial, social and even economic backgrounds; the
wealthy Irish went to Yale. The place seemed, to me, flat.

But to give Holy Cross its due, I must confess that I am grateful to the college for one thing. I was force-fed subjects I otherwise wouldn't have studied and which, in retrospect, I'm glad
I did. If you took premed at Holy Cross you could choose between a B.S. or an A.B. degree, and that was it. I chose the
A.B. route and had to take two years of Latin, two years of
French, Shakespeare and poetry. As did everyone else at Holy
Cross, I also had to study philosophy for two years and religion
for four years. I'm eternally grateful that these subjects were
forced upon me; if I'd been left to my own devices I probably
would have studied only those things which, to my immature
mind, seemed practical for a would-be doctor—things like
genetics and comparative anatomy. I'd have graduated from
Holy Cross without anything even remotely resembling a "liberal" education. I'm indebted to the Jesuits for forcing such
an education upon me.

The Holy Cross experience wasn't a completely miserable one. I played in the dance band, threw the discus for the track team, waited on table for four years—all of which I enjoyed. There were times when I was tempted to quit premed—it was difficult to see the correlation between learning Latin and practicing medicine—and I envied the fellows in business and education who seemed to spend most of the daylight hours in the cafeteria. But the only other career that even remotely interested me was that of a musician, and I knew that, unfortunately, no matter how hard I might work at it I'd never be anything but second-rate. Like 99 percent of the population I've always envied those people who could pick up a horn or sit down at a piano and knock off any song that came into their heads. It's a gift you're born with and I'm one of the many who don't have it. So I stuck with Cicero and organic chemistry, watched Dr. Kildare—in the movies, not on television—and lived for the white coat and stethoscope of the future.

2

Medical School

In contrast to my four relatively miserable years at Holy Cross, I enjoyed, for the most part, the four years at Tufts medical school.

Once a man is accepted by a medical school, the heat is off. The big "cut" in the ranks of the would-be doctors comes at the college level; since only the top ten thousand applicants are accepted, a lot of men who might have made fine doctors are left out. It's too bad, but that's the way it was in 1949, when I started medical school, and that's the way it essentially is, in 1972. (An entire book could be written about the causes, political and social, of this situation, but I haven't got time to write it now.)

For almost the first time in my academic career I was studying material that I knew was going to be of value to me the rest of my life. Anatomy was a course that required mostly brute memory. It wasn't easy to remember where the deltoid muscle began, where it ended, what muscles were next to it, and what blood vessels and nerves nourished it and made it work, but I could see the practicality of having all that information tucked away in my mind. So I studied, not only because I wanted a decent grade but because I wanted to be a knowledgeable doctor.

Like most premed students I had resented the time I spent in college on subjects which seemed unrelated to my future as

a doctor. I know now that my attitude was based on imma-
turity. College is a place where a student ought to learn not
so much how to make a living, but how to live. In the 1970's
we're trying to reduce the time a man has to spend becoming
a doctor. Some medical schools will accept students after three
years of college—others are combining the fourth year of medical school with the internship. It's possible in some programs
to acquire an M.D. degree six years after high school graduation, rather than the usual eight.

The purpose in shortening medical education is to produce
more doctors. Personally, I don't think it will work. With every
year that passes there is more and more knowledge that a doctor should have. How in the world can we expect students to
learn more in less time?

What will happen, I'm afraid, is that we'll start producing
pure technicians. If anything is to be eliminated from the
would-be doctor's education, it won't be biochemistry, anatomy or pharmacology; it will be the course in Shakespeare, the
year of philosophy, the semesters of French. One of the major
problems in medicine now is that doctors tend to have depth
but not breadth to their knowledge. There is a saying, well
known to all medical students, that the G.P. is a doctor who
learns less and less about more and more, until he eventually
knows nothing about everything; the specialist is the man who
learns more and more about less and less, until he eventually
knows everything about nothing. This is the age of the specialist, and because their interests are so narrow, the specialists
tend to see patients as faceless carriers of diseases, technical
problems to be solved, rather than as human beings. What we
need in medicine are doctors who are more the artist and
less the scientist. I don't think that shortening medical education will produce them.

The first two years of medical school were the preclinical
years, the years of anatomy, histology, biochemistry, pharmacology, bacteriology—all the subjects that could be taught in
lecture halls and laboratories. There were occasional forays
into the hospital—rare contacts with practicing physicians;
infrequent opportunities to examine live patients—these were

the high spots, the "ice cream," of the first two years. Most of the time it was a matter of reading, listening to lectures, dissecting and experimenting in the laboratories. It was hard work, but not nearly so difficult as all of us had been led to believe it would be. Anyone who had been able to earn B's in premedical courses could, without working significantly harder, accomplish the same result in medical school.

The last two years were, for most of us, a lot of fun. We had regularly scheduled lectures in internal medicine, surgery, pediatrics, obstetrics—in all the major divisions of medicine—but much of the third and all of the fourth year were spent in hospitals and clinics working with patients. For the first time we had an opportunity to wear a white coat, hang a stethoscope around the neck, and act like "real" doctors. Since most of us had been working for some twenty-three years to achieve this goal, we basked in our glory. It was all a ball.

We were eager. Everything was new to us and exciting. We could spend hours doing physical examinations, listening to garrulous patients, waiting for a woman to deliver a baby, and we were never bored. The first time around, it's stimulating. (I'm not implying that the excitement of working with patients ever disappears completely; it doesn't. But as the years go by we can't help getting a bit used to the routine.)

During all four years our class—and I'd guess we were a reasonably typical group—had a lot of fun. There were only about one hundred of us so we got to know each other well. There were groups within the group, naturally, but because of the process by which medical students are selected we all shared many common interests. We each made particular friends, but we all got along.

We had a lot of parties. After exams we'd meet at someone's apartment—there were no dormitories for medical students—and we'd drink, dance, sing, and generally raise hell. About one-third of the class were married and they'd bring their wives. The rest of us would find dates—not a difficult job for a medical student in Boston. Naturally, a lot of the dates were nurses. Just as naturally, a number of my classmates later married the nurses they met during these years.

Were the parties wild? I suppose that depends on how you define the word. There was no marijuana and nothing I'd call an orgy. We were relatively uninhibited, sexually mature, and since the parties often developed spontaneously the evening after a big examination, we were ready to cut loose. We laughed a lot, loved a lot, and drank a lot. I have fond memories of many of those nights.

Most medical students decide in their freshman year what specialty, if any, they're going to pursue. It's silly, because as a freshman you don't really know what all the specialties are about. Fortunately, no matter what you've decided, you have to spend some time working in each of the specialties, and often an exciting teacher will convert a determined obstetrician to otolaryngology, or a would-be pathologist to dermatology.

At the same time that I decided to become a doctor, at fifteen, I had more or less also decided to become a surgeon. It seemed logical to me that if a man was going to be a doctor he might as well be a complete one. I wanted to be able to cure patients with a knife as well as with pills.

This was, admittedly, an oversimplified view of the profession but it held up pretty well. When in medical school I learned more about the subdivisions of medicine—found out what pathology, ophthalmology, orthopedics and internal medicine were like—I still felt that the general surgeon was the king of the mountain. He treated the whole patient with all the tools that were available; other doctors needed his help but he could usually get along without theirs.

There were times, however, when I wondered if I had what it took to make a surgeon. As early as my freshman year, in anatomy class, I discovered that I wasn't as handy with a scalpel as were some of my classmates. Four of us worked together on one cadaver, and when it was my turn to dissect I was lucky if I could find and peel out the muscles, nerves and blood vessels for which we were looking. Often I'd cut the structure in half before I saw it. Specifically I remember making a shambles of our cadaver's left wrist while one of my coworkers neatly laid out the tendons, nerves and vessels of the right.

In my senior year, after delivering a baby I had a horrible time sewing up the cut or tear that resulted from the delivery. I just couldn't seem to get the proper grip on the holder that held the needle and I dropped a lot of instruments on the floor.

In the operating room, during two months of surgery in my senior year, the intern would occasionally let me help him sew up the skin. If the incision required twenty stitches, he'd have eighteen in before I'd managed to tie two knots. I was really very clumsy; I didn't know, at that time, that clumsiness was something I could and would overcome with experience.

Still, I knew that surgery was what I wanted to do. I liked the hectic atmosphere of the surgical wards and the operating room—I admired the decisiveness of the surgeon who would see a kid with a belly ache, say, "Let's open him up," and get the job done. His style of practice contrasted markedly with that of the internist who would sit around talking for half an hour trying to decide what pill to give a patient. I felt that my temperament was better suited to surgery than to anything else and I knew I'd be frustrated if I couldn't operate. So, even though I knew I might have trouble acquiring the dexterity a surgeon ought to have, I decided to give it a try. In my senior year, when it was time to apply for an internship, I went for a straight surgical year. I was accepted at Bellevue, on the Cornell Surgical Division, and began my surgical training on July 1, 1953.

3

Bellevue

When I graduated from medical school I knew a great deal about the theory of surgery but next to nothing about the practice. If a doctor asked me how I'd treat a bleeding ulcer I could talk for fifteen minutes on the subject, outlining in detail all the methods of both medical and surgical treatment; but if I'd been faced with a patient who was actually bleeding from an ulcer, I wouldn't have had the ability to start a transfusion. I had come to Bellevue to spend five years learning how to practice the science I'd learned in medical school.

I've written about this experience in *The Making of a Surgeon.* It involved five years in which I worked very hard and, step by step, learned my trade. When I walked into Bellevue in 1953 I was lucky if I could put a simple stitch in the skin without stabbing myself or my assistant in the finger; when I finished my training, in 1960, I could perform with speed and dexterity (self-confidence is a trait necessary for surgeons) just about any operation on any part of the body. And I could also guide the patient through the pre- and post-operative periods, and get him safely out of the hospital. I learned at Bellevue how to put to practical use the fund of knowledge I'd acquired in the course of twenty years of formal education.

Surgical training aside, some other important things happened to me between July 1953 and July 1960 (I was at Belle-

vue from 1953 to 1955, and from 1957 to 1960; from 1955 to
1957 I was in the army, and I've written about those years elsewhere in this book).

First, in November 1953 I got married. I was twenty-five
years old and had run around enough. I was ready to settle
down and, fortunately, had found the girl I wanted to marry—
Joan Scheibel.

I had first met Joan during the summer of 1950. I was living
in South Hadley at the time digging ditches for the water department, and a friend offered to fix me up on a blind date. He
mentioned a girl I'd heard of, a girl who was supposed to be
both clever and good-looking, and I agreed to the date. As it
turned out, at the last minute this girl couldn't make it and
Joan came instead. (Joan is clever and good-looking, too, and
she has a sense of humor.)

The four of us went to an amusement park, rode the roller
coaster, listened to a dance band, and ate hot dogs. Joan was
fun to be with, but she didn't bowl me over, nor did I fascinate
her. We got along very well, however, and for the rest of the
summer we went out together two or three nights a week. Usually we went to the movies or played tennis, since we both
liked these things.

The summer ended, I went back to medical school, and
Joan returned to her senior year at Elmira College. We wrote
for a while, but at twenty-two, absence doesn't make the heart
grow fonder; "Out of sight, out of mind" is closer to the truth.
I met other girls, nurses mostly, and Joan spent her weekends
on dates at Cornell.

It wasn't till the summer of 1952, the summer between my
junior and senior years in medical school, that I took Joan out
again. At the time I was fairly heavily entangled with a nurse
in Boston—we'd reached the stage where we were talking
about getting engaged—and I'd suddenly realized that I didn't
want to marry her. What triggered this realization was her inability to let me alone when I was reading. Every time I'd get
absorbed in a book—I remember, specifically, one incident
when I was halfway through *The Caine Mutiny*—she'd say,

"Oh, come on, put that book down and talk to me." I couldn't see a lifetime of that.

Trying to extricate myself I took a summer job as a sort of sub-intern at the Soldier's Home Hospital in Holyoke, Massachusetts—a hundred miles west of Boston. I was on call two or three nights a week, but on the others, naturally, I needed something to do. I called Joan, who had now graduated from college and was working, she told me, "as a sort of janitor at Mount Holyoke College." We started going out together again.

I liked Joan even more on this second go-round. We had a lot of tastes in common—bridge, reading and music, as well as tennis and movies, and we invariably had fun together. This time when I left to go back to Boston for my last year of medical school the relationship didn't end. I wrote and so did she.

However, we didn't, to use a phrase which is probably no longer in vogue, "go steady." She came to Boston for some of our parties, and I visited her in Holyoke on vacations, but I continued to go out with other girls and she had dates with other boys. We hadn't tied each other down formally.

In the spring, just before graduation my medical school class had a big party at a resort on Cape Cod. Joan came to this one, and as usual, we had a wonderful time together; she was then, as she is now, a great party girl. After this blast the idea of marriage seriously entered my head, but I didn't mention it. I did, however, invite her to my graduation.

Still, nothing formal was done. After graduation Joan went back to Holyoke, and I left with a classmate for a last series of swinging parties in New Hampshire. On July 1 I went to Bellevue.

On my free nights at Bellevue I was often too tired to go out; when I was up to it I'd date one nurse or another. Weekends, however, as soon as I could get away, I'd catch a train to Groton Long Point in Connecticut, where Joan spent weekends with her parents. I'd get there about three o'clock on Saturday afternoon and I'd sleep for the next three hours. More often than not, I'd arrive having had only two or three hours' sleep the previous night.

In the fall Joan came to New York to see me on my free

weekends (I had to work every other weekend). We had some very good times, good enough so that I finally convinced her we might as well get married. We got engaged the last weekend in October and were married a month later. We've been married ever since. To each other. Which makes us both, I think, happy.

While I was at Bellevue we knew that I wouldn't be home much; interns and residents were off duty only every other night and weekend. Nevertheless, since we both wanted children, we decided to go ahead and start our family.

Not that we had much choice. In the early 1950's there was no "pill" or intrauterine device available, and even if there were they would have been off limits to Catholics. So, ten months after we were married, Jimmy was born; eleven months after Jimmy, Joan Deborah (Jody) came along; Billy was born eleven months after Jody. Joan and I were married in November 1953; by September 1955 we had three children, all under two. We were very busy.

If we had had a choice, we probably wouldn't have had our first three children quite so quickly, but now that they're grown up—Jimmy's seventeen—we look back on the years when they were babies as hectic, wearing, but wonderful fun as well. Annie was born in 1958 and Julius in 1959, before I'd finished my sojourn at Bellevue, and Mary was born in 1960, shortly after I went into practice. It may sound like treason, now that we're all aware of the overpopulation problem, but Joan and I are happy we have six children.

In 1959, while I was at Bellevue, my father died. He was then fifty-eight and I was thirty.

As we both grew older, my father and I had become good friends. Joan and I lived in New York, and his law practice, which had become a quite successful one, was based in Massachusetts, but he and my mother visited us fairly often. He'd come down on business and then take Joan and me out to dinner or to a show. Often the four of us would play bridge.

When I was a kid growing up my father and I weren't in any sense of the word "buddies." He wasn't the kind of guy who would come out in the backyard and shoot a basketball with me and my brother. He was never a good athlete and he had no interest in sports, though he always came to watch us play in high school games when he could fit them into his schedule.

But I respected and admired him. When I was hanging around the basement of our home with my friends, he'd often come down and talk to us, about anything and everything. Most of my friends never expected to go to college. My father spent a lot of time trying to make them see the importance of more education, and he did what he could—often getting them jobs in Boston—to help them pay for it. I knew he cared about me and my friends. I'd argue with him, like any teenager, when he told me to do something or not to do something, but I knew, deep inside, he was just looking out for me. And I also knew that he was usually right.

As I grew older I found we had a lot in common, which certainly shouldn't have surprised me as much as it did. I didn't give a damn what team was leading the American League, neither did he; I liked to read and play bridge, so did he; I thought I knew all there was to know, and so did he—consequently we argued a lot, but we enjoyed each other's company. I was proud of him and I think he was proud of me.

In 1959, about four o'clock on a Thursday evening, my father phoned me at Bellevue. "Billy," he said, "Mary's [my sister's] two-year-old, Mike, has got some sort of lump in his belly. The doctor thinks it's serious. I'm going to rush him down to Boston Children's. Do you think you could meet us there?"

"Sure," I said, "I'll change and catch a plane as soon as I can." I asked another resident to take my place on call that evening, phoned Joan—who was about to have our fifth child—and flew to Boston.

I met my father, my sister and her husband, Jack, at Boston Children's. My father had figured I could serve as a sort of interpreter for them—laymen often do need an interpreter to talk to doctors—and I did. It looked bad; the chances were excellent that Mike had a neuroblastoma, a relatively rare malignant tumor seen most often in children. The doctors at Children's scheduled special X-rays for the next morning to try and establish a diagnosis.

My father and I went to the Algonquin, a club to which he belonged, to spend the night. Mary and Jack were staying at a hotel near the hospital. We ate, then sat together in the library. We talked about a lot of things: where I ought to practice—he thought I should come back to Holyoke, where the Nolen name would help; about my brother and his future; about what life had been like for all of our family. I remember his telling me that evening, "Billy, you've got to watch out for two things —booze and women. If you don't get into any trouble with either, you should have a good life."

After an hour we were invited to fill in at bridge. "We will if we don't have to play together," my father said. "My son and I play better against than with each other."

I still remember one bid of six diamonds my father and his partner made. I doubled, my father redoubled, and he made the bid. He had a void in one suit where I'd expected to cash an ace. He was delighted.

The next morning, Friday, we met Mary and Jack at the hospital. When the X-rays had been taken I spoke to the doctors, then to my father, sister and brother-in-law. "It looks bad," I said, "Mike has a tumor. They'll have to operate, probably on Monday. They won't know till then whether they can get it out."

Then I called New York and found that Joan had gone to the hospital, in labor. I told my father and he said, "You'd better get back, your first obligation is to your own family."

I dropped him at the Algonquin Club—he was tired and was planning to lie down for a couple of hours—and flew back to New York. I went directly to the Bronxville Hospital, but by the time I got there Julius had been born. Joan was fine. I told her about Mike and then went home to see our other kids.

Ten minutes after I got home the phone rang. It was my brother-in-law, Jack, calling from Boston.

"Bill," he said, "I've got some bad news—about your dad."

"What is it, Jack—is he dead?" I don't know why I expected that, but I did. What other bad news could he have?

"I'm afraid so, Bill. They called his room at two o'clock.

When no one answered, the porter went up and found him dead. He died in his sleep."

He had had a heart attack. I didn't tell Joan; I hated to spoil her day with the news. She and my father had been good friends, but there was nothing she could do now. I told her I had to go back to Massachusetts to help make some decisions about Mike, and that night I drove home to my mother and the rest of our family. It was a sad reunion.

I've always been grateful for that last night with my father. I admired him, respected him, and—to use a word we Nolens rarely use—loved him. I'm sorry he couldn't have lived longer —he enjoyed life and I'd like to have shared more of my life with him—but it just wasn't in the cards. I think of him often.

My father died on July 18, 1959. A few months later Mike died, and a year later, on July 1, 1960, I left Bellevue. Not for Holyoke, Massachusetts, but for Litchfield, Minnesota, where I've lived and practiced surgery ever since.

4
Who I Am—and What This Book Is All About

Having told you where I came from, how I grew up, and the route I followed to become a doctor, it's time to tell you who I am now and what this book is all about. I'm a general surgeon, age forty-four. My wife, our six children and I live in Litchfield, Minnesota, sixty-five miles west of Minneapolis on Highway 12. Litchfield has a population of 5,262. It's the county seat of Meeker County, population 18,349. Litchfield is a fairly typical Midwest community; there will be more about the city a bit later in this book. For the moment the pertinent point about Litchfield is that the county hospital, the Meeker County Hospital, is located here. There are eighty-five adult-patient beds, twelve nursery beds, and two operating rooms in the hospital.

I'm the chief of surgery at Meeker County Hospital, and have been ever since we moved to Litchfield in 1960. Sometimes I suspect that I've been chief of surgery all those years because I'm the only board-certified surgeon on the staff.

The other doctors on the regular staff are all general practitioners. The number varies between ten and twelve. We also have radiology service—there's a group of radiologists in Willmar, a city of 15,000, thirty miles west of here, and one member or another visits our hospital every Monday, Wednesday and Friday morning. He reads the X-rays that have been taken since the last visit and does the special X-rays—X-rays of the stomach, the bowel, and the spinal column—that only radiologists can do. This group of radiologists also provides us with emergency consultations on the rare occasions when these are necessary.

Twice a week a pathologist from Willmar comes to our hospital. He makes certain that the laboratory is being run properly and he also does "frozen sections," if we need them. (A "frozen section" is a procedure in which a piece of tissue, immediately after removal from the body, is frozen, stained and examined through a microscope. Generally it's used to differentiate between cancer and benign disease.)

I'm in group practice with the Litchfield Clinic. There are five G.P.'s in the group and me. I do all the major surgery on all the patients that come to our clinic. I also do all the major surgery for all the other general practitioners who practice at the Meeker County Hospital. In fact, with the exception of some orthopedic, gynecological and genitourinary surgery, for which we bring in subspecialists from Minneapolis, I do all the major surgery that is done in Meeker County. This keeps me reasonably busy. I operate on about three hundred and fifty patients a year; the average general surgeon does a hundred and fifty cases a year.

But I'm not really overworked. I could do more. I'm glad I don't have to, because I have other interests and need time to pursue them. In the spring, summer and fall I play tennis almost every day. In the winter I play hockey three or four nights a week. I read a lot—medical journals, magazines, fiction, nonfiction, and the Sunday *New York Times*, which arrives in Litchfield on Wednesday. I like to watch the Litchfield school teams in action, particularly when my boys or girls are playing or cheer-leading. I enjoy playing bridge, going to the movies and partying.

I also like to write. (Not really; I hate to write. Writing is very hard work. But I like to have written.) Writing has, in fact, become my avocation. I've been at it for ten years. First for the scientific journals, then for *Medical Economics*, a magazine very popular with doctors; next, after collecting a drawerful of rejection slips over a five-year period, for general-circulation magazines. Finally, books.

Which brings me to this book and what it's about. When I wrote *The Making of a Surgeon,* a book about surgical training, I was often asked, "Are doctors angry because you've written this book?"

The answer was Yes. Some doctors—not, by a long shot, all or even most—were angry because I'd told about what it was like to spend five years in a city hospital learning surgery. They didn't think the public had any right to know what this experience was like. They considered me a traitor to my profession.

I couldn't, and still can't, follow their reasoning. We surgeons have no big dark secrets to hide. How could I betray anyone by telling what I thought was a reasonably interesting story? And a true one.

My critical colleagues would have preferred to have me write a book about *The Making of a Lawyer* or *The Making of a Salesman* or—as one wit put it—*The Making of a Nurse.* But if there is one lesson I learned, while acquiring my drawerful of rejection slips, it is to write about what you know.

Oddly enough, until I went into practice I never knew what doctors were really like. In medical school I learned the science of medicine; during my internship and residency I learned how to put my scientific knowledge to practical use; but it wasn't till I went into practice that I learned anything at all about the art of medicine.

The relationship of the doctor in training to his patients is a limited one. At Bellevue we saw and cared for patients only when they were in the hospital. Once they were discharged, once they'd gone back to their homes and families, we never saw them again. We didn't know where they lived or how they lived; once they left the hospital we rarely thought about them again. We didn't relate to them as people, only as patients.

Nor did we really know anything about the doctors in private practice who served as our consultants. We saw them only in the hospital when they came to teach us the science of medicine. We had no idea how much they charged their private patients, how they ran their offices, how they got along with the nurses, their patients and each other. We couldn't conceive of doctors competing for patients, doctors splitting fees, doctors squabbling over who had a right to admit a patient to a vacant bed. We knew next to nothing of what a doctor's business and social life was like.

Nor did we know what it would be like to make a house call, to treat a patient over the telephone, to worry about the patient's insurance coverage. We never had to give any consideration to what would happen to a patient's wife, kids or job while he was in the hospital.

Our only concern, during the years of training, was with the management of the immediate medical or surgical problem—which required, mainly, only a knowledge of the science of medicine. We lived and functioned in an unusual, limited environment.

Once we got out into practice all that changed. Suddenly we had to learn how to live with patients as people and doctors as friends and competitors. We no longer functioned in the protected environment of the hospital; we were out in the "real" world. Now we had to learn the art and the business of medicine.

And that, essentially, is what this book is all about: what I've learned in the last twelve years, about doctors and their lives. How they do their jobs. How they think and feel about patients, malpractice, money, and house calls. How their wives help or hinder them. How the private practitioners feel about the university doctors. About all facets of the life and work of the men who practice medicine.

This book is neither a hatchet job nor a whitewash. Doctors are neither all good nor all bad. Like other men, they're a combination of the two. Sometimes, most of the time, they act decently; occasionally they behave like bastards. They are, simply, human.

What I have to say here is based not only on my own experience in the private practice of surgery, but also on what I've learned from talking to and observing doctors who practice in other communities, in other specialties, in private practice or in salaried positions. When a doctor talks to another doctor it's almost always about his practice; it's a simple matter for one physician to learn what another's life is like.

Though the setting of the book is a real one—I am at the Litchfield Clinic, I do have five G.P. partners, my wife does hate to get up in the morning—the doctors, patients and cases I describe are composites. I've taken characteristics of one doctor and mixed them with those of another, and I've done the same thing with patients and cases. Everything in the book is true, but disguised so that no reader will be able to say, "This is Dr. Smith," or "So that's what happened to Mrs. Brown." I like Litchfield, I enjoy my practice, and I want to be able to live here and work at my profession after this book appears.

Why write the book at all? I could answer, simply, "Because I'm a writer." This would be true, as far as it goes; but it doesn't go far enough. I've written the book because I think people are interested in knowing what the life of a doctor is really like. It's a perfectly natural interest. Doctors deal in sickness and health, in life and death. Nothing matters more.

And the public deserves to know how we doctors work, how we live, how we think, how we behave. They have the right to know our strengths and weaknesses. If men and women have to put their lives, and the lives of their children, in our hands—and they do—they have a right to know what sort of men we are. They have a right to see us clearly, warts and all.

That's what this book is all about.

5

Litchfield—
How I Got There

In July 1960, when I completed five years of surgical training at Bellevue Hospital, I was thirty-two years old, married
and the father of five children under seven. I was ready to begin practicing surgery. The question was, Where?

In most big cities there are too many surgeons. In New York,
Boston, Chicago, Houston, Minneapolis—almost any city with
a population greater than a hundred thousand—the surgeon-
patient ratio is too high. Many of the surgeons sit around the
hospital cafeteria buying coffee for the internists and pediatricians, praying that someone will send them a case. They have
to work hard just to look busy.

That sort of life didn't appeal to me. I'd spent five years
learning to be a surgeon and, by God, now I wanted to be a
surgeon and put my surgical knowledge and experience to
work. I wanted to go where a surgeon was needed.

Joan agreed. She knew I'd be tough to live with if I wasn't
busy—I'm the kind of guy who gets restless very easily—so she
was willing to go anywhere. She liked the idea of living in
New England, because we're both natives of Massachusetts,
but she wasn't addicted to the area. Any place we could live
comfortably was all right with her.

I was ready to get out of New York. During the last three

years of my surgical training, we had lived in Eastchester, a suburb of New York City, in a very pleasant apartment complex. There were lawns, picnic tables, even a small pond for swimming. But I was tired of commuting—the morning traffic on the East River Drive was horrible—and even if I had chosen to practice in Eastchester, we would have had to leave our apartment. There were only two bedrooms, and for the last year Joan and I had slept on couches in the living room.

My training at Bellevue had been interrupted by the draft. From 1955 to 1957 I was in the army, serving as a medical officer in a place called, if you can believe it, Igloo, South Dakota. Sad to say, Igloo is no more; it was closed down completely in 1965 and the land on which it was located is now the site of a pig farm. But when I was there Igloo was an ordnance depot—an ordnance depot is a place where ammunition is stored—with a population of two thousand. It was located out on the plains about thirty miles from Hot Springs, South Dakota, and because the road to Hot Springs was treacherous in the winter, Igloo had been designated an "isolated post in the zone of the interior." Which meant that the army was responsible for providing medical care for all the people in Igloo.

That's why I was there. I, and one other doctor, ran a small hospital. We provided medical care for the sixteen officers, three enlisted men and the two thousand or so civilians who lived and worked in Igloo. We delivered babies, took care of heart attacks, removed tonsils and appendices; we did everything we could within the limits of our abilities and the equipment on hand.

Joan and I enjoyed our two years in Igloo. We had a home of our own; there were wide open spaces where the children could play. It was a welcome break from the hectic life of Bellevue.

The other doctor who served with me in Igloo was a fellow named Don Dille. He and his wife, Bonnie, and their six children lived across the street from us. Don was a general practitioner and a very good one. Until the army grabbed him for a two-year hitch he had been in practice with four other

G.P.'s in the Litchfield Clinic, in Litchfield, Minnesota. Which brings me to the point of this rather lengthy digression.

During our two years in Igloo, Joan and I got to know Don and Bonnie very well. We liked them and we liked their kids. They told us of their life in Litchfield and it sounded as if it might be a pleasant place to live. When Don was discharged, two months before I was, we took a vacation and went to visit them. Their home was on a lake on the edge of the city. They had horses on a farm they owned about two miles from their home. What we saw of their life style, and of Litchfield, appealed to us. When we were leaving, after our three-day visit, Don said, "Why don't you keep in touch with me? Three years from now, when you're through with your surgical training, we might be ready to take a surgeon into our group." We had kept in touch, and now that I was ready to leave Bellevue the idea of going to Litchfield seemed inviting.

But before we definitely settled on Litchfield I felt that I ought to at least look at two or three other places, just to make certain that there wasn't some spectacular opportunity I was passing up. Joan and I picked out three medium-sized New England communities where we thought it might be pleasant to live, and two months before I was to finish my formal surgical training I took a week off and visited them. These trips gave me my first exposure to the business side of surgical practice; it was a most revealing experience.

In the first town I visited (I'll call it Bronxwood), I was told very promptly, by the administrator of the community hospital, that there were no appointments to the surgical staff available. "We've got all the surgeons we need, Dr. Nolen," he said. "We run three operating rooms and there are eight general surgeons on the staff. There's absolutely no room for another man."

"But I'm fully trained," I said. "I'm just about to complete a five-year residency at Bellevue. I'm perfectly willing to compete with the other surgeons for patients. I know I can do the job."

"I'm sure you can," he answered. "That's not the point. We just don't think it's good for the community to have too many surgeons around. It leads to competition for patients, fee-splitting and generally poor practice. There are a lot of other towns that need surgeons. Why don't you try one of them?"

There was nothing more to say. The eight surgeons on this staff had a good thing going, and they weren't anxious to have any more competition. I thanked the administrator, smiling through my clenched teeth, and left.

The next place I visited (a place I'll call Northville) was a city of thirty thousand in which there were four general surgeons in practice. It was a pleasant seacoast community in Maine, and I knew one of the general surgeons, a fellow named Ray Thackeray. We had been close friends in medical school. I decided that instead of going to the hospital administrator I'd talk to him. I called and Ray invited me over to his office. After a few minutes of reminiscing we got down to business.

"Bill," he said, "there's nothing I'd like better than having you practice here—if only you weren't a surgeon." We both laughed; then he shifted gears.

"Seriously," he said, "we've always gotten along well, and from the social point of view I think we could have a lot of fun. But I'll tell you right now, you'd have a tough time making it. There's one guy, Charlie Stark, who has been here for fifteen years. He's an excellent surgeon and he loves to work. He never leaves town and never turns down a case. He does about eighty percent of the surgery. Three of us split up the other twenty percent. I've been here a year and a half and I'm just making expenses. I'd get out tomorrow if Barbara wasn't so hung up on the town. But don't take my word for it. Let me give Charlie a call and you can go over and see him."

I did—and it was essentially the same story. "You're more than welcome to come here, Dr. Nolen. You're well trained and there won't be any problem getting you staff privileges. I'll be happy to recommend you. But, as your friend Dr. Thackeray probably told you, we've already got four general surgeons here and we really don't need another. You'd undoubtedly be able to build a practice, but it might take you two years, three years or even longer. When I quit, things will be different, but I don't intend to quit for at least another ten years."

Dr. Stark was a very confident man. I knew he wasn't afraid of competition. I also knew Ray was right when he said that Stark would be tough competition. I thanked him for his time and left. I also decided not to settle there. We liked the town, but unlike Ray and his wife, we weren't in love with it. I decided to look elsewhere.

The third city I visited, another New England community— I'll call it Hampton—had a population of twenty thousand and not a single general surgeon on the hospital staff. I couldn't understand it; it looked like it might be a surgeon's Shangri-la. I called the hospital, learned that a G.P., a Dr. Hunter, was the chief of staff, and called his office. I introduced myself and asked if he could spare me a few minutes. "I'm very busy, Dr. Nolen," he said, "but I suppose I can arrange it. Drop over to my office about five fifteen," and he hung up. He didn't, to say the least, sound very cordial.

I got to Dr. Hunter's office at five fifteen and at five forty-five his office nurse finally led me to him. He was a big bear of a man in his late fifties, and after shaking hands he asked me to sit down. He smoked a cigarette as I told him who I was, where I'd trained, and that I'd like to live and practice in Hampton.

"So would a lot of other general surgeons, Dr. Nolen," he said, "so would a lot of others. Doesn't it seem strange to you that in a city this size there isn't one general surgeon already?"

"As a matter of fact, it does," I answered.

"Well, I'll explain it to you," he said. "In simple terms—we don't want a general surgeon here. You see, Dr. Nolen, this is a G.P. community with a G.P. hospital. Every member of the staff is a G.P., and we like it that way. We all do some surgery; what we can't handle we send to Boston. Now, if we let you in here, what's going to happen? Very shortly there will be other specialists. And soon after that they'll be running things and they'll squeeze us G.P.'s out. The obstetricians will tell us we can't deliver babies, the internists will tell us we can't read electrocardiograms, and you'll tell us we can't take out any appendices. We'll be left with nothing to do but treat kids with runny noses and women with backaches. It's happened in other hospitals and it will eventually happen here; but we're going to fight hard to keep it from happening for a while yet."

Dr. Hunter was right, and I knew it. The G.P.'s inevitably did get squeezed out of hospitals once the specialists got in. There are very few big cities left where a G.P. can get obstetrical or surgical privileges in a decent hospital; in many communities they can't even get on the staff.

I decided not to fight Dr. Hunter. I thanked him for his time, shook hands and left.

Over the next few days Joan and I talked over the possibilities. Bronxwood was definitely out—a surgeon can't practice without hospital privileges—but despite the discouraging reception, both Northville and Hampton were possibilities. I had confidence in my ability as a surgeon and I couldn't help believing that if I stuck it out a year or two I'd build a practice. The question was, Did I want to live in either one of these towns badly enough to make the fight?

I decided not to bother. The geography of the place I lived in didn't matter as much as the opportunity it afforded. Why go where I was neither needed nor wanted? It was pointless. I could have looked at other places; even in New England I was reasonably sure that if I looked long and hard enough I'd have found a town where I'd have been welcomed. But why bother? I knew I was welcome, and needed, in Litchfield. We decided to go; at the time neither Joan nor I thought we'd stay there more than a couple of years.

As of August 1972 I've been in practice here twelve years.

6

More on Litchfield

In 1920 Sinclair Lewis wrote *Main Street* and told everyone what it was like to live in Sauk Centre, a small Midwestern town fifty miles north of and much like Litchfield. People all over the world read his book and said, "How terrible! So provincial, so unsophisticated, so narrow, how could anyone live there?"

Now, fifty years later, Main Street has changed hardly at all but people have. They've become disenchanted with the cosmopolitan, sophisticated complexity of life in the big cities. Those who can manage it are fleeing to the small towns, if only on weekends. They want to get back to places where they can breathe clean air, swim in unpolluted water, let their kids run free—back to towns like the one in which I live.

It does, however, take a certain amount of self-confidence to live in a small town. Because, though small towns may be cleaner and quieter, the big city is where the action is. It's widely held, by those who don't know any better, that a lawyer or doctor who lives in a small town does so because he can't make it in the big city; that anyone who lives in a place like Litchfield has to be second-rate. I run into this attitude now and then in patients who will allow me to snip off their warts but decide that they'd better go to Minneapolis or the Mayo Clinic when they need their stomachs removed. It used to bug me, but it doesn't any more. I send them off with my blessing. I don't want to operate on anyone who doesn't have complete confidence in me. (I'm happy to report that these episodes occur only rarely now; they were quite common during my first year or two in Litchfield.)

If it isn't fear of the big city that has kept Joan and me in Litchfield, then what does keep us here? Easy. We like the place.

I like it, first, for professional reasons. As I've said, I'm the only board-certified surgeon in the county. Since 1962 I've done all the major general surgery that has been done here, with the exception of cases that are done while I'm out of town. If you need your stomach removed or your hip fracture nailed, and you want it done in Litchfield, I'm the guy who does it. Doing most of the major surgery for ten other doctors gives me plenty to do.

I enjoy having a monopoly practice for another reason; I don't have to play up to anyone to get a case. Some of the big-city general surgeons I know have developed ulcers trying to avoid offending the pediatricians, internists and G.P.'s who send them patients. I have a surgeon friend who is an excellent golfer. I once asked him why he played so often with an internist who was not only a rotten golfer but a complete bore as well. "Bill," he said, "I don't give a damn if he shoots one hundred and thirty and tells me the same story five times every afternoon; he sends me the patients whose fees buy my membership in this place. Without him I'd be on the public course." That sort of stuff has no appeal for me. I'd rather play golf with my friends.

But let's forget about the professional side of life in Litchfield; what about the city itself? Is it an attractive place?

To be perfectly frank—no. Not if you compare it with Greenwich, Connecticut; Bronxville, New York; Lake Tahoe, Nevada; or any of several thousand more towns or cities in the United States. It's not an ugly city, but even its warmest admirers would hardly call it beautiful. It looks about like most of the small cities you see as you fly over or drive through the Midwest.

I've always felt it was a mistake to choose a place to live

primarily for geographic reasons. So you can see the ocean from your front porch or a ski run out of your kitchen window —so what? You certainly aren't going to sit and gaze at either of them all day. If the place doesn't offer you anything but natural beauty you're going to get bored very quickly. Better to visit the ocean or the mountains once or twice a year, and spend the rest of your time living and working in a place where there's challenge and opportunity. That's what I was looking for in Litchfield.

The land in and around Litchfield is flat—there isn't a hill, never mind a mountain—for miles. As a native-born New Englander, I find this flatness very unappealing. The flatness leads to one characteristic of the Midwest that constantly confused me when I first moved here. It still does. When you ask a native of the area how to get to some place, he'll invariably say something like, "Take the highway east [or north, or west, or south] for three miles. Then go south for two miles to the intersection. Drive west another mile and you're there." Everyone gives directions in terms of the compass, because the roads, unlike the twisting roads of New England, run in straight lines. Before I can follow these directions I always have to translate them from east and west into left and right.

Litchfield is split by the railroad tracks into two sections. There's a saying in the Midwest (possibly elsewhere too; I don't know) that if the railroad tracks run at right angles to the main street, the city will continue to grow and flourish; if the main street parallels the tracks, the town is doomed to dwindle and die. I don't know how true it is, but there are a couple of small towns around here that seem to be breathing their last; their main streets parallel the tracks. Litchfield's main street is at right angles to the tracks, and our census in 1970 was 5,262; up 200 from 1960. Not exactly what you'd call a boom town, but at least we're not fading out.

The business section of Litchfield runs for three blocks on the north side of the tracks (see how Midwestern I've become?). The south side of town is almost purely residential. On the south edge of town is Lake Ripley. There's a public beach and park on the lake—the lake is about a mile in diameter—and the golf club is situated on the edge of the lake. There's a road around the lake and on weekends there are always people "taking a drive around the lake." It's a narrow, bumpy road so you have to go slow, but there's really no reason to hurry.

There are bass, northern pike, walleyes, crappies and sunfish in Lake Ripley, and every summer evening there are men, women, and kids fishing from boats or shore on and around the lake. In the winter the lake is dotted with fish houses from late November till March. Since the farmers have more leisure time in winter, winter fishing is even more popular around here than is summer fishing. They move fish houses, small wooden houses, out onto the lake, cut a hole in the ice and sit in them and angle for or try to spear pike. The fish houses have heaters and gas lights or oil lamps; some even have carpeting. They can be quite elaborate.

All the residential streets in Litchfield are lined with trees, mostly oak and elm. They are quite attractive.

There's a park, with two tennis courts, on the south side of town, and another park with an old-fashioned bandstand at the edge of the business district on the north side of town. Every Friday evening in the summer, from 8 till 9 P.M., the city band gives a concert in the park. People sit in their cars and blow their horns in appreciation after each number; a lot of kids and quite a few adults sit in the park and listen to the concert. Joan and I often go to them when we're in town. The stores are open till nine on Fridays.

The biggest business in Meeker County, of which Litchfield is the county seat, is farming. Most of my patients, and most of the customers of the merchants here, are in farming in one way or another. They run a farm themselves, work on a farm or work for someone who supplies farmers or buys their products —feed salesmen, farm-implement dealers, milk processors, that sort of thing. Even some of our industry—Anderson Chemical, where they produce chemical products for cleaning milking equipment, and the Land O'Lakes plant, which converts whole milk to the dried form—are basically farm-oriented; but we do have a few other fair-sized businesses, like the Litchfield Woolen Mill. If the crops are good, we all thrive; if not we all suffer.

Which is why a favorite topic of conversation in Litchfield is the weather. I realize that people talk about the weather everywhere, but not as intently as they do in a farm community. Here a prolonged dry spell can mean bankruptcy. In most places all it means is that you'll have to water your lawn every evening.

Oddly enough, it's difficult to find any two farmers who will agree on what kind of weather we need at any given moment. One will say, "We sure could use a good rain"; another, on a neighboring farm, will say, "I hope the hell it stays sunny; the corn needs a chance to dry." What they want depends to a certain extent on the kind of soil they have—sandy, clay, or plain old dirt—and on the crops they're raising. But it also depends, to a large extent, on pure orneriness.

You learn very quickly that no farmer is ever completely satisfied with the weather. It is always too wet or too dry, too hot or too cold, never just right. I've decided after looking, casually, for twelve years for a farmer who felt the weather on any particular day was perfect that he doesn't exist. I think a possible explanation is that a farmer is afraid he'll jinx himself if he says, "The weather is wonderful and I'm going to have a great crop." He's afraid the Lord will rain hail down on his head and on his corn. I think I'd probably harbor the same fear if I were a farmer.

The second biggest industry in Litchfield, as it is in most small towns, is the school system. I've yet to meet anyone from a small town who didn't say, "One thing about our town, we've got a great school system." I'll say the same thing.

The people of Litchfield are willing to spend money on education. We moan and groan about taxes, but when the school bond issues are on the ballot, we vote them through. There are some people, of course, who complain loudly about "the huge salaries those damn teachers get for working twenty hours a week, nine months a year," but by and large we're for education.

What I like best about having my kids go to school in Litchfield is that I know the teachers and the principals, and they know me. I can call up Roland Scharmer, the math teacher, and say, "Roland, what about this D you gave my son. Is it just that he's no good at math, or is he goofing off on his homework?" And Roland will tell me.

If Julius raises hell in class, as he occasionally does, I'll get a call from his teacher, who will tell me, "Dr. Nolen, you're going to have to get after Julius. He's getting to be a wiseacre. He's always smarting off at me and he disrupts the class with his corny jokes." So I ground Julius for a week.

In Litchfield the teachers are much more a part of the community than they are in most big cities. I play basketball, hockey and poker with teachers (the males); Joan and I know the female teachers through social contacts with them and their husbands, or just through school activities. I feel confident that the schoolteachers in Litchfield offer my children not only the courses they need but the help and guidance that can make a great difference in how much they get out of their education. I think my kids are getting a better education here than they'd get if I sent them away from home to private schools.

Another nice thing about living in Litchfield is the relationship of professional trust that exists among those who work here. When I lived in New York and something went wrong with my car I never knew when I brought it to a garage whether I was getting fair and honest treatment. I was always afraid the repair men would fleece me. I didn't know them and I didn't trust them. I'd heard too many stories about unreliable work and overcharging, and I'd been stung on a couple of occasions myself.

It's not like that in Litchfield. I know Clint Olson, who runs the repair department at Fenton Chevrolet, and I trust him. Just as I trust Al and Dick Fenton, who own the business. I'm sure they're going to see that my car is properly repaired and that I'm charged a fair price. We all live together in this little town, and mutual trust is something we have to have.

I can't think of anyone in Litchfield whom I wouldn't trust to deal with me honestly. When I call Jerry Beckman because

something has gone wrong with the television set I bought
from him, I know Jerry will show up and fix it promptly; when
I ask Al Nelson, who manages Ideal Lumber, if he can send
someone over to add another bookcase to the cabin he built
for us, I don't worry about the details. I don't have to. I know
Al will do a good job at a fair price. When I phone Wayne Rick
because the drain in the sink is plugged, I'm sure he'll respond
as quickly as he can; he knows us, knows we have six children
and can understand that a plugged drain is a major catas-
trophe.

In Litchfield you couldn't stay in business long—whether
your business is repairing cars or removing gall bladders—if
your customers didn't trust you. You can't get away with
shabby work in a small town. Unfortunately some people can
—and do—in bigger cities.

In Litchfield it's even possible to get along with the police.

Twice I've had to go to the police station at night to pick
up one of my kids. The first time it was Billy. He was thirteen
then, and he had sneaked out of the house after we'd gone to
bed, met a couple of his buddies, and gone to call on his "girl
friend," whose parents were out of town. They were raising
hell, just "goofing around" as he said, in a vacant lot, when the
local patrolman spotted them. He brought all the kids to the
station, called us parents, and we picked them up. It scared
them plenty—which was the point of bringing them in.

Another time, Jimmy was involved in an automobile accident shortly after he got his driving license. He wound up at
the jail. John Rogers, our sheriff, called me and asked me if I'd
come down. In my presence and with my blessing, he gave
Jimmy a good chewing-out for careless driving. Jimmy has
since been a much more cautious driver.

These are little things, I know, but they make a lot of difference in our lives. I sleep better knowing that Chief Fenner, or
one of the patrolmen, will call me promptly if they see one of
my kids hanging around a spot where marijuana is occasionally
available. (Drugs, at least as of June 1972, have been a relatively minor problem in Litchfield, for which I'm also most
grateful.) I like the idea that, with luck, I'll be warned before

my children get into serious trouble, because the police in Litchfield know and care about them. The city is small enough to allow that sort of personal relationship.

I'm afraid I'm beginning to sound like a tout for the Chamber of Commerce, so let me admit now that there are a number of things about life in Litchfield that are decidedly unappealing.

Its small size, for example, is a mixed blessing. It's nice to know the teachers, the police, the merchants, but it gets to be rather boring when you see the same people all the time.

In Litchfield it's easy to get tied into a very, very restricted social life. There are couples who are with the same three or four other couples all the time. If I say to Joan, "I saw Jack and Barbara Robertson at the golf club," she doesn't have to ask me whom they were with. She'd know. It would have to be either the Bronsons or the Leiders. They're all part of the same small clique.

When we first moved to Litchfield we almost got tied into one of these packages. Couples Clubs were all the rage then, and still flourish locally. These aren't the wife-swapping kind; these clubs are nowhere near that lively. Four or five couples get together, usually on a Saturday night, every other week. The members take turns acting as hosts. First there are drinks, then dinner, and finally everyone plays bridge or whist.

We were invited the first time as "substitutes" for a couple that were out of town. It wasn't a bad evening—the conversation, as usual, ran to sports, cars and politics among the men; to school and children in the women's division—Joan and I were new in town, we didn't know anyone well, and we found the talk relatively interesting.

Two weeks later we again acted as "subs." This time the party seemed less fascinating. If you enjoy bridge there's nothing worse than having to play the game with someone who neither knows much nor cares about it. In this group none of the men liked bridge; the wives did. So after drinking and eating heavily, the men would invariably all but fall asleep trying to play cards. I didn't mind the eating and drinking, I carried my own in both divisions, but the cardplaying was sheer agony.

Finally we were asked to become full members of this particular club—one couple had moved out of town—and, like jackasses, we accepted.

In the next few months I got so I could hardly get out of bed on the Saturday when the club was scheduled to meet. Every chance we got we'd run off to Minneapolis to avoid, gracefully, the meeting. We were the most unreliable members this club had ever seen.

Fortunately, we never had to resign; to do so would have been an insult to the other members, all of whom we liked. The club just fell apart. Probably the other couples became tired of the repetition too. One postponed meeting followed another, and without any formal proclamation the club dissolved.

It has, of course, been replaced by another; there must be a dozen such clubs still flourishing in town. They come and go.

But even though we avoided that particular trap, in Litchfield it's impossible to have a really wide variety of friends. The town is just too small. When we go to the golf club the chances are excellent that we'll know everyone there. We'll also be able to guess pretty well what they'll have to say on any subject; just as they know how we feel about things. We see each other so often that we can't help getting to know each other well. Too well. There are very few surprises. Which is as nice a way as I can think of to say that social life in Litchfield, if indulged in too intensely, gets to be awfully boring.

Living in Litchfield we miss diversity in other ways. The golf-club food is fine, but we know the menu, the sauces, the hors d'oeuvre tray by heart. We'd like to eat someplace else once in a while, but it means a thirty-minute drive to Hutchinson or Willmar, and even these towns haven't got anything really different—no Chinese restaurant, no real seafood. For that we've got to drive sixty-five miles to Minneapolis.

And it would be nice to be able to go, on impulse, to a decent movie; to pick up the paper and say, "Let's go to *Carnal Knowledge* tonight, it's at the Plaza, or would you rather see the Bogart revival at the Strand?" We've only got one movie theater, the Hollywood, and the owner, Fred Schnee, a very nice man, would have to close its doors if he ran *Belle de Jour.* People would stay away in droves. *Love Story* is what it takes to sell the popcorn. I'm delighted that Fred manages to keep the theater open. Many small-town theaters have folded.

Our kids are missing the opportunity to know people with different backgrounds. There are no blacks in Litchfield, nor any Jews. We're top-heavy with Scandinavians; there are one hundred Andersons and ninety-nine Johnsons listed in our phone directory, but not one Stein. It's easy to find someone who can fix lutefisk, but it's impossible to buy a bagel.

I'm sure there are a lot of other things, major and minor, that we miss by living in Litchfield. We know all this and accept it. After weighing the pros and cons, we've decided the pros win, and by a large margin. Litchfield is the right place for us. At least for the present.

7

A Typical Day

One of the joys of practicing surgery is that every day is different. When I get up in the morning I know, roughly, how I'm going to spend the next twenty-four hours, and I'm sure they're not going to be too much like the previous twenty-four. I know, too, that at any time of the day or night my "routine," to use the term loosely, may and probably will be interrupted. There's one thing the practice of surgery isn't, and that's boring.

My day ordinarily begins at 7 A.M. There's a whistle in Litchfield that blows every morning, precisely at seven, and as soon as it goes off, my two youngest daughters, Annie and Mary, come running down the stairs. They are our early risers.

Annie immediately takes our dog, Sammy, a mongrel we've had for seven years, for his morning walk. Sammy usually sleeps at the foot of Annie's bed, so he gets up when she does.

I generally lie in bed for ten minutes after I hear the whistle, then get up and put the coffee on. We always drink Sanka at home; I'm sensitive to caffeine and "real" coffee makes me "hyper." I'm hyper enough as it is.

After I brush my teeth I decide what to give the kids for breakfast. The only thing they'll all eat is pancakes, so when I don't fix pancakes I have to arrange a smorgasbord. Canned hash for some, eggs (scrambled only) for some, cold or hot cereal for the rest. They're too damn fussy, but Joan and I let them get away with it earlier, and now it's too late (and too difficult) to change.

So I fix breakfast. Mary and Annie eat first and then wake up the others. Usually I get them all fed by seven forty. I leave the dirty dishes in the sink.

Which brings me to Joan. The reason I make breakfast is a simple one. Joan hates to get up in the morning. She's a night person. When she does get up early—that is, before eight— she's barely civil. She sits at the dining-room table, smoking a cigarette and drinking coffee, and doesn't utter a word.

I decided long ago that getting the kids their breakfasts would be my job. I don't mind getting up early in the morning. Even if I did mind I'd have to get up because I usually start operating at eight. Since I have to get up anyway, and since night people don't get along with day people in the early morning, why not let Joan sleep? Not meeting till at least 10 A.M. has been the salvation of our marriage.

After the kids have eaten and while they're getting ready for school I take a shower and get dressed. I leave for the hospital and they leave for their respective schools at about seven fifty.

Our house is an old one, by Litchfield standards; it was built in 1918. It's not much to look at—plain stucco—but it has two things going for it. First, it's roomy. We have five bedrooms, a decent basement where the kids and their friends can hang out, and plenty of general living space. Even with eight in our family we're not crowded.

The second big plus to this home is its location. We're only two blocks from "downtown" and not more than four blocks from any of the schools the kids attend. We don't have to spend time chauffeuring our children; they can walk or bike to any place where they have any business going. These are two big reasons why Joan and I have been content to live in this house for the twelve years we've been in Litchfield.

I get to the hospital, and into the operating room, by seven fifty-five; the hospital is a five-minute drive from my home. I say hello to my first surgical patient, who by that time is on the O.R. table, and while I'm changing into a surgical scrub suit

Sam Longworth, our nurse anesthetist, puts the patient to sleep. Whichever doctor has referred the patient to me will act as my assistant, and while we scrub up, the circulating nurse paints the abdomen or chest or whatever it is we're operating on with Merthiolate.

Then I do the case. An hour or so for a gall bladder, two or three hours for a stomach, half an hour for a hernia. The length of time the case takes depends on the nature of the disease, how severe it is, and—if it's in the belly—how fat the patient is. Any operation on a fat patient takes longer than the same operation on a thin person. It's not just the few seconds it takes to cut through the blubber, it's the depth of the hole the surgeon has to work in. It's harder to get proper exposure so you can see what you're doing when you're working in a deep hole.

As soon as I finish the operation, after I help the nurses get the patient off the table and onto the stretcher, I write the postoperative orders. These tell the floor nurses, who will be caring for the patient, what medicine they can give for pain, and how often; what intravenous fluids, if any, I want the patient to have; and which antibiotics, if any, I want given. These orders tell, briefly, how I want the nurses to take care of the patient for me.

Next I sit in the doctors' dressing room, drink a cup of coffee—the one cup of real coffee I drink every day—and dictate a record of the operation which will be put on the patient's chart. The record tells what kind of an incision I made, what sort of disease I found, what operation I performed, and what suture materials I used. It also includes negative findings—for example, if I take out the patient's gall bladder I'll probably examine his stomach, since it's nearby, and I'll note that he didn't have an ulcer or a hernia of the stomach. This information may come in handy if the patient becomes ill six months, a year or even five years later. It all goes on the operative note. For those who might be interested in reading a typical operative note here's an example from the record of a patient whose gall bladder I removed.

By the time I get the operative note finished and my coffee

drunk, the nurse will probably have arrived with my second surgical patient, if I have a second case scheduled for that particular day. The second case, and the third, if there is one, are usually less formidable problems than the first. I like to do big cases first when I'm freshest, and follow them with less serious problems. I can relax and enjoy repairing a hernia if I've got a tough stomach already behind me.

After I've finished operating, around ten or ten thirty, I "make rounds" on all the patients I have in the hospital. First, I stop at the nurses' station and look over the charts on each of my patients. On each shift the nurse who has been responsible for the care of each patient writes a note about the patient: "slept well," "complained of pain in leg," "didn't finish lunch"—whatever she considers pertinent. These notes often tip the doctor off to something that may be going wrong; for example, if I read a note which says, "complained of pain in leg," when I go in to see the patient I'll check carefully to be certain he or she isn't developing phlebitis. If the patient "didn't finish lunch," I'll want to know why his appetite is gone. It may be a sign that his gall bladder disease, which had been subsiding, is flaring up again.

The other pages of the chart contain the reports from the laboratory, the X-ray reports, a running record of the patient's temperature, pulse and respiration, all the data about the patient and his particular illness that we've accumulated during his hospital stay. I glance at it all.

After I've looked through the charts, checking some quickly, others more thoroughly, depending on the current stage of the illness, I visit each patient, taking the charts with me.

On a typical day, the first patient I visit is a fellow named Vince Jarrett, a twenty-two-year-old man whose appendix I had removed five days earlier. Vince is sitting in a chair when I enter.

"How's it going, Vince?" I ask him.

"Not bad, Doc," he says. "Still a little stiff when I walk but it's getting better. When can I get out of here?"

Vince's temperature is normal. He has had an uneventful

RECORD OF OPERATION

Name Rose Murphy Age 56 Room No. 215 Date 7-20-71

Dr. Nolen   Assistant Dr. Roberts

Preoperative Diagnosis Cholelithiasis [stones in the gall bladder]

Postoperative Diagnosis Same

Name of Operation Cholecystectomy [removal of the gall bladder]

Description of Operation

PATHOLOGY AND OPERATIVE FINDINGS: On exploration this patient was found to have a gall bladder which contained many small stones, a very small cystic duct, and a common duct which was not enlarged. The stomach was mobile and there was no evidence of an ulcer.

PROCEDURE: With the patient in the supine position, under general anesthesia, the abdomen was prepared and draped in the usual manner. A right subcostal incision was made, bleeding vessels were clamped and ligated with plain catgut, the peritoneum was opened and pathology as described was noted. The gall bladder was put on traction with a carmalt clamp, the stomach was packed medially and the colon inferiorly using sharp and blunt dissection. The cystic duct was exposed. It was ligated in continuity and then divided, as was the cystic artery, and the gall bladder was then dissected free from its bed in the liver. There was no apparent bleeding. Two drains were left in and brought out through a stab wound in the right flank. One drain was placed in the Foramen of Winslow and one in the right gutter. The wound was then closed in layers using o chromic on the peritoneum, interrupted oo silk on the linea alba and fascia, plain catgut subcutaneously and a running locked ethilon on the skin. A dry dressing was applied and the patient was returned to her room in good condition.

SPECIMEN: Gall Bladder with stones.
CULTURE: None.
DRAINS: Two penrose.

W. A. Nolen, M.D.

Dictated & Typed 7-20-71/km

postoperative course. "Probably tomorrow," I answer. "I'll see you in the morning and take your stitches out. If everything's O.K. you can leave around ten thirty."

"Fine, Doc. I'll be ready."

I leave Vince and move down to room 264. Here I have Louise Summers, a sixty-two-year-old woman, a segment of whose bowel I removed yesterday. The bowel had cancer in it.

Louise is in bed and she has a hollow rubber tube—a Levin tube—coming out of her nose. The lower end is in her stomach and the other end is attached to a bottle to which suction is being applied. We're keeping Louise's stomach empty so that her bowel won't have to work for a few days. Louise also has fluids dripping into a vein in her arm from a bottle hanging by her bedside.

"How are you this morning, Louise?"

"Not too bad, Dr. Nolen, considering. I've got some pain, but the shots help." As I listen to Louise I feel her pulse and examine the dressing on her abdomen. Then I check the Levin tube to make certain that it hasn't become plugged.

"How long do I have to have that tube down?" she asks me.

"Probably one more day, Louise. I want to give your bowel a rest. If that tube wasn't down you might be vomiting. Does it bother you a lot?"

"It's a little sore in the back of my throat, that's all. I can put up with it."

"Good, Louise, I know you can. Everything's going fine. You should be up and around in a few days. The first day's the worst and if you have too much pain just ask the nurse for a hypo. Don't be a martyr. And I'll see you later this afternoon." I usually make rounds twice a day, for the first day or two, on patients on whom I've performed major surgery.

I make a mental note of the fact that Louise didn't ask me what I'd found. She knew before the operation that X-rays had shown a probable cancer. She obviously suspects the cancer had spread—and it had. To her liver. If it hadn't spread, if I had been able to get it all out, I'd have volunteered that information. Since I didn't say, Louise will guess. I'll leave it up to her to decide if she wants me to spell out the bad news. Probably she won't. Patients rarely do.

The next patient I visit is Fred Racine. Fred is fifty-eight, a high-powered businessman. He owns a fleet of trucks and he's been having union problems recently. He's also been having stomach problems.

"How's it going, Fred?" I ask him. He's sitting on the edge of his bed, smoking a cigarette. There's a glass of milk on the bedside stand near him.

"Lousy. Goddammit, Bill, I'm sick of this place. When can I go home?"

"Look, Fred, let's not get antsy. I just got the report on your stomach X-rays. You used to have one ulcer; now you've got two. The old one in your duodenum, a new one in your stomach. And you know as well as I do that if I let you go home you'll be back, bleeding, in a month. It's time you and I had a chat. You've got a decision to make."

For the next fifteen minutes I sit and talk to Fred about his ulcer problem. It boils down to the fact that he's not doing well on medical management. He refuses to do what I advise. He continues to smoke, drink and eat irregularly. He's in trouble most of the time with pain or bleeding, and, in my opinion, it's time to operate on him and take out part of his stomach. I give him the facts, make my recommendations, and leave the decision up to him.

"What's the chances of me making it through surgery?" he asks me.

"Excellent, Fred. You're in good shape except for your stomach. I don't anticipate any problems."

"All right," he says, "I'm sick of being sick. Let's get the goddam thing over. How soon can you do it?"

"It'll take another day to get the barium out of you. We'll plan on Thursday."

"O.K. I leave it up to you. I'll call Alice and let her know."

"Right, Fred. I'm sure you're making the best decision. You'll feel like a new man when we get this operation over."

So it goes for a half hour or so. I have, generally, five or six patients on each of the two floors of the hospital. Some require a lot of time, others just a quick hello. But each has to be seen every day. Skip one patient and, sure enough, it will be the one who is showing an early sign of a complication. It never fails.

When I finish visiting my patients I take the charts back to the desk and spend a few minutes writing on each. For Louise I have to order the intravenous fluids to be given over the next twenty-four hours; the laboratory will have to put two pints of blood on reserve in case he bleeds during the operation I've scheduled for Thursday; another patient needs a laxative; still another a sleeping pill. I write all these orders, and then, on each chart, on a page labeled "Progress notes," I make a brief, dated entry about the patient's condition that day: "Wound looks fine"; "X-ray report shows gastric ulcer, will need surgery"; "Satisfactory first postoperative day." These notes give me a running record of the patient's progress, useful if something goes wrong. I can't trust my memory when I've got a dozen or so patients to see every day.

By the time I've finished rounds it's usually about eleven o'clock. I leave the hospital and drive to my home, which—another great convenience—is only two doors from our clinic building. I stop in at the house, check the mail and visit for a few minutes with Joan before I walk to my office.

My office is in the basement of our clinic building. When our group expanded from four to six we were short of space, so I took over what used to be our library. Since my office practice is not very great I don't need much room. I'm comfortable in the library, and when patients come in I see them in one of my partner's examining rooms upstairs.

I never see patients in the morning except for emergencies—patients who have cut themselves, have fallen and broken a bone, or have suffered some other sort of injury. If none of these drop in, my time is my own till noon. I usually write for the hour or so that remains of the morning.

We take a two-hour lunch break, from noon till two. In the spring, summer and fall, as long as the weather is favorable, I play tennis during this interval. It keeps me from eating much of anything for lunch. When I don't play tennis or get some other form of exercise I'm inclined to overeat and then I'm sleepy for the first part of the afternoon. I make my own lunch—usually soup and a sandwich—since Joan never knows when I'll be home or what, if anything, I'll want to eat.

At two I head back to the office. I see patients by appointment, and schedule most of them for Wednesday or Friday afternoons.

After moving to Litchfield, one of my concerns was that I might not keep up with what was going on in surgery elsewhere. I intended to read the monthly surgical journals, but I thought that might not be enough. Discussion of problem cases with other surgeons was, in my opinion, the best way to make certain I didn't stagnate intellectually.

So I arranged my afternoon off to coincide with the weekly surgical conference at Hennepin General Hospital in Minneapolis, and made a practice of attending these meetings whenever I could get away.

Hennepin General is the city hospital in Minneapolis. It's like Bellevue in New York on a smaller scale. The indigent people who comprise the bulk of its patients usually have, as did the patients at Bellevue, not one but several diseases. Malnutrition, alcoholism, lung disease—these problems, the diseases often found in the poor and the homeless, are common in patients who come to General with a primary complaint of hernia, stomach ulcer, gall bladder disease. The combination of diseases makes the management of city hospital patients particularly challenging.

Hennepin General is a teaching hospital, affiliated with the University of Minnesota. Third-year medical students spend two months at General, getting their first exposure to clinical surgery. Most of the surgery is done by interns and residents, under the direction of the salaried surgeons who supervise the training program. In addition to the clinical surgery, the surgical director and his staff run a very active research program in which each of the surgical trainees spends a minimum of six months and usually a year.

At the surgical conferences any patients who have died during the preceding week are discussed. The intern or resident describes the patient's course—what signs and symptoms he had, what the laboratory tests on his blood showed, what his X-rays demonstrated, what operation (if any) he underwent, everything that happened to him from the time he entered the hospital till the time he died. As the intern or resident describes the case the attending surgeons—myself and other practicing surgeons in Minneapolis—ask questions and suggest alternative methods of treatment. These case presentations aren't given for the purpose of criticizing the hospital staff, but in order to learn from the cases. Occasionally the discussions get rather heated, which is all to the good; the more interest each man takes, the more all those in attendance learn.

New cases and problem patients are also presented to the audience of practicing surgeons and medical students. The hospital staff looks for suggestions on how to manage them. Since the hospital is research-oriented, there are always new methods of diagnosis and treatment discussed. The conservative surgeons and the adventurous surgeons frequently have divergent opinions on how to manage cases, and, again, the discussions often get heated and stimulating.

Regular attendance at weekly surgical conferences—even though, for me, it means a seventy-mile drive to Minneapolis —seems like a good way to stay abreast of surgical progress. I have a chance to discuss cases with other surgeons, to pick their brains, to find out how they're managing their cases and to compare their problems and procedures with mine. If it weren't for these conferences I'd have to resort solely to formal surgical meetings, such as the annual five-day meeting of the American College of Surgeons. These meetings consist of lectures, closed-circuit televised operations, and surgical movies, without the provocative discussions and arguments that make the Hennepin General conferences so stimulating.

But most afternoons I'm in my office in Litchfield, and the patients I see are usually postoperative patients. I check them three weeks and six weeks after surgery to make certain that their wounds are healing well and that they haven't developed a late complication such as a hernia or stitch abscess. These checkups don't take more than five or ten minutes each.

Other patients I see are those referred either by my partners or by the other doctors. These are patients who may or may not need operations. They're sent to me for my opinion.

Typical is Mrs. Barbara Simon. A G.P., Brian O'Connor, referred her to me as a possible candidate for a thyroidectomy after doing some thyroid tests. Brian had felt a lump on her thyroid gland when he did an insurance examination on her a few weeks earlier. After I introduced myself to her I started asking questions.

"How old are you, Mrs. Simon?"

"Thirty-five."

"When did you first notice this lump in your neck?"

"I never did notice it," she says. "Dr. O'Connor found it when he examined me."

"When was that?"

"A week ago. Last Wednesday."

"Has anything else been bothering you?"

"Like what?"

"Have you lost any weight? Have your bowels been working normally? Have you been more nervous than usual?" Weight loss, diarrhea and nervousness are all symptoms of a toxic (overactive) thyroid gland.

"No. I've felt just fine."

"Good. Now I want to examine you."

I feel Mrs. Simon's neck, asking her to swallow so that her thyroid gland will move under my fingers. She has a firm nodule—a lump—in the lower portion of the left lobe of her gland.

I feel the entire neck area looking for other lumps; thyroid growths, if they're malignant, usually spread first to the small bean-shaped lymph nodes in the neck. There are no enlarged nodes.

After I've examined her neck I examine the rest of her. A thyroid which is not functioning properly can cause changes in the eyes, the skin, even the nervous system. But none of these changes are present in Mrs. Simon.

Having completed my examination I say, "Mrs. Simon, you have in your thyroid gland a small lump which isn't causing any symptoms. It's a localized overgrowth of thyroid tissue. Now we have to decide what to do about it.

"The chances are about ninety-nine out of a hundred that it's a benign nodule, a little lump that will never bother you unless it increases in size. If that should happen, and it became unsightly, we would take it out at that time.

"There is, however, the one-in-a-hundred possibility that this could be a form of cancer. Now, if you were sixty I'd say don't worry about it; but you're not. You're thirty-five years old and you've got a long time to live. I'm afraid that if we leave that lump in there you're going to worry about it and, frankly, so will I. The risk of the operation you'd have to go through to have the lump removed is far less than one in a hundred. I'd say, since you're so healthy, that it's less than one in a thousand. So I'd recommend having it removed. What do you say?"

"I guess I'd like to get rid of it. To tell the truth I have been worried about it. When do you think it should be done?"

"There's no rush," I tell her. "We can schedule it at your convenience. I'll call Dr. O'Connor and tell him I agree with him, and then, after you've talked it over with your husband, you go and see Dr. O'Connor. He'll call me and we'll work out a suitable time."

"Fine, Dr. Nolen," Mrs. Simon says, "and thank you." She leaves.

The way I dealt with Mrs. Simon demonstrates two things I always consider.

First, I assume that every patient, no matter what his problem, is concerned either that he has cancer or that what he has "may turn into cancer." So, even when the patient doesn't bring up the subject, I do. I tell them, when I can, "Don't worry. Your problem is not cancer." Many patients are elated when I make that statement. Even patients with hernias or hemorrhoids worry that cancer may be their real problem. Where I can't be positive, as in Mrs. Simon's case, I try to give the patient the best estimate, on a percentage basis, that I can. But whether the odds are good or bad, I tell them. I know the question is on their minds.

The second point: I always try to say something nice about the referring doctor, and I make certain that the patient goes back to him. I don't want to steal patients; I don't want to take the slightest chance that the patient will switch to me or one of my partners as a family doctor. I want more referrals from Dr. O'Connor.

As soon as Mrs. Simon leaves I call Brian and tell him what I've found. There's nothing worse for a doctor than having a patient return to him before he has heard what the consultant's opinion is. He doesn't know how to treat the patient and he has to try to track down the consultant to find out what his recommendations are. It's happened to me, when I've sent patients to other consultants. I don't like the situation when it comes up and I don't want to inflict the same problem on the guys who refer to me. That's why I call right away.

Next, I see Mrs. Sue Warner. I know Sue and her husband, Paul. We play bridge with them. They're good friends.

"This is a pleasant surprise, Sue," I say. "What can I do for you?"

"You may think it's pleasant, Bill," she says, attempting a smile, "but I don't. I was just in to see Steve [one of my partners] for my annual checkup and he found a lump in my breast. He wants to see what you think about it."

Breast lumps are serious business, and although I'm still cheerful I make certain that Sue knows I'm concerned. I leave while my office nurse puts a gown on her and then I come back in and examine Sue's breasts. She has a lump, about an inch in diameter, in the upper outer portion of her left breast.

There are a lot of things about breast lumps that may suggest malignancy: if the skin over the lump is shriveled (the so-called *peau d'orange*, or orange skin), if the lump is stuck to the underlying muscles, if it is very hard or large—all these things make the possibility of malignancy in the lump more likely. But even when these findings are absent, and there are no enlarged glands in the axilla suggesting spread, the surgeon still can't be certain. Sue had none of these suggestive findings;

this was encouraging. Still, the lump would have to come out.

"Sue," I said, after I'd completed my examination and she had dressed, "that lump you've got doesn't feel like a bad tumor to me. I think it's a cyst. But you know—you've read enough—that I'll have to take it out to be certain."

"I was sure you would, Bill. I'll have to talk to Paul, of course, and arrange for a baby-sitter, but that shouldn't be a problem. When can you do it?"

One of the nice things about practicing in Litchfield is that generally we have no bed problem. I can schedule cases for any day I choose, with the exception of weekends when we limit the O.R. schedule to emergencies. I knew Sue would want the lump out as soon as possible; any woman would.

"I've got a gall bladder and a hernia to do tomorrow," I tell her, "but if you can come into the hospital tonight I'll get to you by eleven in the morning."

"I'm sure I can arrange it, Bill. Let's plan on it."

"Right, and, Sue, tell Paul to call me if he'd like. I'll be glad to talk to him if it will ease his mind."

Sue thanked me and left the office.

I hadn't bothered to explain to Sue how I'd approach this operation. She's an intelligent woman, and like most intelligent women, she knew what would happen. I'd take out the lump and give it to our pathologist. He'd freeze it immediately and examine it under the microscope. If it was benign I'd close the wound and Sue would be back in her room ten minutes later; if it was malignant and if Sue agreed I'd probably do a more extensive operation. I'd talk with Sue and Paul later about the various operations I might do. I'd let them know what choices we had. This was not the time for that sort of discussion.

So the afternoon goes. Take out some stitches, talk to a possible gall bladder case, sew up a laceration, possibly even run over to the hospital to do an emergency appendectomy. I keep reasonably busy most of the time.

When I'm not, when there's a lull between patients, I go down to my basement office, drink Sanka and read. There are always surgical journals to peruse—keeping up is a never-ending problem—and when I'm tired of reading medical literature I turn to general magazines or books. I always bring whatever book or magazine I'm currently reading to the office with me.

By five o'clock, unless it's an exceptionally busy day, I've seen the last of my patients. I drive over to the hospital, visit any particularly ill patients, and briefly check the patients I've operated on earlier in the day. By five-thirty I'm home. And the evening begins.

8

Nights in Litchfield

During the school year, unless we're going out for the evening, we eat about six fifteen. We can't eat earlier because there's always at least one child involved in some school activity, like football practice or rehearsal for a school play, which keeps him or her tied up till at least six. Joan refuses to prepare two dinners. I don't blame her.

We have a rule, frequently broken, that the children are to stay out of the living room between five o'clock and dinner time. During that interval Joan and I talk, read the paper, and may have a drink.

After dinner the kids study or watch television. Joan and I read. I get to bed about ten; Joan, since she's a night person, stays up till twelve or one, or two, depending on how engrossing her book or the TV movie is.

Once or twice a week I get called to the hospital in the evening, to sew up a cut, see some kid with a bellyache or set a fracture. Occasionally I have to operate—take out an appendix, repair a perforated ulcer or fish a clot out of an artery. It might happen three times in a week, or I might not be called for a month. I'm not pestered anywhere near as often as the G.P.'s who see kids with earaches, men with heart attacks or women in labor. Most of the G.P.'s average at least one trip to the hospital a night, and the popular ones are called even more often.

What I've described, briefly, is a typical evening in Litchfield. It applies only to weekday nights in the school season. Over a calendar year I'd estimate that only about one-third of our evenings are "typical." (I realize that this makes a "typical" evening untypical, but you know what I mean.)

At least two nights a week Joan and I go out. Almost invariably there's a party somewhere on Saturday night—often at our house—and at least one other night a week we'll go out to dinner at the golf club, play bridge or go to a movie.

The social life in Litchfield is very active. It can get to be too active if you let it. This is one of the traps you have to avoid if you live in a small town.

For example, whenever Joan and I go out to the Golf Club for dinner, we find, quite naturally in a city of five thousand, that we know almost everyone who is there. It's impossible to walk in without someone inviting us over for a drink. And we go; we're very weak-willed. We have a drink, dinner and wind up staying out till eleven or twelve. We waste a lot of time having "fun."

If you get the impression that liquor plays a role in the social life in Litchfield, you're correct. About as it does everywhere else. People are no different about alcohol here than they are in New York or Los Angeles.

Actually, though we and our friends often have a drink or two in the evening, no one in Litchfield—with the exception of the out-and-out alcoholics—does any significant drinking during the day.

There's no opportunity. The only places in town that serve liquor are the Legion Club, the Vets Club, and the Golf Club, and none of these open till 4:30 P.M. If you're going out to lunch you have to choose between the Litchfield Hotel, the Truck Stop Cafe, The Farmer's Daughter, and the Traveler's Inn. None of these has a liquor license so in Litchfield the three-martini lunch is an impossibility.

Of the three watering spots in town—only the Golf Club is open continuously from 4:30 P.M. till midnight. The Legion and the Vets Club are open from 4:30 till 6:30, during which time they pour a lot of liquor, but they close from 6:30 till

7:30. This forces a lot of men to interrupt their social drinking and go home for supper. After eating, only the hardy ones
with exceptionally tolerant wives return to the bar to continue
their drinking. That one-hour hiatus undoubtedly saves a lot
of Litchfieldites from themselves.

During the school year school activities take up about one
evening a week. Anyone with six kids can understand why. In
the fall, for example, we see three football games a week.
Friday nights we watch Jimmy play football with the varsity;
Monday nights Billy plays with the tenth-grade team; Julius
plays at five on Thursday with the seventh grade.

During the winter we get involved through our kids in
watching hockey and swimming. We also go to the band
concerts and choral-group recitals, though we haven't a single
offspring who can carry a tune in a bucket. (Which is sur-
prising since I'm a very enthusiastic singer. I know all the
words to almost every song written between 1941 and 1947,
and will sing one or all of them whenever requested to do so.
Not a common occurrence.) We see most of the high school
plays.

Two or three nights a week and on Sunday afternoons, from
early December till March, I play hockey. There are a dozen
of us more mature individuals (I hate the word "older") who
still like to skate, and we scrimmage among ourselves or
with the high school and college kids. We play three or four
games every year against teams from other towns, and if I do
say so, we play pretty well. I come home from these games, or
scrimmages, completely exhausted. But I love it. And it keeps
me in reasonable shape till the tennis season returns.

I've mentioned the Litchfield house parties, at which we
spend most of our Saturday nights. Now let me elaborate.

They're about like most parties we've been to in the other
cities where we've lived. Starting time is seven or seven thirty.
Cocktails for two hours, give or take a half hour, and then
dinner. After eating, if the meal has been fairly light, there
may be enough people who aren't half asleep so that we start
dancing.

Ordinarily, after dinner we sit around drinking coffee and

talking—soberly, as opposed to the pre-dinner drinking chatter. After drinking and eating I get awfully sleepy and I'm usually ready to go home. But Joan never wants to leave until the last gun is fired. She's always wide-awake, even after a heavy dinner. So if the party is in my home I often excuse myself after dinner and go to bed. If it's at someone else's house I occasionally go home alone. Joan gets a ride from some other couple later.

Sometimes, at a Litchfield party, there's a little hanky-panky, but rarely anything serious. When Sally Bannister gets tight she likes to dance with whomever she's with into a dark corner and kiss him rather heavily, but nothing more. It doesn't seem to bother her husband, Sid. He figures if that's her way of having fun, what the hell. He'd just as soon sit and drink.

There are in Litchfield, just as there are in every other city, certain women who exude sex. If the party begins to swing a bit, and some husband starts to bird-dog one of these sexy wenches, the appropriate wife may get up-tight and look daggers at both her husband and the sexy one. But there's rarely anything said—till they get home, that is, and I can't report on that.

In the twelve years I've been here there has been damn little scandal in Litchfield. No husband, to my knowledge, has been caught in bed with another man's wife, or vice versa. If there's a lot of that stuff going on, I'm unaware of it; and I don't think I'm unaware of much that's happening here. Either *Couples* was an exaggeration, or the Midwest has got a long way to go—downhill—to catch up with the Eastern towns. Or another possibility: the husbands and wives here may be cleverer than those elsewhere. I wouldn't rule that out.

While I'm on the subject of party nights I may as well mention the Golf Club parties. They're held on the first Saturday of every month. There's always a theme—the luau in August, complete with the pig on a spit; a Halloween costume party in October; Las Vegas Night in February, with paper money for gambling: the same themes country clubs all over the country use as an excuse for parties.

Basically all the Golf Club parties here and, as far as I've been able to determine by talking to friends and relatives, elsewhere are the same. Everyone gets boozed up, the men with temperate wives eat, those with drinking wives don't, or at least not till about midnight. Everyone dances. Once in a while a husband, whose wife isn't watching, manages to hustle a wife, whose husband is otherwise occupied, outside for a few passionate kisses; otherwise, it's just like a house party.

Frequently, when the bar closes at 1 A.M., someone will suggest, "Everyone come to my place for bacon and eggs." Usually a man makes the suggestion; the wife, depending on her mood, will either agree jovially or snarl and accept her fate. Another drink may precede the coffee, bacon and eggs—sometimes there's a little dancing—and everyone leaves at about 3 A.M. Fortunately there is little traffic in Litchfield at that time (or at any time, for that matter) and in the twelve years I've been here no one has had a serious accident on the drive home. Usually, unless the husband is one of those guys who insists, "I'm perfectly sober and, goddam it, I'm going to drive," the wife acts as chauffeur.

Sunday, for the vast majority of those who attended the party, is pure hell.

I've recapped the Litchfield Golf Club Saturday-night party scene because, on more than one occasion, we've been part of it. Not as often in the last few years—how many Las Vegas parties can any man take?—but often enough. It's part of our "way of life."

A point that seems to fit well here, and that's pertinent to my role as a surgeon, is that when I do get a bit tight at a Golf Club party in the presence of a large segment of the Litchfield population, many of whom are my patients, it doesn't seem to bother my practice. Actually, on those occasions when Joan gets angry and chews me out for drinking too much—which she does every time it happens—other people at the party invariably come to my defense. "Let him alone, Joan," they'll say, "he's always under an awful lot of pressure and he needs to blow off some steam. It's good for him." Their reasoning is really a lot of nonsense, I shouldn't get boiled any more than anyone else. But it's nice to have people come to my aid. (But it really makes Joan mad. She knows this excuse is nonsense.)

A few more points about the Golf Club, since it's the center of social life in Litchfield.

Membership is relatively inexpensive. For twenty-five dollars a couple can buy a social membership for a year; for a hundred and twenty-five dollars you can get a full golfing membership for the entire family. There's no swimming pool, nor are there any tennis courts, but the food, the drinks and the nine-hole course are fine.

One of the results of the relatively low charge for membership is that just about anyone in Litchfield can afford to join. We have teachers, farmers, lawyers, postmen—men from every walk of life—who belong to the club and play in the golf league. In big-city private golf clubs, the high membership fees and the quotas make the clubs extremely homogeneous—mostly professional men and executives with incomes of thirty-five thousand dollars or more. The Litchfield Club is much more heterogeneous and democratic. I like it that way.

What else do we do at night? Sometimes, usually on weekends, we go to Minneapolis. We go to the Guthrie Theatre, to the North Star hockey games, to an occasional jazz concert. We like movies and once in a while we'll drive to Minneapolis, see a film in the afternoon, have dinner, and go to another film in the evening. Sometimes we go to three different films, mostly foreign or X-rated movies that won't play in Litchfield's one theater.

Living in Litchfield, we find that we see as many movies, as many sporting events, as many concerts, as do our friends in Minneapolis. More than most. And by going to New York for a few days every year, we see as many musicals and plays as do the majority of our friends in the East. (Admittedly, it takes money to fly to New York once a year; but it would cost us a lot more to live there.)

Summer evenings are even less organized than they are during the school year. Our kids have a wide variety of interests and it's difficult to get them all together for meals. So we don't. Meals in the summer are strictly a seat-of-the-pants affair.

We've got a cabin on Lake Minnie Belle, six miles out of

town. Joan spends most of the day there and at five o'clock I join her. Any of the kids that want to come out with me can; those that don't stay in town. If there's one thing that can ruin a day or an evening at the lake it's some offspring moaning, "There's nothing to do around here." Usually it's the older kids who want to stay in town with their friends, and we let them eat TV dinners, hamburgers, hot dogs or anything else they can fix themselves. Their diets are anything but balanced, but they seem to be quite healthy.

At the lake I take a short swim, fix a drink and read. We don't eat till nine or ten. After dinner Joan or I go back to Litchfield to sleep. We trust our kids within limits, but not enough to leave them in town alone. Our philosophy is, basically, "You trust your children but you cut the cards."

We often entertain at our lake place. Nothing fancy—hamburgers, hot dogs, potato salad—but the chance to swim and water-ski (which bores me to pieces) gives our guests, and us, something different to do.

That's about it. Our lives aren't exceptionally exciting, but they are full and, for the most part, enjoyable. We like Litchfield—it's a nice place to live—but I hope my children will leave here, at least for a few years, and live in other parts of the country or the world. I want them to be able to compare life in Litchfield with life elsewhere. Then, if they choose to come back and settle here, they'll know what they're passing up.

9

My Writing Career

One of the major reasons why Litchfield is "right" for me is that it gives me a chance to pursue two careers: to be a writer as well as a surgeon.

If I were living in a big city where there were a lot of surgeons, I'd have a very difficult time holding on to a practice. When a doctor writes frankly and openly about medical issues like malpractice, fee-splitting, unnecessary radical surgery, as I've been doing for several years, he's apt to rile the conservative segment of his profession to which the vast majority of doctors belong. They don't want anyone rocking the medical boat and they aren't apt to send patients to a surgeon who upsets them.

Since I'm the only surgeon in the county I've got a captive clientele. As long as I do my surgical work well and act like a decent person, the local doctors aren't going to send their business elsewhere. In Litchfield I can speak my mind; I couldn't do that, and survive as a surgeon, in most other places.

Anyone who thinks I'm exaggerating ought to read the mail I get from doctors after I've said something they don't like.

It's much easier to earn a living as a surgeon than as a writer. In my role as a surgeon I can get out of bed, go to the hospital, take the gall bladder out of one patient and the appendix out of another, and be five hundred dollars richer by ten in the morning. I can spend two weeks writing an article; when I've finished, it may earn me five hundred dollars. On the other hand, it may earn nothing. I never know.

A gall bladder operation—any operation—has a well-defined beginning and end. Once you've become a surgeon, most operations are relatively routine. Open the abdomen, take out the organ, close the abdomen; step one, step two, step three. After a while it becomes rather like baking a cake, following a recipe you've used hundreds of times.

Writing, on the other hand, never becomes routine. Every time a writer picks up a pencil and a blank sheet of paper he faces a completely new challenge. There are no guidelines to follow, no step-by-step routine. He's never sure that he's going to be able to get the job done in a decent fashion. It's frightening.

I'd never have the courage to try to earn a living solely as a writer. The pressure would be too great for me. I don't think I could stand the strain of waiting for the mail every morning, hoping that somebody will send me a check for something I've written; dreading the sight of a manuscript, returning in its self-addressed envelope, with a form letter that reads, "Thank you for submitting this to us. Unfortunately it does not meet our present needs. The Editors." Even now I hate the sight of a returned manuscript, and if I had to depend exclusively on writing to feed my family, I'd probably beat up any editor who turned me down. As it is, I can go to the hospital, operate and earn a living. My admiration of the courageous men and women who work solely as free-lance writers knows no bounds.

Since 1968 I've devoted about two hours a day to writing. Since this book is at least in part about my personal experiences, it seems reasonable to include a chapter on my writing.

When I was in surgical training in Bellevue I co-authored my first article, a little gem entitled "Carcinoma of the infrapapillary portion of the duodenum." It was the report of a patient we'd operated on, a woman with the disease mentioned in the title. Carcinoma, i.e., cancer, is very rare in this portion of the intestine. When we encountered it in this patient we did an operation which failed to cure her; as a matter of fact, she died of the operation. Since there were only eighteen other cases like this in the world literature we "wrote it up," reasoning that perhaps someone would read the article, benefit from our experience, and do a different operation than the one we had done if he ever ran across a case. The article was published in *Surgery*, February 1956.

Ham that I am, I got a big kick out of seeing my name in print, even as co-author of a minor article in a tiny journal. By the time it was published I was in the army, and since I had some spare time, I decided to write another article.

This one was entitled "Inadequate Operation for Pyloric Stenosis," and was a case report of another failure. The patient in this instance was a three-week-old boy with a benign tumor at the lower end, the pylorus, of his stomach. It's not a rare disease and the operation isn't terribly difficult, though it is a bit delicate. The surgeon cuts through the thick muscular coat of the pylorus down to the inner lining, the mucosa. He then spreads the muscle fibers apart, unblocking the end of the stomach. The trick is to cut all the thickened muscle, but not to nick the inner lining. If all the muscle isn't cut, the lower end of the stomach won't unblock; but if you cut too deeply and open the mucosa the patient may get peritonitis.

I had never seen the operation done, but I thought I could manage it. I did it under local anesthesia, after looking up the technique in a book, and everything seemed to go well. The baby, however, continued to vomit. Three weeks later, when he was six weeks old and still weighed only six pounds, I re-operated on him. Thinking back on it, I'm amazed that I had the courage—perhaps "stupidity" would be a better word. I found that the muscle fibers had healed together, reblocking the end of the stomach. I hadn't spread them sufficiently. I redid the operation and the baby made an uneventful, rapid recovery. This was a very strong baby.

I reported the operation; the point, such as it was, was to warn other surgeons to be sure to spread all the muscle fibers. The article was published in the *Archives of Surgery*. It's amazing, the amount of insignificant junk that clutters up the medical literature.

Again I enjoyed the thrill of seeing my name in print. I was driven on to even greater heights. I did some research and "authored," as we doctors say, two more medical articles, "The Use and Abuse of Antibiotics in One Small Community" and "The Incidence of Drug Resistant Pathogenic Staphylococci in an Isolated Community." You've probably read both of them; they were published in the *New England Journal of Medicine*. But if you haven't just write to me; I've got hundreds of reprints of each. (Medical journals, like most scientific journals, not only don't pay their authors, they charge them for reprints, which the author can then send to anyone who requests one.)

By the time these last two articles appeared I was back at Bellevue, working very long hours, and though I had the inclination I didn't have the time (not really; I know now that I could have found the time) to write. It wasn't till 1960, when I went into private practice in Litchfield, that I ventured into the writing game again.

My first effort, published as an editorial in *Surgery, Gynecology and Obstetrics*, was entitled "Surgery and the Pursuit of Happiness." At the time I wrote it I had been in Litchfield about six months and was very bitter about the fact that I wasn't being sent many patients. Happiness, to me, was a great big waiting room full of patients who needed operations. My article was a diatribe against the blindness and selfishness of all the doctors who wouldn't send their patients to young, eager surgeons, like me. Judging from the flock of requests that I received for reprints, there were a great many young surgeons who felt as I did.

Since *Surgery, Gynecology and Obstetrics* is *the* surgical journal, I felt that I had reached the top in the field of non-remunerative writing. After publishing, as sole author, an editorial in this prestigious journal there was nowhere to go but down. Now, to make any measurable progress with my writing, I had to sell something.

Medical Economics is one of the many journals that are dumped at regular intervals, gratis, on the desk of each practicing physician. It is, according to regularly conducted surveys, always among the readership leaders. This seems reasonable; all doctors, regardless of specialty, have one interest in common—money. *Medical Economics* tells them how to earn as much as possible and what tricks may help them hang on to what they earn.

But the magazine treats a multitude of subjects; it's possible, when you think about it, to relate any and everything to money. As a regular reader I noted that some of the articles were written by practicing physicians. The magazine even solicited, in occasional advertisements, contributions from doctors. I decided to contribute.

I wrote a piece entitled "What's Wrong With Small Town Practice?" By this time, 1962, I had become established as the first and only specialist in Litchfield, and I wrote the piece to say that disgruntled specialists in the big cities might find professional satisfaction if they moved to small towns.

The idea wasn't bad, but the article was horrible. I didn't know it at the time, of course, but I do now. I had written a lengthy essay without a single personal touch; I had written as I had for medical journals, rather than in the style of *Medical Economics*. It didn't work.

Fortunately my manuscript reached the hands of a *Medical Economics* editor who was kind enough not to throw it directly into the wastebasket. Instead, he returned it to me with some suggestions to guide me in rewriting it. Encouraged, I went back at it, and the second time around they bought it.

I was delighted. I had earned my first check—for seventy-five dollars—as a writer. I could have picked up twice that by snipping out an appendix in one-tenth the time it had taken me to write and rewrite the article; but this was different, this was special, as anyone who has ever sold a line knows.

My spirits were dampened a bit when the piece was eventually published; it appeared as a picture essay, with perhaps twenty lines of my original prose—but by that time I had a fairly severe infection with the writing bug. I had learned in this first venture that if you wanted to sell to a magazine, it wasn't a bad idea to write in the style that was characteristic of their articles. I caught on to the *Medical Economics* style and quickly sold them two more pieces.

These two articles, on fee-splitting and malpractice, were published under pseudonyms. They were, I thought, honest articles, but they were critical of the medical profession and I was afraid I'd feel the wrath of organized medicine if I put my name on them. (I subsequently said, "To hell with it," and haven't used a pseudonym in six years. I've occasionally been rapped on the knuckles by organized medicine but it has never bothered me. When I write, I'm right.)

Now it was 1963, I had sold three articles to *Medical Economics*, and on the strength of these, I was invited to become a contributing editor. I was expected to produce one publishable article every two months. At this point I developed the habit which, to my way of thinking, allowed me, finally, to classify myself, albeit loosely, as a writer; I started writing every day. (William Faulkner once said, when asked when he wrote, "I write every time the spirit moves me, and the spirit moves me every day.")

This was a difficult habit for me to acquire. I'm a day person —I function best between 7 A.M. and noon—so, naturally, that's when I prefer to write. But I could hardly say to my patient, "I'm sorry, Mrs. Wilems, I have to write this morning while I'm fresh. This afternoon, when I'm sleepy and not really much good at anything, I'll take out your gall bladder." That just wouldn't work.

So I had to devise a system that allowed me to both write and operate in the morning. It wasn't as difficult as it sounds. I simply stopped wasting time.

Mornings, after I fed the kids, I'd sit and write—even if it were just between seven thirty and seven fifty. It's amazing how much a man can write in twenty minutes. If I didn't have to operate till eight thirty I'd get an hour of writing done.

I started bringing a pad with me to the hospital. If I had made my rounds and had ten minutes between cases, I'd write. Once I had an idea and had the article started, I could make progress even in these brief interludes.

I stopped seeing patients electively in the morning. As a

surgeon I don't have a big office practice. Instead of seeing patients now and then all day, I prefer to see them one right after the other in a shorter period of time. Without morning appointments I could finish operating, return to my office and often have an hour of writing time left.

I gave up watching Laurel and Hardy. I'd have to say that this was the sacrifice I found most difficult to make. I think their films are hilarious. But their old movies are on television, in Minnesota, from ten to eleven on Sunday morning, and Sunday morning is prime writing time. I could get a lot done on Sunday, so Laurel and Hardy had to go.

Now, let me admit—any writer will know this to be true without my saying it—I don't write three hundred and sixty-five days a year. No one has that much self-discipline. I still sneak an occasional look at Stan and Ollie—I can't resist. But the point is that I began in 1963 to write damn near every day. I acquired then that bit of self-discipline that is the single most important quality that any writer must have. As someone said, "The most difficult thing about writing is applying the seat of the pants to the seat of the chair." There are dozens of aphorisms in the same vein, such as, "No one likes to write—everyone likes to have written." They are all true. I stuck at writing regularly till I reached the point when any day I didn't write I felt guilty as the devil. I still do.

If I were writing *The Seven Storey Mountain*, I'd say that at this point in time I had reached the base of the third and most difficult peak. I started trying to sell to the general-circulation magazines.

I made all the usual mistakes. I failed to study my market; I didn't even read some of the magazines to which I was sending my stuff. I never checked to see if the subject about which I was writing had been covered recently in one magazine or another. I didn't even know enough, till I lost a few articles, to include a self-addressed stamped envelope so that the editor would return my article rather than just toss it in the wastebasket.

These were all bad enough, but my worst mistake, by far, was that I wrote on subjects about which I knew nothing. I still remember the first thing I sent out. It was a short story called, heaven help me, "Momma Wouldn't Like It," about a Jewish mother. I'm one hundred percent of Irish ancestry, so you can imagine what this story was like. I sent it, of course, to the magazine to which every innocent beginning writer sends his fiction, *The New Yorker.* I still cringe when I think about it. I can just imagine the editors passing my manuscript around the room, each doubling up in laughter as he or she read it.

I wrote on politics for the *New York Times Magazine,* wrote light verse for *Look,* and even wrote a nifty little number called "When He Cut Out My Appendix, He Stole Away My Heart" for *True Confessions.* I think *Cavalier* still has the original manuscript of my pornographic short story, "Booby Trap," all about this luscious tomato with big boobs. (If the editor does have it please contact me; I'll pay well just to get it back.)

For five years I sent manuscripts out, and for five years they came back. Two weeks, to the day, for a round trip to *The New Yorker;* three weeks, give or take a week, for *Esquire.* When a manuscript I had sent to *Playboy* didn't return for six weeks, my hopes soared. I refused to leave my home for the clinic in the morning till the mail was delivered. I knew I shouldn't be overly optimistic, but I couldn't help myself. As it turned out, when I finally wrote asking if the editors had reached a decision, I was told the manuscript had simply been misplaced. They returned it with their apologies.

I read somewhere that George Bernard Shaw wrote six pages a day for six years, and had completed six novels, before he ever sold a line. Then, it wasn't one of the novels that he sold, but a play. Shaw had great faith in himself.

I'm not certain that I would have had enough self-confidence to sustain me through five years of rejection slips if I hadn't been selling regularly to *Medical Economics.* I just figured that if I could sell to them, I ought to be able to sell elsewhere. So I stuck at it.

After the first four years I came to the conclusion that I had better stick with medical or paramedical subjects. These were the things I knew something about; and having learned by then to read the magazines to which I was trying to sell, I could see that there was a market for medically oriented pieces. Nearly every one of the mass-circulation magazines ran a medical article almost every month. Diets, the pill, cancer—people wanted to read about these things.

In November 1967 I had my first near miss.

My brother-in-law, a thirty-eight-year-old businessman with five children, had recently choked to death on a piece of steak while attending a banquet. He had died, in the prime of his life, in otherwise excellent health, just because not one of the thousand other men at that banquet knew how to perform a tracheotomy, a relatively simple operation that anyone, with an average I.Q., could be taught to perform. His life had been needlessly lost.

I was frustrated and furious. Damn it, I thought, why the hell don't we doctors teach the lay public how to do a tracheotomy. We teach artificial respiration, cardiac massage, all sorts of other first-aid techniques; but we refuse to teach them how to do the one thing, the only thing, that will save a choking victim.

I looked into the subject, wrote an article entitled "How to Perform a Tracheotomy," and sent it off to *Esquire*.

They kept it a month, and I got hopeful, but it finally came back. Not, however, with the form rejection slip. Instead, there was a long, encouraging letter, which said, "Although we are not going to publish it, we're certain you'll be able to sell it elsewhere."

Esquire was, I suppose, afraid of the legal ramifications. It's a gutsy magazine, but I imagine the lawyers could envision some guy grabbing a knife and laying someone's neck open, after shouting, as he came to the rescue, "I read how to do it in *Esquire*." In retrospect their fears may have been reasonable.

Subsequently, through a free-lance writer whom I knew at *Medical Economics,* I placed this article with an agent. He tried it on a dozen other magazines, without success. The *Reader's Digest*'s refusal, as I recall, said, "Though it's a fascinating piece I find it hard to believe this sort of thing is for the amateur." The piece never sold.

However, I now had an agent, and a few months later, I got an idea for another article. I decided to write about the first appendectomy I'd ever performed. I could remember the entire event most vividly—I subsequently learned that most surgeons have vivid memories of their first appendectomy—and, I reasoned, if the operation impressed me to that extent, possibly it might also interest lay readers. The point of telling the story was to let the readers know that all surgeons must begin somewhere, that for each of us there is a first operation, and that when we perform it we are not dexterous, self-confident, polished surgeons like the Caseys and Kildares of television fame; we are nervous bumblers who can hardly tie our own shoelaces. I wrote it and sent it off to my agent, with the suggestion that it might sell to the *Reader's Digest*. I was impressed by the twenty-five hundred dollars that the *Digest* advertisements offered for true first-person stories.

My agent read it and sent back a note which said, "If it doesn't sell to the *Digest* it won't sell anywhere. It's frightening."

It didn't sell to the *Digest*—I should have realized, and certainly my agent should have realized, that it wasn't their style. My agent returned it to me.

One of the unwritten laws of the author–agent relationship is that the author must have trust in the agent's judgment. If the agent says an article won't sell, the author puts it either in the wastebasket or on his shelf. He doesn't try to sell it on his own.

In 1968 I didn't know this. When my agent returned the article I thought, What the hell, I went to all the trouble of writing this, it may as well be in the mail as on my desk, and I sent it off to *Esquire*. I had no strong feelings about the piece. I liked it, naturally, but I had liked others. I was no more hopeful about "The Appendix Is Where You Find It" than I had been about dozens of other things I'd written.

I mailed it on a Saturday. Two weeks later, on Saturday morning, I was home, having a cup of Sanka before going to the office, when the mail arrived. Among other things the mail included an envelope from *Esquire*, manuscript size, the same sort of envelope in which they had returned others of my manuscripts.

I suffered through my usual few moments of depression—I was almost used to them now—and proceeded to open the envelope and remove the manuscript, wondering where, if anywhere, I should now send it. Lo and behold, clipped to the manuscript was a small, typewritten note. I could quote it verbatim, but I'll spare you; the essence of it was, We'll buy it.

I'm still unable to write well enough to tell anyone how elated that brief note made me. I'd guess I might have had the feeling a woman has when she gives birth. I wouldn't trade that moment with Neil Armstrong for the chance to be "first" on the moon.

I woke Joan—it was only nine thirty in the morning—and she got out of bed to savor the news with me. I called a couple of close friends who I knew could appreciate and wouldn't resent my success. That evening we opened a bottle of champagne that we'd had in the refrigerator for more than two years; I'd been saving it to celebrate with when I sold my first article to a general-circulation magazine.

A few weeks later I sent two more articles to my agent and, in the cover letter, I mentioned—very innocently—the sale to *Esquire*.

A week later he returned the articles to me with a terse note, the gist of which was, I am not the proper agent for you. I didn't understand his reaction till I learned, later, about the niceties of the author–agent relationship.

The *Esquire* sale opened a new door for me. From Dan Brennan, a Minneapolis novelist, I got the name of another agent. I wrote to him, told him about the *Esquire* piece, and asked if he'd consider reading my articles. He agreed, but said, "I prefer to sell books. If you think you have a book or two in you, we can start with the articles."

It had never occurred to me to try a book; the sheer bulk of the writing required was enough to discourage me. It didn't seem like the sort of thing I could turn out between operations —in less than ten years, that is. But my new agent's suggestion made me reexamine the possibility, and after he had sold two articles for me, I got a book idea. First I thought I might write about Bellevue Hospital, the scene of my first appendectomy; but gradually this idea evolved into the idea of writing, for the layman, a book about what it's like to go through five years of surgical training. I thought that if readers could enjoy an article on my first appendectomy, they might like to read about all the experiences a man goes through on his way to becoming a surgeon.

The idea lent itself to a logical subdivision—the training took five years, each with its own special demands—and I began to write about year one. I had finished the first fifty pages and had sent them off to my agent when my article about the appendectomy appeared in *Esquire* in November 1968. (There may still be a few copies available, though I think I bought most of them myself.)

At this point I got a real break; the editor in chief at Random House read the article, liked it, contacted my agent and asked if I was thinking of writing a book. My agent sent the fifty pages to him and we got a contract for my projected book. I had been very lucky.

Writing a book was different from writing an article. I won't go into it in detail; suffice it to say that the thought of the two hundred and fifty unwritten pages I had contracted to write made me extremely tense. I'd wake at night to scribble ideas on pads; in the middle of a conversation I'd suddenly grab my notebook out of my pocket and dash down a thought. I was rather rapidly driving Joan and my kids out of their minds. I finally took a week off, checked into a motel in Litchfield and did nothing but write. This precipitated a lot of local gossip— "Has Joan finally thrown him out?"—but it did the job. I wrote seven hours the first day, five the second, three the third. At that point I could hardly stand the sight of a blank sheet of paper, but I had enough of the book written so that I felt I was in control. I went back to two hours a day, which, for me, is about as long as I can write without going stale.

I finished the first draft, rewrote and rewrote again. Someone said—I'm full of these quotes—"The secret of good writing is good rewriting." He or she was right. Toward the end I would become almost physically ill at the sight of my manuscript, back from Random House "for a few more touches," but the editor kept after me and I'm glad. I'm sure it helped.

The book came out and I learned something else; it's almost as hard to sell a book as it is to write it. (Publishers have known this for years, as have experienced writers, but it was a great surprise to me.) Helping to sell it was a new experience, exhausting but stimulating, and though it wore me out, I enjoyed it.

That experience—I could write reams about it—took me through the winter of 1970–71. Since that time I've been back here in Litchfield, living my life.

Which, as of today, includes working as a surgeon, enjoying myself as a husband and father, and bleeding a little every day as a writer.

I've got a nice life, and I wouldn't want to give up any part of it.

II

10

The Litchfield Clinic

The first decision a man has to make when he goes into practice is whether to stay solo or join a group. I chose the latter. The Litchfield Clinic, of which I'm a member, is fairly typical of the group practices that have existed for years in small towns around the Midwest and that are now becoming common everywhere.

As I said before, in our group there are six doctors, five G.P.'s and me. Our ages range from thirty-five to seventy-two and, naturally, we all have our own outside interests. Some of my partners like to hunt and fish, one is interested in architecture, another is a ham radio operator. We're all friends, but once we leave the clinic building we lead our own social and business lives.

Professionally, however, we all have similar goals. We want to practice good medicine and earn a decent living, but we're not interested in dying prematurely of overwork in order to leave a pile of money to our heirs. As soon as we find that there are more patients coming to the clinic than we can comfortably handle we start looking around for another partner, even if it means a temporary drop in income, as it usually does. The group has grown from two to six in about twenty years, which is consistent with the growth of the county.

Harold Wilmot is our senior man, seventy-two years old. He started practicing in Litchfield in 1927. In the last few

years he has delivered the grandchildren of mothers he delivered when he first came here. Now the babies are delivered
in the hospital; in 1927 most of the babies Harold delivered
were born at home.

Dr. Harold, as he's known (to distinguish him from his
brother, Dr. Cecil Wilmot), remembers patients dying of scar-
let fever, pneumonia, infected wounds—ailments that we cure
now with a couple of shots of penicillin. He remembers when
doctors didn't have an awful lot to offer patients except compassion. Now he gives them all the newest remedies—he has
kept up with medical progress—but unlike some of us, he gives
them compassion too. He'll still make house calls to farms,
miles out of town, just as he did forty years ago, and he'll drive
his patients in to the hospital or the office if they need a ride.
I'm sure he never worries about whether the patient can or
can't pay him; he just tries to help his patients out.

Harold is an able doctor. When I have a patient with an
abdominal problem—someone who I suspect may have a perforated ulcer or a hot appendix but can't be certain about—
Harold's the doctor I bring in as a consultant. Harold has
examined an awful lot of abdomens in his lifetime and his
clinical judgment is excellent.

His patients are the most loyal I've ever seen. When Dr.
Harold is gone his patients refuse to see anyone else unless
they've got a problem that just can't wait for his return.

Cecil Wilmot—Dr. Cecil—is sixty. His biggest problem is
keeping patients away. He commands a following about as
loyal as Harold's.

Cecil is the most considerate man I know. He never rushes
a patient, calmly listens to long, involved rambling histories
of their illnesses, and always takes the time to explain to them
exactly why he's ordering the pill or treatment he thinks appropriate. He has the warmth that used to be considered
characteristic of the true family doctor. He numbers among
his patients people whom the rest of us avoid at all costs, people whose style and personality would irritate any other doctor
beyond endurance. Cecil treats them all as if they were his

best friends. Cecil likes his patients. His patients love Cecil. Cecil has heart.

Fred Schnell is our worker. He sees more patients most days than I see in a week. He has difficulty saying no to anyone; as a consequence his schedule never has an opening and he has patients sitting in the waiting room hoping to fill any vacant moments that a cancellation might bring.

Even with this heavy load, Fred never slights anyone. True, he doesn't spend too much time with any one patient—most of the patients he sees, and this is true of any general practitioner, have minor ailments, easily and quickly diagnosed and treated—but his patients don't expect much time. They know he's busy, they're happy that he'll see them, and they figure two minutes with Fred is worth ten with anyone else.

Fred is the perfect example of the adage, "If you want something done, take it to a busy man." He serves on more civic boards, does more for Litchfield, than almost anyone else in town. He has a knack for organizing, for building, for raising money, and he throws himself into civic projects—productive ones, not just "busy work"—with the same enthusiasm and ability he applies to his medical practice. I get tired just watching him work.

Dan Johnson is thirty-five. He grew up in a small town— Tyler, Minnesota, population 1,138—where his father was the doctor. With his background he was a natural for our group.

Dan hustles as Fred does, has the tolerance of Cecil, keeps up with things, like Harold. He got into medicine, as I did, in the "new" era, so he's reluctant to chase out into the country on house calls; but when asked, he goes. He'd never shirk the call off on one of his partners—as I might.

Dan is the kind of doctor, the dedicated G.P., that medical schools produced in quantity thirty years ago, but rarely now. He's the kind of doctor the public is crying for.

Cecil Leitch is our swinger. At thirty-five he centers the first line on our city hockey team, is turned on by the same music as the college kids and at parties can outdance any one of them, plays golf and tennis and hunts a lot. During the duck season he and Dan don't often get to the hospital before nine;

they head out to some pond and knock down a couple of mallards before work.

Cec is the kind of guy who can cheer up a patient just by walking into his room. He jokes with his patients, treats them like buddies, makes them smile. He likes life and it shows.

But he's no clown. He's the one who prodded us into setting up a coronary care unit, taught the nurses how to run it, and supervised the entire operation. On his weekend off he'll help any other doctor manage a bad coronary. He doesn't like it when his work interferes with his play, but he accepts it.

Cecil's the guy who keeps me alert. I operate on his patients, as I do on the patients of all the other doctors in town, and he always "reads up" on the operation before we do it. When he assists me he'll ask me questions just to make sure I know what the hell I'm doing. I've gotten so that whenever I work with Cec I read over the technique before I step into the operating room even if I've done similar cases hundreds of times. I don't want him to catch me not knowing something I should know. He's good for me.

I have faith in Cecil. At one time or another every doctor in the clinic has taken care of me, Joan, or one of my kids. I trust them all.

But, as Fred is Joan's doctor, Cecil's mine. We play on the same line on the hockey team (I have to concede he's better than I), we battle on the tennis court often, and we get into the same sort of trouble with our wives when we raise a little hell at parties. We're on the same wavelength in almost every dimension of life. We understand each other.

Once he caught me in a trap that every doctor falls into on occasion. My son, Billy, was playing quarterback for the ninth-grade team. In a game against Willmar, our traditional rival, he played well in the first half, but in the second he didn't look good. His passing was off. At home, after the game, I asked him what had happened.

"I banged my wrist in the second quarter," he said. "After that, it hurt every time I threw."

I examined the wrist. There was no swelling, no deformity,

no limitation of motion. "It'll be O.K.," I said. "You've just bruised it."

Two days later Billy said, "It still hurts, Dad." I looked at it again and told him, "Use a little heat, it'll get better."

When he complained the next day Joan finally said, "I'm going to call Cecil. I think something's the matter."

So she did. Cecil came over, ordered an X-ray, and sure enough, the wrist was broken.

He's never let me live that down.

The rest of the doctors on our staff are solo G.P.'s, not part of our clinic group.

Lennox Danielson worked with his father, Karl, until Karl died at age eighty-six, when he was still doing a fine job for his patients. Since Karl's death, all of us in the clinic have worked closely with Lennox. He's a great guy. At sixty-five he's still the best shot in town; he lets everyone in his hunting party unload their guns at a duck, then brings it down with one shot. He can catch bass on a day when everyone else, on the same lake, strikes out. He has the biggest vegetable garden in town, grows fantastic roses and mows about an acre of lawn himself. I can't keep up with him.

As a doctor, he's the personification of common sense. He recognizes nonsense when he sees it; his patients never get a flock of medicines they don't need. He knows what's essential and what isn't.

Lennox was the first guy outside our group to refer a patient to me when I came to Litchfield. I helped him remove a gall bladder; he's a damn good operator himself. He liked the way I worked and from that time on he sent me his major cases, cases he wouldn't handle himself. He never worried about my stealing his patients. He had self-confidence—and justifiably so.

When some doctors call me to see a patient, I never know till I get there whether they really need me or not. With Lennox there's never a doubt. When he calls and says, "Bill, I've got a guy here you'd better see; I think he needs his abdomen opened," I move. Lennox is always right.

He never gets in over his head. The one essential a good

G.P. must have is the ability to know what he doesn't know. Lennox never panics, never calls for help on routine cases, but neither does he ever get into a mess trying to manage some problem he hasn't the training or experience to handle.

If I had to choose the one most important characteristic that a good doctor ought to have, I'd say it was good judgment. Lennox has it.

Don Dille is the "fatherly" type of doctor—the kind of guy who, even in the 1970's, might actually be found sitting by the bedside, holding the patient's hand, the family all around him. His favorite patients are those who need counseling and help with their emotional and social problems. He thrives on "heart to heart" talks.

And he's good at it. He's only fifty, but for twenty years he was the county coroner, and when he had to "sign out" the victims of accidental deaths and suicides—a big part of the coroner's job—he spent many hours consoling the families of the deceased. When a doctor can anticipate a death—when the patient has cancer or severe heart disease, for example —he can at least partly prepare the family for what's coming. When the death is totally unexpected, as accidental deaths are, it's not unusual for the bereaved husband or wife or parent to go completely to pieces. Don usually knows just what to say to help these unhappy people through the shock of their loss. He is a compassionate man.

When it comes to working long hours, Greg Olson, another one of the solo G.P.'s, is the undisputed champ. At two o'clock in the morning, on any given day, the odds are about two to one that he'll be at the hospital, working on charts (he's always behind with his paper work; so am I), caring for an injured patient or waiting for a woman to deliver. The nurses often find him asleep at a desk with a pen in his hand. Once he even fell asleep while sitting on a stool, sewing up a laceration. He had the needle holder and the forceps in his hands, the stitching was half completed, and the nurse had to wake him up; he'd fallen asleep out of sheer exhaustion.

Greg acts as if he were personally responsible for the health and welfare of every person in every little town within reasonable driving distance of Litchfield. His practice in Litchfield keeps him in his office till at least seven most nights, and till two or three on Saturday afternoons, and yet he insists on running an office in Watkins, a doctorless town of five hundred, twenty miles west of Litchfield, and in Cosmos, eighteen miles south, whose three hundred residents are also without a physician. By himself. He figures he can do the job if he gives up almost everything else, and he feels an obligation to do it. Greg's dedication makes Albert Schweitzer look like a playboy.

Dave Allison, who practices alone, drives around Litchfield all summer long with a canoe tied to the top of his station wagon. He keeps thinking that some afternoon he'll be able to put it into a lake and paddle around, but he rarely makes it. Just as he's ready to take off, another of his pregnant patients goes into labor.

Most of the doctors in town examine their obstetrical patients when they're first admitted in labor and then, if it looks as though it's going to be several hours before delivery, they go home.

Not Dave. Any patient of his knows that barring emergency calls, Dave won't leave the hospital till her baby is safe in the infant nursery. He manages a woman in labor as I manage an operation; he's completely involved from the first contraction of the uterus to the last. Women love this attitude, naturally, and Dave has the biggest obstetrical practice in town.

There isn't however, any calculating behind his approach; on an hourly basis I'm certain he earns far less from his obstetrical patients than from any of his other general-practice clientele. He spends those hours with them because that's his way; he never rushes, never seems harried, walks around as if he had all the time in the world, and he gives his patients as much of it as they want. His pregnant ladies want a big share; they get it.

I admire Dave's attitude. I couldn't and wouldn't do it. I give my patients what I think they need—not, necessarily, what they want. That's why I'm a surgeon and Dave is a fine G.P.

Joe Houts is the only doctor in Dassel, a town of about one

thousand. He delivers the babies, removes the appendices, treats the flu and manages the heart attacks of almost everyone in the town. If I had his job I'm afraid I'd leave. But Joe is loyal to the patients he serves. He gets angry when his meals and sleep are continually interrupted, but he sticks at this job. He's a conscientious careful worker and an excellent G.P. surgeon.

Now, having told you about all the doctors who practice in Meeker County Hospital, I'm not going to mention any of these names again.

The doctors I write about in this book are composites. They have the characteristics of doctors I know in Litchfield and elsewhere. The traits I attribute to them can be found in physicians in almost any community. They are traits that fortunately in some instances, unfortunately in others, are part of the nature of that beast—the doctor. I expect that any doctor, from any city, who reads this book will be able to say, "Stu Nielsen could be——" naming an acquaintance; "George Engel could be——" naming another. I expect they'll even be able to say, "Bill Nolen could be——"; because the doctors I've written about, though not specific people, are very real.

Some of the things I have to say about the medical profession are uncomplimentary. I'm sorry. I wish that doctors deserved nothing but praise. Unfortunately, that isn't the case.

But though I take some cracks at the profession—cracks it deserves—I'd like to emphasize one thing: almost all the doctors I know are nice guys. Even those who overcharge, operate unnecessarily or refuse to make house calls are not bad people. They would deny that they are behaving dishonestly; they wouldn't believe it. Because doctors, like other men and women, have blind spots, they refuse to see themselves as others see them. It's easy to get caught in the trap of self-deception.

We doctors have built a medical system that works wonderfully in some spheres, poorly in others. The fee-for-service system, by its very nature, may lure the unwary physician into behavior that is economically motivated, less than admirable, even unscrupulous. But the physician who, for example, orders unnecessary tests has no difficulty rationalizing his position so that he feels neither guilt nor remorse. He convinces himself that everything he's doing is for the good of his patient. An objective observer could only say, "Hogwash."

The system stifles self-criticism. The surgeon who accuses an internist of prescribing unnecessary medications will receive no more referrals from that internist; the orthopedist who tells a general practitioner that he has mismanaged a fracture will never see another of that G.P.'s patients. Silence, even in the face of flagrant wrongdoing, is the only safe policy. If you want a thriving practice, keep your mouth shut. The medical profession does not tolerate traitors.

Fortunately I'm able to convince myself that in writing what I think is an honest book about doctors, I'm not being a traitor. I know that I may be called a traitor by some doctors, but I hope not by many. As the only surgeon in the county where I live I'm protected, at least partially, from the economic reprisals to which another doctor might be subjected. If I were living in a wealthy suburb, competing with a multitude of other surgeons, I too might be afraid to speak out. That's the way the system works.

The patients who come to our clinic make appointments to see specific doctors. People in Litchfield—people everywhere, I suppose—like having one doctor they can see regularly. They'll see someone else only if "their" doctor is away.

We all work on an appointment basis, though up until about three years ago one of my partners saw patients in the order in which they showed up at his office. That policy, which used to be common, has now died out almost everywhere.

Patients who don't have an appointment but simply drop in are seen by the first doctor who becomes available, provided that doctor isn't me. I don't mind seeing surgical problems, injured patients or even a kid with an earache, if everyone else is busy. But it's a waste of time—both mine and the patient's—when I have to look at a rash, check a patient with heart disease, or examine a possibly pregnant woman.

When I first came to Litchfield I got into a little squabble over this policy. Helen Ames, the girl whose job it is to assign patients to doctors, asked one of my partners, "Will Dr. Nolen be seeing all kinds of patients when he's not busy with surgical patients?" My partner said yes, and a few minutes later a child with a bad cough and a rash was delivered to my office. I took one look at the little girl and strolled out to the admitting desk.

"Miss Ames," I said (it was my first day at work and I wasn't on a first-name basis), "that little girl you sent back to my office hasn't got a surgical problem. You'd better have someone else see her."

"I'm sorry, Dr. Nolen," she said, "I sent her back because Dr. Brogan said you'd be seeing any patients that came in."

"That must be a misunderstanding on his part," I said. "I'll see only surgical patients. If everyone else is tied up I might see some others, but let me know first what kind of cases they are. I'm not in general practice."

That, happily, ended that. Miss Ames gave the message to Tom Brogan, and I guess he decided to let it ride. He also spread the news to my other partners and they apparently accepted my decision. At least no one ever insisted I see general-practice patients.

This was a bit of self-assertion that I felt was absolutely necessary. There had never been a specialist in Litchfield before and both the doctors and the public had to learn to live with one—as I did with them. I had heard, before I came to Litchfield, of other surgeons who had gone to small towns to practice surgery, and had wound up doing general practice. It was a trap I didn't want to fall into; not after spending five years learning a specialty.

Which brings me to one big advantage of group practice: a guaranteed income. If I had come into Litchfield solo I would have had a difficult time building a surgical practice. Before I could have gotten enough referrals to earn a living by operating, I would have probably been tempted to start treating any and all patients that came to my office. With rent to pay and eight people to feed and clothe, I'm sure I wouldn't have had the courage to turn down any five-dollar

office calls. I would have had to either leave Litchfield or
become a general practitioner. And once I became a general
practitioner, I could have said good-bye forever to any surgical referrals; G.P.'s don't refer surgery to competing G.P.'s.

As it was, working in a group, I knew that even if I weren't
busy my partners were, and I'd have money to take home at
the end of the month. I didn't have to worry about going
hungry.

In our group all the full partners take home an equal share
of the income. For the first year I was on salary; over the next
four years I received an increasing percentage; then I became a full partner. All six of us are now full partners; at the
end of the month we pay our bills and divide what's left six
ways.

This system is simple, but it will only work successfully if
all the partners are reasonably flexible as far as money is
concerned. In our group, for example, there is one partner
who almost always brings in more income than the rest of us.
He works fast and has a big practice. If he was in solo practice,
he'd undoubtedly be taking home more money than he does
as a member of our group. But he never complains; at least
not so we can hear him. I've discussed the matter with him
several times and he always says, "Look, I'm content. If I
were alone I'd have to take calls every night and weekend,
would have problems getting away on vacation, wouldn't have
consultation available. Alone, I don't think I could do as good
a job for my patients as I do now. And even though I might
earn more money, I don't think I'd have time to enjoy my life
as much as I can now."

I'm inclined to agree with him. Working as a group we can
arrange a call schedule, see hospital patients for each other,
take plenty of vacation time. With six of us in the group we
try never to have more than two doctors, and preferably only
one, gone at a time. But even so, we each manage to take
thirty days of vacation a year plus a half day off every week.
That's a lot of free time—more than most of us would be able
to take if we were alone.

The ready availability of consultation is a real plus for the doctor in group practice, as well as for his patient.

If I'm doing a preoperative examination on a patient and I notice a heart murmur, I call Carlo Germain in to listen and evaluate it. If one of my gall bladder patients shows up for a postoperative examination with a rash, I have Charlie Thompson look at it. Dermatology is one of his big interests; I can't tell measles from chicken pox.

And my partners call me in to look at any potential surgical problems their patients have. A woman thinks she has a breast lump; if Carlo can't find it he has me examine her. A man with a stomach ulcer not getting better on the usual medicine —Charlie will ask me to see him and decide whether or not he needs surgery. Every day at our clinic I see two or three patients for my partners, and they do the same for me.

Of course, the solo doctor can refer patients to a consultant too. Unfortunately, he often doesn't when he should, just because it's too much trouble for the patient and himself. If Stu Nielsen, a solo G.P., doesn't know what's causing a rash, he's apt to try some treatment he has guessed at. Then, if it doesn't work, he'll refer the patient.

There's a money thing involved here too. Often, in our group, we don't make any charge for seeing each other's patients, so the patient gets two doctors for the price of one. But if the consultation takes a lot of time, we do charge; and the fee stays with our group. When Stu refers a patient he loses the money, so for financial reasons there's a temptation to treat the patient himself.

The one big problem for doctors in group practice is that of getting along with each other. Whenever you work closely and interdependently there are bound to be sources of friction.

In our group we're remarkably lucky. The six of us get along pretty well together, even though no two of us are alike. It isn't that smooth in many groups.

I know one group of eight men that has problem after problem. A couple of years ago they had to kick one guy out because he wasn't producing. Everyone in the group took home one-eighth of the net each month, but this particular fellow was bringing in only half of what each of the others was earning. He just didn't want to work. You can only take that sort of thing for a month or two; then it's bound to rile people. The ants won't subsidize the grasshoppers indefinitely.

On the other hand, if you're the sort of guy who insists on getting the lion's share if you do the lion's work, you don't belong in a group; or at least not the sort of group I'm in.

As a general surgeon I can fix a hernia ($175), remove an appendix ($175), take out a stomach ($450) and be home for lunch; I've earned $800. One of my G.P. partners would have to see 160 patients at $5 an office call to equal that.

So, generally, the surgeon who is in a group with either a bunch of G.P.'s, as I am, or with a group of medical specialists —an internist, a pediatrician, perhaps a dermatologist—ordinarily brings in more income than the other doctors. (I don't, but that's because one of my partners is so extremely busy.) Surgery pays better than any other specialty. If a surgeon is going to lie awake nights swearing that he's being "taken," then he doesn't belong in a group like ours.

Of course, he doesn't have to join a multispecialty group; a surgeon can form an alliance with two or three other surgeons. There are groups composed of doctors who are all in the same specialty. Even here, however, he may run into trouble. He may be the guy who operates fastest, gets the most referrals, does the biggest and most expensive operations. If so he'll probably bring in more each month than his surgeon colleagues; if he's taking home the same amount of money it may bug him. It may also, as often happens, bug his wife. She'll tell him he's being exploited.

There are dozens of ways to solve money problems without busting up a group. You can make each partner's share dependent on what he brings in, seniority, hours worked; there are several formulas that may be used. Personally, I've always felt that if you have to resort to complex formulas the group is in trouble. Once you start basing take-home income on what a doctor puts on the books each month the partners start vying for patients and cases. Instead of harmony and a spirit of helpfulness you've got disunity and competitiveness.

You've lost half the benefits you expect from being in a group. You might just as well be solo. But I'll admit there are many groups—usually big multispecialty groups—which have been functioning with relative tranquillity for years using these complex formulas.

In our group, admittedly things aren't always smooth. Now and then Steve Charrah gets sore because Carlo Germain isn't getting to the hospital till nine in the morning; occasionally Gordon Landers gets up-tight when he sees me sitting in my office, reading a book, while he can't get any relief from the constant flow of patients; every once in a while Paul Hauser gets upset if he has to go on more than his share of house calls. When these things happen the guy who is sore stops in and bitches to another one of the partners. Word eventually filters back to the partner at fault. Ordinarily, it all works out without any major confrontation.

There are, naturally, some doctors who start out solo, find they can't stand it, and join a group; and vice versa. There are times, for example, when I wish I were as free as Stu Nielsen. When he wants an afternoon off he takes it; just signs out to one of the other G.P.'s in town. When he feels like working hard he does; when the pace gets too hectic he slows down. He's completely his own boss.

I can't act as impetuously as Stu. If I want a vacation I have to arrange it with my partners. And I can't slow down. If I pass up a gall bladder or a stomach in order to spend a lazy morning, I'm not being fair to my partners. Since we split our total income six ways, I'd feel guilty if I freeloaded off the other men in our group.

What it boils down to, I think, is this: there are doctors (I'm one of them) who function best in a group. Others, like Stu Nielsen, are happier in solo practice. It would be ridiculous, and possibly disastrous, to force one sort of arrangement on every doctor. We weren't all made in the same mold.

11

The Salaried Surgeon

One guy who wasn't made in the same mold as I is a friend of mine from my medical school days, a doctor I'll call Phil Flanagan.

When Phil finished his surgical training, in 1960, he went into practice in a New England city of fifty thousand. Phil didn't do very well. There were more surgeons in the city than were needed and there was a lot of fee-splitting going on. There was also a lot of surgery being done for reasons that Phil considered something less than valid. He's the kind of guy who speaks his mind, and consequently he acquired many enemies. After two years he was barely making expenses and he decided to pull out.

He went as far from New England as he could get—to California. He signed up with a Kaiser-Permanente group and became a salaried surgeon. Kaiser-Permanente is the name of the biggest prepaid medical-care plan in the United States. It has several hospitals, chiefly on the West Coast. Phil and the other doctors in his group provide all the medical care for subscribers to the plan; the patients prepay a specified sum each year. Phil had gotten as far as he could from the fee-for-service system of private practice.

Phil liked the life. He didn't have to compete with other surgeons; he didn't have to worry about his patients' ability to pay; and he worked a forty-hour week. Once a month he took a weekend call; the other weekends he was free. He wasn't earning a fortune, not as much as he might have earned if he had built a very successful private practice, but he was making more than he had in New England. He was able to live very comfortably.

Now that he was settled, Phil decided to join the American College of Surgeons. He had all the necessary credentials and he couldn't imagine that there would be any trouble. But he told me when I met him at a surgical meeting in San Francisco, "The bastards wouldn't let me in. They gave me a big run-around; nothing specific, just told me they'd prefer to defer my application for a while. The same thing happened to other guys—all of them working in the Kaiser group. The College doesn't like the prepaid system, and they keep us out. They're narrow-minded conservatives."

That was eight years ago. Now, because of pressure from all sides, organized medicine—the A.M.A. and all its subdivisions and allies—is beginning to talk and act more liberally. Phil has been accepted by the College of Surgeons.

We doctors love the fee-for-service system. We like getting paid item by item for each of the things we do. We think that a warm, effective doctor–patient relationship is important for the patient's well-being. We think it can only exist when the doctor is directly responsible to the individual patient for providing medical care, and the patient is directly responsible to the doctor when it comes to paying the bills. That's the way it has always been and, by God, that's the way it always should be. So we say.

"We," as I'm using the pronoun here, refers to organized medicine and is, I think, a fair statement of its point of view. And there are grounds for making such a statement; the fee-for-service system has some merits that other systems lack. The patient who goes to a man in private, solo practice will usually get warmer, more personal care than he'd get from a member of a group—even a small group.

Take me, for example. I worry about my patients, am concerned about their jobs and families, try to be a friend as well as a doctor to them. Still, if it's inconvenient for me to follow a patient postoperatively, I have no compunction about turning him or her over to one of my partners. I feel as though a partner is sort of an extension of myself. Unfortunately, I forget that often the patient doesn't feel that way. He or she has come to me, rather than to one of my partners, because he likes and trusts me. I'm the one that he expects to walk into the room every day. When I don't show up, he's disappointed.

Because our group is so small this doesn't happen very often. Even if one of my partners is managing the postoperative care, I try to look in on the patient every day. But in a big group it's not unusual for the patient never to see his surgeon once the operation is over. It's possible that some patients don't care; but from my experience I'd say that most of them do.

If you go to a solo doctor you're never—or almost never—going to have this problem. If he's the guy you want taking care of you, you'll have him. Every morning it will be his smiling face, looking in to reassure you. He'll follow you through every step of your illness because you're his responsibility, and his alone.

In salaried groups, this business of responsibility is a major problem.

Let's assume a surgeon on salary takes half your stomach out on Wednesday and two days later, on Friday night, a blood vessel in the remaining portion of the stomach gets loose and starts to bleed. (Most surgeons have seen this sort of complication at one time or another.)

Now the management of your case becomes a very delicate problem. Is it safer to transfuse you and wait for the bleeding to stop, or should the surgeon reoperate immediately and tie off the bleeding vessel? The man who is best prepared to answer that question is the surgeon who did the original operation.

If that surgeon is a solo practitioner, a member of a small group, or part of a group where he gets paid on the basis of what he does, the chances are excellent that he'll give up his weekend off, or postpone his vacation, to stick around and see the patient through his crisis.

If the surgeon is a full-time salaried man whose work week ended at five o'clock on Friday, he may still stick around—but I wouldn't count on it. It may even be that the surgeon who is covering for him—taking the responsibility for his patients over the weekend—may not even call him. Off is off in a lot of these salaried groups.

Even if the doctor is the sort who will stay around on his off hours to see a critical patient through an illness, he will almost certainly do nothing more than is absolutely required of him when it comes to treating routine problems. Most doctors are bored by colds, backaches, women who are "all tired out"; if they weren't getting paid for seeing these patients, they'd avoid them. The salaried doctor, who gets paid whether he sees these patients or not, will do his damnedest to avoid work in the out-patient clinic or the office in which these routine problems are treated. Even at Bellevue, as an intern and resident, I dodged this sort of assignment whenever I could, as did every other doctor on the house staff.

It's too bad it has to be this way, but it's almost inescapable. The guy who chooses to join a big clinic on a salaried basis may do so for a variety of reasons; but one of them is often the appeal of a forty-hour week. He knows that a great many doctors, most doctors, work more than forty hours. He also knows that even when the doctor in private practice isn't actually working—seeing patients or operating—he's on call. I know that I've been waked at two in the morning, pulled off the tennis court, called on my weekend off—hundreds of times. I never get used to it. I curse every time the damn phone rings. But it's all part of the private-practice game; and from the patient's point of view I think it's the best system.

Why can't doctors act with as much dedication, whether they're salaried or not? They can, of course; some do, and it would be grand if they all did. But often they don't. Why? Because they're human.

The satisfaction a man gets from caring for the sick is one of the big rewards in medicine. I'd say, and most doctors would agree, that it's the biggest. But it isn't the only reward; money is another. And, like most people, doctors often equate the quality and quantity of the job they're doing with the size of the check they bring home each month. See a lot of patients, relieve a lot of misery, earn more money. In our society we're all conditioned along these lines.

Once you get into a pure salaried position, then the money incentive disappears. Extra hours sitting by the woman in labor, more time spent talking to the kid on drugs, piling out at 2 A.M. to sew up the man injured in an auto accident—none of that is going to bring you any more money. That incentive is gone.

Still, most doctors would continue to work hard just for the extra ego gratification, the satisfaction they get from making someone well, if this reward were just as available to them in a salaried group as it is in solo or small group practice.

Unfortunately, it isn't. When a patient goes to a place where all the doctors are salaried—or even to a big group private practice—the one-to-one doctor–patient relationship disappears. Ask some patient who has lost a gall bladder how he liked his surgeon. If he went to a solo doctor he'll say, "Dr. Ramsey is a great man. He did a wonderful job for me." If he went to a big group he's apt to say, "It was done at the White Clinic. They do fine work there." Chances are he won't even know the name of the surgeon who operated on him.

I'm not defending the doctor who lets money and the gratitude of his patients motivate him, I'm explaining him. He's human. It would be nice if we were all completely altruistic, working only because we want to help our fellowman, but this simply is not so; to paraphrase the old show-biz slogan, if we don't get paid for what we do we'd certainly like the applause. Even doctors don't work well without one or the other.

So what's the poor patient going to do—go to the private practitioner, the big group, or sign up for prepaid care from salaried doctors?

Where my family is concerned, if any of us need care, we go to a private practitioner. If one of my G.P. partners can't handle the problem, he'll send us to the appropriate private doctor in Minneapolis. When my son, Jimmy, tore a tendon in his hand playing football Carlo sent him to an orthopedist in Minneapolis. When I had an unusual case of hepatitis a few years ago one of my partners referred me to an internist in private practice. I like the idea of having one individual responsible for my care. I think the personal responsibility gives him an extra incentive to do a good job.

If I needed, God forbid, some extremely complex treatment —an open-heart operation, for example—I'd go to one of the big clinics where a lot of this sort of surgery is done. I'd sacrifice individual responsibility for the experience, equipment and sophisticated care that I could get at the big clinic. I wouldn't like to make this choice, but I'd have to. You can't have both.

The last place I'd go, or send my family, is to a prepaid clinic with salaried doctors. For all the reasons I've mentioned, I don't think the treatment would be as good as what I'd get elsewhere.

I am, however, willing to concede that what I think is ideal treatment isn't available to everyone. I know that as a surgeon I earn a hell of a lot more than the average man; yet I'd have difficulty paying for some kinds of complicated medical care. And I know that even routine medical care is out of the financial reach of many people. You can get wonderful medical care, the best in the world, in the United States—if you can pay for it. Unfortunately, a lot of people can't. They'd be better off with almost any other system of medical-care delivery —even the care they'd get in a prepaid plan.

I expect something will be done and soon. We shouldn't tolerate the situation as it is; it's not fair to the poor and not even all that great for the middle-income population. We'll need to modify our health-delivery system so that everyone can be assured of good medical care, even if it means that great medical care may not be as easily available to the wealthy. I hope it can be done without destroying all the incentives that stimulate doctors to provide the best care they can. We'll see.

12

The Big Hospital versus the Small Hospital

When I decided to live in a small town I had to accept, as part of the package, the knowledge that I'd be practicing in a small hospital. I knew that in our eighty-bed Meeker County Hospital we couldn't have all the facilities that would be available in the big metropolitan hospitals. I thought that at one time or another I might miss those "extras," and I have; but over the years I think I've been able to give my patients better care in our small hospital than I could have in a bigger one.

Patients don't get lost in a small hospital. In big hospitals they sometimes do. Not literally, of course, but figuratively. The patient becomes a number rather than a person. It's easier, when you're dealing with hundreds of patients, to think of a woman as "the gall bladder patient in room 824," rather than as "Mrs. Leona Rush, forty-eight years old; wife of a fifty-three-year-old auto salesman with a drinking problem; mother of four children, ages six to seventeen; etc., etc." It's impossible for the nurses, the laboratory and X-ray technicians, the nurses' aides—all the people with whom a patient comes into contact—to really get to know a patient as a human being when they're seeing hundreds of new patients every week—particularly when they're seeing most of these patients for the first, and probably only, time.

In our little hospital most of the patients know one or more of the people who provide their care. The aide who comes in to make the bed, the nurse who gives them their injections, the laboratory technician who draws the blood samples—if the patient doesn't know them all personally, he or she usually knows them by sight. It's consoling, when you're ill, to be among familiar faces.

Sometimes this familiarity can be a great help from the medical, as well as psychological, point of view. On one occasion, for example, I had as a patient a woman, Mrs. Wilson, with severe abdominal pain. Her symptoms suggested appendicitis, but not everything fit the picture. Her pain seemed to be out of proportion to the rest of her symptoms. I couldn't decide whether or not to operate.

While I was sitting at the nurses' station looking over her chart, the head nurse, Mrs. Gedney, said to me, "Excuse me, Dr. Nolen, but I wonder if you know that Mrs. Wilson's daughter, Lois, her eighteen-year-old, left home last week to marry the Andrews boy—the one who quit college?"

I didn't know, Mrs. Wilson hadn't mentioned it; it was an important piece of information. It explained Mrs. Wilson's pain. If she had her appendix removed perhaps her daughter would come home, so Mrs. Wilson wanted an operation. Armed with this new information I was able to talk away, rather than cut away, Mrs. Wilson's symptoms. Because a nurse knew Mrs. Wilson's family, because Mrs. Wilson was a person and not a number to her, she was able to prevent an unnecessary operation.

I get all sorts of information about my patients from the ancillary help at the hospital, and even from other patients. I hear things about their families, their jobs, their drinking habits—things the patients wouldn't tell me or any other doctor—and it enables me to do a better job when I'm treating their illness. Every bit of information a doctor can get about his patient helps.

To be fair, let me admit that there's another side to this particular coin. If you want privacy or secrecy when you're ill, you aren't going to find it in a community hospital. Everyone, from the woman who does the laundry up through the chief of the medical staff, is going to know what illness you have and how it's progressing. Hospitals are full of nosy people.

A friend of mine once told me about a coffee party she attended with a half dozen other women, one of whom was a nurses' aide at the hospital.

"Say," Mrs. Allen said, "what happened to Jean Reilly? She was pregnant, you know, and I heard she was in the hospital last week. Did she lose the baby?"

"I don't know," said Mrs. Lewis, "but I have to work tomorrow and I'll find out."

The next day, during her coffee break, Mrs. Lewis went through Jean Reilly's chart, looked over the doctor's notes, and that evening called all the women who had been at the coffee party to report that Jean Reilly had indeed had a miscarriage.

There are darn few secrets kept in a small community hospital.

The experience of being in a hospital is a very disturbing one to most patients. Illness that requires hospital care comes as a shock to most of us—I dread it myself—and patients are often intimidated by the experience. They don't behave as they normally would.

I had one patient, for example, whom I referred to a big medical center because she had a nerve disorder that we couldn't explain. As part of the evaluation the doctors ordered a myelogram, an X-ray study of the spinal cord done by injecting dye into the spinal column.

Unfortunately, as occasionally happens in any hospital, but most often in a big institution, the patient was mislabeled. Instead of being sent to the department where the myelograms were done, she was sent to the area where they did intestine X-rays. My patient had a barium enema and an X-ray study of her large intestine instead of her spinal cord.

Why didn't she say anything to the X-ray technician or the radiologist? She didn't feel that she should. She wondered why this study was being done, but she figured the people in the hospital knew their business. Who was she to object?

In Litchfield, where she felt at home, she'd have spoken up. She wouldn't have felt lost, as she did at this big hospital. She would have had the proper X-rays.

It's impossible to overestimate the value to a patient of being in familiar surroundings at times of stress. I've had patients who, I'm sure, survived serious illnesses because they had the support of their friends, their relatives and their clergyman when they were fighting for their lives. Without that sort of support they'd have given up; and every doctor knows that when a patient gives up, the battle is usually lost. The patient who has lost the will to live rarely survives.

It's in the big hospitals that the patient ordinarily runs the greatest risk of receiving highly scientific but highly impersonal care, not only from the nurses and technicians but from the doctor as well. In big hospitals there are solo practitioners who take full personal responsibility for each of their patients, but it's also in the big hospitals or clinics that the patient is most apt to encounter the "professor" who is so busy with a flood of patients that he hasn't got the time to apply anything but the bare essentials of his skills to the individual patient. The results of this "cut and run" policy can be disastrous.

Here's an example. One Monday evening, as I was walking past the X-ray viewing room at the hospital on my way to see a preoperative patient, Carlo Germain called to me. "Come in and take a look at this chest X-ray, Bill," he said. "Worse damn case of pneumonia I've seen in a long while."

The X-ray did look bad. The entire lower half of the chest on the right side was dark. "Whose film is it?" I asked. "Anyone I know?"

"You sure do know him," Carlo answered. "It's Bart Lewis' film. He just got back from the White Clinic this afternoon. He didn't feel well, so he called me as soon as he got home. His temperature was a hundred and four and I couldn't hear a sound on the right side of his chest, so I sent him over here for an X-ray. He's up in room 215. Why don't you stop in and see him?"

"I'll go up right now," I said.

Bart and his wife, Mary, were and are close friends of ours. We'd met them shortly after we arrived in Litchfield and since that time we'd seen a lot of them. They liked movies, bridge and skiing, and Joan and I often went out with them socially. Bart had had problems with an ulcer for several years before I arrived in Litchfield and he had been referred to the White Clinic by one of my partners. When we got to know each other he asked me if I wanted to take over his care. I said no. I figured that the White Clinic doctors had followed him for a long time and had a thorough understanding of Bart and his stomach. He was a hard-driving businessman and I was certain he'd be a tough ulcer patient to manage. Since the doctors at White weren't involved with him as personal friends they could probably treat him more objectively, and more strictly, than I could.

Over the next few years Bart was in and out of the White Clinic. Sometimes it was pain; sometimes, obstruction of the end of the stomach; finally a hemorrhage. When he got over that episode Bart finally agreed to let the surgeon at White operate on him and remove part of his stomach. It was from this operation, performed four weeks earlier, that Bart had just returned and called Carlo.

When I walked into Bart's room I could hardly believe what I saw. Despite his ulcer problems, Bart had always been a rugged, handsome, strong-looking guy. Now, as he sat back propped up on pillows, he looked like a refugee from a prison camp. The flesh hung loosely on his cheekbones, his eyes were sunken, his skin yellow; he looked sicker than hell.

"Bart," I said, "how are you feeling?"

"Gee, Bill," he answered, and his voice had the weak, high-pitched, shaky sound that goes with chronic illness, "it's good to see you. Frankly, I feel awful. It pains every time I take a breath, and I'm so weak I can hardly make it to the bathroom. If I'd known that goddam operation was going to leave me like this, I'd never have had it."

I couldn't believe the White Clinic would have let him come

home as sick as he obviously was, so I asked him, "Bart, did you get sick like this suddenly?"

"No," he answered, "what happened was this. I was operated on about four weeks ago. Ten days after the operation I was feeling pretty well, so Dr. Gray, the guy that operated on me, let me out. But he suggested that Mary and I stay at a hotel near the clinic another two weeks so that they could check me in the out-patient department every other day. A couple of days after I got out of the hospital I began to notice this pain when I breathed. I told the doctor in the out-patient department, but he didn't think much of it—said I had to expect some pain after any operation. It kept getting worse, but he insisted it wasn't anything to worry about. Finally, he told me I could go home. So I got the hell out of there. As soon as I got back I called Carlo, and you know the rest."

Since Bart was Carlo's patient and he had suggested I stop in and see him, I didn't think he'd mind if I examined Bart. I looked at his incision, listened to his chest and finally pressed on his abdomen and flank. When I did, Bart winced. "Damn, Bill," he said, "that really hurts."

"Sorry," I said, standing up, "I just wanted to check something. I'm going to talk to Carlo now, Bart, and we'll probably get some more X-rays. I'll see you a little bit later."

"Do whatever you have to do," Bart said. "I just want to get well."

I found Carlo out at the nurses' station. "Carlo," I said, "I think Bart has got a big abscess up under his diaphragm. His history is just right—it takes about three weeks for these things to get so big they show up on X-ray. Let's get a side view of the chest and another X-ray with him lying down. That may tell us. But even if it isn't definite I think the odds in favor of an abscess are so high that we ought to operate on him."

"You know," Carlo said, "I considered the possibility of an abscess. But I couldn't believe they'd have missed it at the White Clinic."

"I'm sure Dr. Gray wouldn't have," I answered, "but Gray never saw him after he left the hospital. Gray was probably out of town—maybe speaking somewhere—and apparently one of the interns or residents followed Bart in the out-patient department. He shouldn't have missed it either, but he did."

An hour later I put in a person-to-person call to Dr. Gray at the White Clinic, and I told him what we suspected. "I'm sorry to hear it," he said, "but I agree you'd better operate on him. Nothing else to do. Let me know how it goes."

Bart was a sick man. An abscess under the diaphragm is a damn serious complication—many of the patients who get it die—and I was reluctant to operate on Bart myself. The operation was a simple one—just open the abscess and stick some drains in—but I decided to call a friend of mine, an older surgeon in Minneapolis, and ask him to come out and scrub on the operation. I had been in Litchfield long enough now so that I wasn't worried about appearing to be "chicken"; I didn't hesitate to ask someone to share the responsibility for operating on a close friend.

The next day we drained Bart's abscess. There was over a quart of creamy greenish-yellow pus up under his diaphragm. We washed it out and put five rubber drains into the abscess cavity, bringing them out through the incision. Bart tolerated the operation very well.

Happily, he made a rapid recovery. With the pus drained, his temperature dropped quickly to normal, his chest pain went away, and his appetite returned. In two weeks we had him out of the hospital, and six weeks later he was back at work. He has been well ever since—and that episode occurred in 1965.

I've described Bart's case at length because his case demonstrates so well the sort of screw-up that is more likely to occur in a big hospital than in a small one. Our little eighty-bed hospital here in Litchfield isn't perfect, but in some ways, and for some problems, it's a better, safer place than a larger hospital.

If, for example, I had operated on Bart in Litchfield, I certainly wouldn't have left town till he was well. Or if I'd had to leave, I'd have left him in the care of one of the other doctors in town who knew Bart well. Then, when Bart started complaining about the pain in his chest, he wouldn't have gotten the brush-off.

This is one of the weak spots in going to a big hospital for care. The patient isn't well known to his doctors. If he or she complains the doctor doesn't know how to take it. If the patient is a stoic, as Bart was, any complaint of pain is significant; if he had been a chronic moaner, then it wouldn't have been necessary to spend hours tracking down the cause of an ache. There is no substitute for a thorough knowledge of the patient—of what his home, his wife, his job, his personality are like—when it comes to providing medical care. And that kind of knowledge takes years to accumulate, so it's usually unavailable to the doctors in a big hospital.

Nor is it reasonable to argue that this was an exceptional case, that if Dr. Gray hadn't left town he would have been following Bart's postoperative care, and everything would be all right. Nonsense. Dr. Gray is a "big daddy" of the surgical establishment. Most of the time he spends in the hospital he spends in the operating room; the postoperative care is left to the resident surgeon who helps him on the case. Gray wouldn't have time to do all the operating he does if he had to run around from bed to bed every day, asking his postoperative patients how they slept and if they had moved their bowels. So he delegates the responsibility for those chores. (Which, by and large, the resident does as well as Gray would anyway.)

My point is that, admittedly with exceptions, you get better continuity of care and more personal attention when one man takes responsibility for the total patient, as is true in a small, community hospital.

One of the statements that I hear once in a while—and if *I* hear it once in a while, chances are it's said often—is that the Meeker County Hospital can't possibly be as good as a big hospital in New York, Chicago, Los Angeles or even Minneapolis, because we don't have all the equipment they have. The answer to that argument is yes and no. Yes, we don't have the equipment; no, that doesn't make us inferior.

Ever since the development of the heart-lung machine,

about 1954, a lot of people—doctors as well as laymen—have gotten a fixation on equipment. If a hospital doesn't have a heart-lung machine, an artificial kidney, a cobalt-therapy X-ray machine, it can't be any good; conversely, if the hospital has the equipment, it must be good.

What everyone seems to forget is that though we might need all or some of this fancy equipment on occasion—say, to treat about 2 percent of the populace 2 percent of the time—98 percent of the ailments of 98 percent of all patients can be treated perfectly well by a doctor working with the basic equipment all hospitals have. Patients don't often have strange holes in their hearts, kidneys that won't work at all, tumors that require treatment with a cobalt machine; most patients have pneumonia, heart attacks or hernias. When and if they develop these other strange ailments, there's time to transfer them to a hospital which has that equipment.

In our operating room in Litchfield we have all the basic anesthesia equipment, all the necessary tools, to operate on the brain, the chest, the abdomen, the extremities; on any part of the human anatomy with the exception of the open heart. We don't have a heart-lung machine because I don't do open-heart surgery. (Not because it's awfully difficult, from a technical point of view—it isn't—but because it requires a team of technicians and the full-time devotion of the surgeon. Deliver me from the guy who does an "occasional" open-heart case—and since "heart" surgeons are the glamour boys of the moment, there are a lot of "occasional" heart surgeons around.)

What does it take to practice the most modern obstetrics? A pair of trained hands and two or three sets of forceps, the latter to be used with discrimination. We've got that equipment in our little place.

For medical diseases, until recently, it was again only a matter of having intelligent doctors and a decent laboratory. We've always had these. In the last few years, the "coronary care" unit, a special area in the hospital with electronic equipment for "monitoring" and treating patients with heart attacks, has come into vogue. When statistics became available which showed that such equipment was of value in saving lives, we bought it, as did other even smaller hospitals near Litchfield, because a heart attack is a problem that often has to be treated immediately, and the closer to home the better. If you have a heart attack your care in Litchfield will be just as good—if not better—than that you'll get anywhere else.

I have a good reason for suggesting it might be better—based again on hospital size. Patients with coronaries, sitting in bed with wires leading from their chest and extremities, intravenous fluids running into their arms, an electrocardiograph ticking away by the bedside, are bound to be nervous, no matter how much sedation they have. If there's another patient in the next bed, he's nervous too. And if patient A has a complication, requiring a flurry of activity—possibly even some drastic measures, like shocking the heart or doing an emergency tracheotomy—patient B's anxiety will increase.

In our hospital there is usually only one patient, occasionally two and rarely three patients in the entire unit; so the chances of an upset of this type are remote. If there were six or nine such patients around—as may be the case in a bigger hospital—the chances of someone getting into trouble double or triple. The patient with a coronary, other things being equal, is better off in a small unit.

One problem that often occurs in big hospitals is a lack of communication. The superspecialists on the staff are each interested in only one part of the patient's anatomy; there's no doctor who is concerned with the patient in his entirety—with the patient as a human being—and so the patient can't find any doctor to whom he can talk and from whom he can get any practical information.

This is extremely frustrating for the patient. When Lee Rossitter came back after having a heart operation at the White Clinic, he told me, "Bill, it was awful. I'd ask a doctor when I'd be able to get out of bed and he'd say, 'I'm the surgeon, you'd better discuss that with your internist.' I'd ask the internist when I could go back to work and he'd say, 'That's up to your surgeon.' I couldn't get a straight answer from anyone."

Relatives find the problem even more difficult. A wife who

wants to know how her patient-husband is progressing will probably have to call the doctor's office if she's ever going to get the information—if she can discover which doctor she's supposed to call, and if she can ever get him on the phone. The fragmentation of care that has come with superspecialization has created a tremendous communication gap. Everyone's patient is really no one's patient.

Now, let me admit, there are times when a patient in a small hospital is at a disadvantage.

One evening I was called to the hospital to see a sixteen-year-old boy, Derek Smith, who had fallen off the back of a pickup truck, landing on the pavement. He had bruised his shoulder and the back of his skull, but he didn't look particularly ill.

"How are you, Derek?" I asked him.

"Not too bad, Dr. Nolen," he answered. "Shoulder hurts a little when I move it and I've got a sort of a dull headache. Otherwise all right."

"Were you knocked out?"

"I don't think so. I was dazed for a minute. The truck hit a bump and suddenly I found myself lying on the ground. I can't remember it too clearly, but I wasn't really out."

I examined him. His pupils reacted to light, his reflexes were O.K., he knew the date, his name, where he was. X-rays showed a minor separation of the shoulder but no evidence of a skull fracture.

"I'm going to keep you in here overnight, Derek," I said. "I don't think there's anything serious but you've gotten a couple of good bumps and I think you'll be more comfortable here." I talked to Derek's parents and sent him upstairs, with routine orders to the nurse to keep an eye on his blood pressure, pulse, respiration and state of consciousness. I went home to bed.

At two in the morning the phone rang. It was Mrs. Rawlings, the nurse on second floor. "Dr. Nolen," she said, "you'd better come right over. The Smith boy doesn't look very well."

Ten minutes later I was at the hospital, examining Derek. He was completely out, unresponsive even to pain. His pupils were dilated, one slightly more than the other, and his breathing was irregular. His extremities were held rigidly. All this was evidence of brain damage—probably fluid in the brain tissues, possibly a hemorrhage.

"I came in to see him half an hour ago," Mrs. Rawlings said, "and he seemed to be all right. His blood pressure was up a little, but he was sleeping quietly. Then when I came back he was like this."

This sort of thing can happen in head-injury cases, not often, but once in a while. Instead of a gradual decline in condition, the patient deteriorates rapidly. The question, now, was what to do. Most times it's better not to operate—just use medicine to try and get rid of the swelling of the brain; but if there's bleeding in the skull, it's best to let it out. I couldn't be certain in Derek's case.

At that moment I'd have given a lot to have a neurosurgeon available, someone who had seen more cases like this than I had, someone who could relieve me of the responsibility. In a big hospital in a larger city a neurosurgeon would have been available. In Litchfield I was on my own and Derek was dependent on me.

I called a neurosurgeon I knew in Minneapolis, described the situation to him and said, "I'm afraid to send him to you. I don't think he'd survive the trip and I doubt that there's time for you to come out. What do you think I ought to do?"

"It sounds bad whatever you do," he said. "I don't think the boy will make it. But I guess you'd better put a couple of holes in his head on the remote chance that there's a blood clot in there. If there isn't, you haven't lost anything. Let me know how it comes out."

So we took Derek to the operating room, shaved his head, and for the next half hour I became a neurosurgeon. Not that in this case that was such a big deal—simply a matter of drilling holes in the skull and taking out a piece of bone—but I didn't like the role. It wasn't familiar to me.

As it turned out, the venture was futile: no blood, just swelling. And despite all the routine measures, Derek died the next day. His brain damage had been fatal.

I don't think a neurosurgeon would have made the diagnosis earlier; and even if he had, as it turned out, there was nothing that he could have done to save Derek. But, another time, having a neurosurgeon available might be lifesaving. When you go to a small community hospital you have to realize that all the specialties won't be represented, and that once in a great while this can be critical.

But, to repeat, for 98 percent of patients 98 percent of the time the small community hospital is just as good, if not better than the bigger institution. When you have a problem that your local doctors can't diagnose, or that they haven't the equipment to treat, time enough then to go to the bigger institution with the flock of specialists and the fancy equipment. Your local doctor, provided he knows enough to know when he doesn't know enough, will send you to the proper place at that time.

Any doctor worth his salt ought to be able to practice good medicine without all the fancy equipment and superspecialization that so many consider essential in the 1970's. One of my surgical mentors used to say, "Nolen, if you can't do any operation with a rock and the top of a tin can, you're no surgeon." After twelve years in Litchfield, I'm inclined to agree with him.

13

Nurses

No matter what size the hospital is, the people who run it are not the doctors, the administrators, or the members of the hospital board; hospitals are run by nurses.

Nurses play an extremely important role in patient care. They are the actual providers. The doctor stops in and sees his patients for five minutes in the morning, writes a few orders and leaves. For the remaining twenty-three hours and fifty-five minutes of the day the nurses are with the patients. If the nurses don't do their jobs efficiently the patients aren't going to get well. Every doctor relies of necessity on the nurses.

Naturally, not all nurses are reliable in every respect; who is? What the doctor has to know is which nurses can be dependent upon to do what jobs. He then tries to arrange things so that he and his patients benefit from the nurses' strengths and aren't hurt by their weaknesses. It's a matter of getting to know the nurses well.

We have one retired nurse here in town, Sarah Germain, who will still come in to "special" for us once in a while. Sarah's seventy years old, gentle and very pleasant. When I have a patient who isn't really very sick—some elderly woman, say, who has had a breast lump removed—I'll ask for Sarah. The patient doesn't really need a special nurse, but if she wants one I'll get one like Sarah who will hold her hand, talk to her, treat her nicely. That's the kind of nurse she'll appreciate.

On the other hand, when I've got a very sick patient, one who is desperately ill, I ask for Janice Moriarty, a woman who is really capable.

Janice has saved the lives of several of my patients. One of them was Al Lacey, who runs a laundry here in town. Al came into the hospital one Sunday afternoon with a big hole in his left chest. He'd been out hunting with a couple of buddies and one of them accidentally blasted him with a 12-gauge shotgun. Fortunately, they'd just gotten out of the car so they were able to load Al back in quickly and rush him to the hospital.

As soon as I could get the blood cross-matched I hustled Al to the O.R. I took out a rib and looked around his chest. A few pellets had grazed the pericardium (the sac around the heart), but the heart itself was all right. The major problem was his left lung. The lower lobe had been blown to shreds. While Sam Longworth, our anesthetist, pumped the blood into Al I took out the shot-up lung. I left two tubes in the chest, one to drain off any blood that might seep from the raw surface of the lung, the other to take care of any leaking air, and we got Al off the table. His blood pressure was stable at 100 over 60 and his pulse was running about 110. I figured he needed about two more pints of blood. Barring complications, he'd make it.

I called Doris Levine, who was the nurse in charge, and said, "Doris, get me a special for Al Lacey—and get me a good one. He's going to be critical for the next eight hours. Try Janice Moriarty first; if you can't get her try Molly Risner. If you can't get either, call me back."

Half an hour later, while I was checking Al over back in his room, Janice walked in. "Hi," she said, "what's up?"

"Plenty," I answered. "Al Lacey got a shotgun blast in his chest and I've just taken out the lower lobe of his lung. He's still oozing some and we're about two pints behind. He's going to be rocky for a while. You'll have to make sure his chest tubes stay clear and his I.V. keeps running. Keep an eye on his breathing too. You may need to suction out the back of his throat once in a while. He's going almost entirely on one lung."

"Shall I sweep the floor too?" she asked. Janice is a wiseacre.

It was midnight by the time I left the hospital and I was tired. By twelve thirty I was in bed and asleep. At two o'clock the phone rang. It was Janice.

"Dr. Nolen," she said, "I think you'd better come over here and take a look at Lacey. He's had the two pints of blood and his pulse is up to a hundred and thirty. He doesn't look good."

"Are you sure those chest tubes are open?" I asked.

"Yes. There's some bloody drainage from the lower tube, but not much. There's still an air leak, but it's not as active as it was an hour ago. I don't think it's his chest. He keeps complaining about pain in his belly. You don't think he could have something sour down there, do you?"

"I doubt it," I said, "but I'll be over." Janice wasn't an alarmist. If she smelled trouble she was probably right.

Ten minutes later I was pushing on Al's belly, trying to figure out what was wrong. Janice had been right; his chest seemed O.K.

The trouble seemed to be in the left upper part of his abdomen. He was tender there and he kept his muscles rigid. These findings, together with the fact that his blood pressure was low and his pulse fast, made me wonder about his spleen. The spleen sits right under the diaphragm. Maybe one pellet had gone through and nicked it. I hadn't seen a puncture in the diaphragm, but I'd been so concerned with the lung that I could have missed it.

I called Janice out in the corridor. "I think I'd better take him back to the O.R.," I said. "I'm not certain, but he may have a bleeding spleen. Better call the lab and have them cross-match four more pints."

"What do you think I am?" she asked. "An imbecile? I called the lab fifteen minutes ago."

So we took Al Lacey back to the O.R. This time I opened his belly and, sure enough, his spleen was bleeding. There were three pints of blood in his abdomen. I took out his spleen, mopped up and closed. We gave him four more pints and he made the grade.

Most nurses and a great many doctors would have missed the second diagnosis. Admittedly, I did the surgery, but if

Janice hadn't called as quickly as she did, if she hadn't spotted trouble early, Al would have bled out. It was Janice Moriarty who saved Al Lacey's life.

It goes without saying that nurses like Janice Moriarty are invaluable. In most private hospitals there are no interns or residents, and during all the hours when no doctors are around, the nurses take the responsibility for acting for them. Sometimes the responsibility is awesome.

Take our coronary care unit. This is a two-bed ward, next to the nurses' station on our third floor, where patients with acute coronary thrombosis are admitted. While they are in the ward, usually for at least the first four days after a coronary, they are constantly attached to an electrocardiograph. On the wall, over the patient's head, there is a running tracing of what the patient's heart is doing.

The nurse in the coronary care unit provides all the routine nursing care for these critically ill patients. This means close observation of pulse and blood pressure, extreme care in administering medications, and applications of liberal amounts of T.L.C.—tender, loving care.

In addition, she has to keep one eye constantly on the E.K.G. She has to look for changes in rhythm or in the shape of the waves. Alterations in the pattern of the E.K.G. are often the first indication that something new has happened to the patient's heart. If so, he needs immediate—and by "immediate" I mean within two or three minutes—attention.

If there's no doctor around, who's going to give that care? The nurse. She can tell the floor nurse to put in a call for "Dr. Blue"—"Dr. Blue" being the page signal which means "Any available doctor, come immediately to the coronary care unit" —but until "Dr. Blue" shows up she's on her own.

I'm a lousy Dr. Blue. I know less about E.K.G.'s now than I knew when I was in a medical school, and I didn't know much then. Fifteen years of concentrating on surgery have given me a sort of tunnel vision, and coronary patients aren't in my line of sight.

I have been caught. One afternoon, just as I was leaving the hospital after setting a wrist fracture, the call for Dr. Blue came over the page system. I hustled to the coronary care unit, hoping madly that some other doctor would already have arrived, but to my dismay no one had. It was two thirty and there was no other doctor in the hospital.

Helen Ames was on duty. When I arrived she was suctioning mucus out of the mouth of an elderly man. He was blue, gasping for breath, with bloody froth on his lips. Above his head the E.K.G. machine was churning out its tracing. All I knew about it was that it sure as hell looked strange.

"What's the problem, Helen?" I asked.

"Take a look at that E.K.G.," she said. "He's gone into ventricular tachycardia. What shall I do?"

I hadn't the foggiest notion. I knew ventricular tachycardia was dangerous, the heart races along out of control till it becomes exhausted and collapses completely in a matter of about five minutes—and I knew there were lots of strange new drugs that could be given to slow the heart and convert it to a normal rhythm. But how much of which drug to give, and when, were beyond me.

"The first thing we've got to do," I said, "is to send for help."

"Miss Ralston," I shouted to the floor nurse, "put in a call for Dr. Germain."

"Now, Helen," I said, "what do you suggest we do now?"

"I think we ought to give him fifty milligrams of Xylocaine," she answered.

"Give it," I said. She filled the syringe with Xylocaine solution and injected it into the tubing of the intravenous solution that was running into the patient's arm. I watched the E.K.G. After about thirty seconds the heart slowed and the rhythm became normal.

"You've cured him," I said, grinning like an imbecile.

"I hope so. Let's wait a minute."

Sadly, before the minute was up, the heart began its race again and Mr. Lawrence, the patient, again turned blue.

"Now what?" I asked. I was beginning to perspire.

"I'd suggest pronestyl, intravenously."

"Are you sure you know what you're doing?"

"I'm sure," she replied.

"O.K. Shoot." She gave him the drugs. Again Mr. Lawrence responded. This time the improvement seemed to be permanent. His pulse came down to 90—it had been about 160—and he began to breathe easily. His blue skin gradually became pink. I turned to Helen to congratulate her; as I did I heard a sudden gurgle. I wheeled around just in time to see Mr. Lawrence again begin to fade. His E.K.G. now looked, difficult as it was to believe, even worse.

"He's fibrillating," Helen said. "We'll have to shock him."

Fibrillation is a dreaded complication. The heart muscle fibers, instead of contracting as a unit, quiver individually. The heart stops working as a pump and the blood stops circulating. It lies stagnant in the heart and blood vessels.

The only way to restore rhythm to the heart is to put two electrodes on the patient, one on the chest in front of the heart, the other on the back of the patient, and then turn a switch which shoots an electric current through the chest. On the way, it passes through and jolts the heart. Sometimes this shock gets all the muscle fibers beating as a unit again—by electrocuting the patient, so to speak.

I'd never used the defibrillator, though I had watched demonstrations, and I didn't want to use it now; but there was no way out. Carlo Germain still hadn't arrived and Mr. Lawrence would be dead in another two minutes if we didn't stop the fibrillation.

"All right, Helen," I said, "let's go."

She quickly slapped one electrode on the chest and handed the other to me. I placed it against Mr. Lawrence's back.

"Push the switch," Helen said.

"Which one?" I asked—there were two on the machine.

"The one on the right," she answered.

I pushed it. As the shock ran through his body Mr. Lawrence's muscles went into spasm. His entire body went rigid. In a second it was over.

I looked up at the E.K.G. It had worked. His heart was beating with a regular rhythm. We watched for five minutes, and the beat never faltered. It was then that Carlo Germain walked into the room. He looked up at the E.K.G.

"What the hell's the idea of yelling for me?" he said. "I had an office full of patients. That E.K.G. looks perfectly normal."

I could have hit him.

When I'm called at night, after I've fallen asleep, to come and see a patient, I do what a great many doctors do—I snarl. I realize that it's not the fault of the nurse that I have to get up at night and go to the hospital, but often I'm nasty to her. It's rather like the policy of killing the messenger who brings bad news to the king; I have to take my vexation out on someone.

Fortunately, the nurses, after twelve years, have learned to understand. Even though I snarl—may even curse a bit—I make the trip; and by the time I reach the hospital I'm civil again. I treat both the patient and the nurse gently. As I should.

Almost every day I spend two or three hours operating, so I have to work very closely with the O.R. nurses. Mostly, we get along very well together.

I'm a very impatient person, and I hate delays. When I get to the O.R., about five minutes before eight, I expect to find the patient on the table, the intravenous solution running into the vein, the instruments ready and the scrub nurse scrubbed. I look in on the patient, let him know I'm wide-awake, and then while I change into a scrub suit and wash my hands, Sam Longworth puts the patient to sleep and one of the O.R. nurses paints the skin of the operative area with Merthiolate. By the time the drapes are on the patient I'm scrubbed and ready for my gown and gloves. I don't have to stand around, and neither does the rest of the team.

Here in Litchfield I've never had any problems; the O.R. staff doesn't like to waste time any more than I do, but at one hospital where I used to operate there was a nurse working in the O.R. who just could not get herself organized. I'd come in in the morning and she'd still be running around putting instruments on the table. Which meant that she would start scrubbing only about two minutes before I did. I'd get into the O.R. and have to stand around with my arms dripping waiting for her to get her gloves on and hand me a towel.

She would never catch up. I'd say, "Give me a number 2-o silk tie," and she'd have to call to the circulating nurse, "I need some 2-o silk." Then I'd have to stand and wait till she opened the package, laid out the sutures, and handed me one. It doesn't sound like much of a delay, but, believe me, in the middle of an operation a one-minute interruption seems like a half hour. You can't read a book or have a cup of coffee. All you can do is stand fidgeting, looking down into the open abdomen, waiting impatiently for the damn silk ties.

Sometimes she'd delay us, literally, twenty minutes. I'd get halfway through an orthopedic case, ask for a screwdriver, and find that she hadn't remembered to put one in. So we'd all get to sit down for twenty minutes while the screwdriver was sterilized. The unnecessary prolongation of the operation was bad for the patient, and bad for me. Sometimes, while I was sitting there, I'd have the circulating nurse bring me some milk which I'd sip through a straw. Without the milk I'm sure this nurse—I'll call her Susie—would have given me an ulcer.

After a while, every time Susie saw me come through the door she'd get very jumpy and nervous; I'd get worse. If I knew in advance that she was going to be "helping" me the next day, I'd spend a very restless night. She probably didn't sleep at all. I tried not to let my dissatisfaction show, but I suppose it radiated through every pore. I'm not good at masking my emotions.

One of us had to go, and after six months Susie quit. She took another job in the hospital on a floor where she could work without my constantly breathing down her neck. She's an excellent nurse and does a fine job caring for patients. Now, whenever I visit that hospital, Susie and I get along very nicely.

Since our hospital is small, and we run only one O.R. at a time, I get to know the scrub nurses well, and vice versa. All the O.R. nurses know how I do most cases: what retractors I use, when I want silk and when I'll use catgut, how I'll close the skin. They anticipate all my requests and most operations go very smoothly. Surgery isn't funny, but with a good team, it is a lot of fun.

We're not, in contrast to what you might gather from watching a television operation, all up-tight in the O.R. A lot of operating time is devoted to opening and closing the abdomen, and to paraphrase Spiro Agnew, when you've seen one abdominal wall you've seen them all. Unless the patient has two or three old scars, in which case the surgeon has to be very careful not to inadvertently open the intestine when he's opening the abdomen, opening and closing are fairly routine. So while we're doing those portions of the operation we talk about whatever is of current interest—the high school football team, the approaching school board election, Vietnam. It's quite possible to cut and sew while discussing other things.

Even the definitive part of the operation—removal of the stomach or gall bladder or spleen—is largely routine. Clamp a blood vessel, tie a blood vessel, clamp another, tie another. It's a good time to discuss the current film at the Hollywood.

During sticky parts of the operation, while trying to peel the ulcer of the pancreas or fish a stone out of the common bile duct, we're all business. There are a lot of vital structures packed into the abdomen, and a false move can get a fellow into a lot of trouble fast. It's at these times that I don't want to ask for an instrument or a suture and find it's not immediately available. I expect the O.R. nurses to be just as well prepared as I am, and, frankly, I'm always damn well prepared. If I wasn't I wouldn't be operating.

It's fun working with good O.R. nurses. I'm glad we have them.

The O.R. supervisor, the nurse in charge of the O.R., is treated like a queen in most hospitals. (We treat ours like a queen too, but because we like her, not because we have to.) In big hospitals her power is awesome.

She is the one who decides what nurse is going to scrub on which case. She can assign some girl with two left hands to help on a stomach removal, and ruin a surgeon's day. Or if she likes a doctor, she can give him the best nurse on the staff to help him fix a simple hernia, and he'll have a delightful morning. It's very wise to stay on the right side of the O.R. supervisor.

Her greatest power resides in the small loose-leaf pad on which the surgical cases are scheduled. Most surgeons prefer to operate in the morning, at seven thirty or eight, when the O.R. schedule begins. Not only is it nice to operate when you're fresh, but if your case is first you know exactly what time you'll start. If you have to follow someone else your starting time will depend on how well the first operator's case, or cases, go.

In Litchfield, for example, I will never—except in the most dire emergencies—schedule a case to follow one of Pete Morrison's. He can take hours to do the simplest things. When he puts a bilateral vein stripping (an operation to remove varicose veins) on the schedule, I know the O.R. will be tied up for at least six hours. Fortunately, he knows it too, so he'll usually do only one leg. He does the other leg a month or so later.

In our hospital, since I'm the only guy doing major cases, I have very little scheduling trouble. But in the big hospitals the competition for "prime" time is vicious.

Supposedly it's first come, first served—but it doesn't always work that way. The chief of surgery ordinarily has little difficulty getting his cases on the schedule at eight, but the new man on the staff will rarely be that fortunate. He'll get to follow two or three other cases, some time around two in the afternoon.

Unless—he can get on the right side of Miss Janson, the O.R. supervisor. Remember her birthday, but not her age; ask her opinion about politics, art, cooking or whatever it is she's interested in; possibly, if you're really desperate and she's the sort that appreciates it, give her a little pat on the behind now and again. After all, she may be 90 percent dragon but she's still a person. Treat her like one.

It really does the trick. At a hospital where I once worked —not in Litchfield—there was one guy who stepped on the O.R. supervisor's toes shortly after he got on the staff. He criticized the method she used to sterilize the skin—a picayune thing—the sort of criticism only a guy fresh out of residency would make. And the sort of thing that really burns a sensitive O.R. supervisor.

That surgeon was doomed. He couldn't get a case on the schedule before noon to save his soul. And the help he got! He'd have been better off doing the cases alone.

He finally went to the chief of surgery and complained. "Miss Janson is giving me a tough time, Dr. Fischer," he said. "I know there are days when she could give me decent operating time, but she won't. She saves the time for her favorites."

"Look, Bruce," Dr. Fischer said (underlings address the chief as Doctor; the chief calls underlings by their first names), "what do you want me to do? Speak to Miss Janson? If I do, you're through. Sure, she'll give you an occasional hour in the morning if I ask her to, but she'll make your life miserable. She'll start canceling out your cases for emergencies that aren't real emergencies. You're operating in the afternoon now; if I speak to her, you'll be operating at night. Take my advice and be nice to her. That O.R. is her whole life."

Bruce ate a lot of crow for the next three weeks. He complimented Miss Janson on how smoothly she ran the O.R., on her appearance, on just about everything he could think of. He made a point of chatting amiably with her every day. He never griped about the rotten hours he was assigned.

It paid off. In a few months he was getting as much prime operating time as most of the senior men on the staff. In fact, one of them started complaining to the others about Bruce's privileged status. But Bruce didn't care; he had Miss Janson on his side.

The head nurses on the floors don't have quite the clout that the O.R. boss has, but they have enough.

For example, if things get busy—several new patients coming in, patients to prepare for surgery, critically ill cases on the floor—some of the nice but inessential chores may not get done. Maybe some patient won't be lifted out of bed into a chair; possibly a bed bath or two will be skipped; perhaps the "hypo" for pain will have to wait a bit. Which patients will be the ones to have to put up with these omissions or delays? In our hospital they'd be Dick Hopkins' patients. Why? Because Dick continually gives the nurses a hard time. The nurses won't skip the essentials on any patients, but if any patients are going to get the short end on the frills that can mean the difference between real comfort and a so-so situation, they'll be his.

Nurses are just like anyone else with a job to do; they like to start out in the morning with a clear picture of what has to be done so they can organize their time. There are always little emergencies, sometimes big ones, but even allowing for these it's possible to arrange things so that work can be done in a relatively relaxed style if—and this is crucial—the doctors on the staff visit their patients relatively early in the morning and write their orders at that time.

Dick Hopkins doesn't do that. He wanders into the wards anywhere from 11 A.M. to 2 P.M. and writes things like: "Give soap suds enema stat" ("stat" means immediately); "Send patient to physiotherapist today"; "Change dressings on leg three times a day." It takes him just a few minutes to write orders that may require three hours to carry out. When he writes them at two in the afternoon there just isn't time, before the shift changes, to get everything done. Unless some nurse works overtime; which is often the case.

Dick doesn't bother to consider the nurses' problems. Nor does he consider the situation in the laboratory; he'll order a barrage of blood chemistries to be done on a Sunday morning, when there's only a skeleton crew on duty. He calls them "emergency" studies, but nine times out of ten they could just as well wait till Monday. Is it any wonder that the nurses and the lab workers hate to see him coming? He's a very inconsiderate guy.

The ego trip some doctors are constantly on shows up most flagrantly in the hospital setting. Like Dick, they can't get it through their heads that the nurses, though they admittedly haven't had as much medical education, may still have something constructive to contribute to patient care. Instead of treating nurses as fellow professionals, asking their advice and requesting their help, the doctors treat them like servants. It's a great mistake.

There are, naturally, some nurses who are just not very competent. I know one whom I wouldn't trust to empty a bedpan, let alone distribute medications. But these women don't get jobs as head nurses; they stay under the supervision of the head nurse, and she sees to it that they keep out of trouble. There are a lot of bed baths to be given, and this keeps them busy.

Hospitals are little cities unto themselves. There are a lot of jobs to be done, and most of them aren't done directly by the doctor. He writes the orders; someone else carries them out.

If he wants to give his patients the best in medical care, if he wants to save himself time and energy, he is wise if he treats with respect the nurses, the laboratory workers, the X-ray technicians—any and everyone who works in the hospital. It takes a team effort to make patients well. The doctor may be the quarterback, but he needs an awful lot of blocking if he's going to score a touchdown. If he's not a nice guy, if he insists on acting like a prima donna, he won't get the help. His patients will be the ones to suffer.

14

Doctors and Sex

A great many people, men particularly, suspect that doctors lead very full extramarital sex lives. They know that we spend a lot of time working very closely with nurses, and that we sometimes have as patients women who are frustrated one way or another. The female patient who "falls in love" with her doctor is a cliche; and like most cliches, she is based on reality.

I'm no Dr. Kinsey, so I can't give you any figures on the percentage of doctors that carry on extramarital affairs, but I suspect it may be rather high—probably higher than it would be in the population at large. There are some solid reasons for this state of affairs.

Suppose, for example, some woman has designs on a physician. It's no problem to find out whether he feels the same —and wants to take the appropriate action. All she has to do is call him some night when her husband is away. She can wait till the kids are in bed and then ring him up because she has "a terrific migraine." If he tells her to take two aspirin and come to the office in the morning, then he's not interested and there's no harm done. But if he decides to make a house call she can get into bed in her negligee and it won't take long to find out how he plans to treat her headache. If he insists on a complete physical before he gives her the "hypo," they're in business.

I don't want to suggest that this sort of thing happens often —it doesn't. At least not to me. But it has happened to friends of mine and I mention it just to show how easy it is for a doctor. Let an insurance man make a house call at 2 A.M. and his wife will be waiting with the frying pan in hand when he gets back home; the doctor's wife just rolls over and goes back to sleep when her husband drives off in the wee hours.

What most doctors can't get away with is the long afternoon or the two-day trip. It's been done, of course; one guy I know goes to so many medical conventions—to keep up with medical progress—that if he were really going to all the lectures he should know enough by now to cure cancer, arthritis and asthma. The fact of the matter is that when he decides to take in the meeting of the "Society of Pediatric Allergists" in Cincinnati he takes his faithful office nurse with him. His office nurses usually last about a year—time enough for three or four conventions.

But most doctors can't sneak away for more than an hour without running the risk of getting into trouble. If a doctor has any sort of practice there are constant calls for him—from patients, from the hospital, from other doctors. And he has to be reachable. If the patient he operated on in the morning goes into shock after lunch, and the hospital can't find him because he's off somewhere with his paramour, both he and his patient are in trouble. It's a nervous situation not conducive to relaxed love-making.

That's why some doctors concentrate on either a nurse or the office help. A friend of mine told me about one group of eight doctors in which, after a business meeting, the surgeon asked the internist, "Are you going to bed with our receptionist?"

The internist said, "No."

"Good," said the surgeon. "Then you can fire her."

Office help works out beautifully for the doctor, just as it does for men in most businesses. The wife can hardly complain if her doctor husband is late getting home in the evening. Doctors are supposed to work late; they have a lot of patients who need help. And, naturally, the office nurse can't leave till the doctor has seen his last patient. Devotion to duty and all that sort of thing.

The only bad feature involved in affairs with the help is that, quite often, things get sticky. Let's assume you're paying your office nurse a hundred and fifty dollars a week. She knows you're grossing fifteen hundred dollars. If you're having an affair with her on the side she may figure that she deserves a raise. A substantial one.

Worse, she may even decide she wants you, lock, stock and barrel. Here she is, your good and faithful servant, at the office bright and early, keeping your patients moving on schedule, bringing you coffee when you want it, even staying late and making love to you. Unless she has a husband who is pulling down fifteen hundred a week—highly unlikely if she's working for you—she may decide that as long as she's spending all this time and energy on you, she deserves to go home with you in the evening to that big $80,000 mansion, rather than to her little $15,000 bungalow. A lot of nurses—and office girls—have gotten ideas like this. And a helluva lot of doctors have had their practices, to say nothing of their family lives, ruined because they mixed their social and professional lives.

A psychiatrist recently suggested another reason, other than the simple proximity to women which men in many walks of life have, for the apparent superabundance of affairs between doctors and nurses. He said, "A nurse often shares a doctor's life in moments of crisis, at times when his wife can't be there. An internist works all night trying to pull a patient with a bad coronary through a crisis; who's with him when the man's heart finally starts beating regularly? The nurse in the coronary care unit.

"A surgeon takes a woman with a ruptured uterus into the operating room, works like hell to stop the hemorrhage and get the uterus out, and who's working side by side with him when the patient finally comes out of shock? The scrub nurse.

"A pediatrician spends six months trying to keep some child with a malignancy alive and comfortable. Who's around to share his grief when the little girl dies? The nurse.

"Is it any wonder that after working through so many crises

together, sharing so many moments of elation and despair, a doctor and nurse might get emotionally involved with one another?"

There is something to this emotional-crisis theory. I know one surgeon, for example, who is a real hell-raiser. Not all the time, but sporadically. And I can just about predict when he's going to cut loose: when he loses a tough case.

Like Rose Curtis. Rose went to this surgeon—I'll call him Ed Mathews—to have her gall bladder out. Rose was forty, had three kids, and except for gallstones and being moderately overweight she was in good health. So Ed took her gall bladder out.

Postoperatively Rose got pancreatitis. This is inflammation of the pancreas. It comes on sometimes after gall-bladder or stomach surgery for reasons which are obscure. Most times the patients recover in a few days, but once in a while the inflammation runs wild, and despite everything you do, the patient dies.

For ten days after Rose got sick Ed worked constantly. He had me see Rose, had an internist in to see her, even called one of the big daddies at the university to see if he had anything to suggest. None of us came up with any brilliant ideas. Rose died.

The same night Ed went on a tear. He told his wife he was going to a medical meeting and he took off with one of the local floozies for two days. Then he came back and went to work.

What happens to Ed—to all of us at one time or another—is that when we're confronted with these tragic sudden deaths, we think, What the hell. If life is like that, if we may be cold tomorrow, then let's live it up as if there isn't any tomorrow, because there may damn well not be.

The other cases that set some of us off are the cancer cases. Cancer can be so awfully insidious. Jim Lewis comes into my office and says, "Bill, I noticed a little blood when I moved my bowels this morning. Probably nothing much—I've had hemorrhoid problems for years—but maybe you'd better check me out."

Jim is a lawyer, forty-two years old, and a good friend of mine. I check him out and find he has cancer of the rectum. At operation I find the tumor has already spread to the liver. Jim's number is up. How do I react? I go out and live it up. Maybe tomorrow it will be my turn.

I'm aware of the fallacy inherent in going from the particular to the general, the danger in saying, "This is the way I react, so it's the way all doctors react," but I can't help believing it's true. We doctors are reminded constantly of the unpredictability, the brevity, the cruelty of life. It's harder than hell to get up-tight and all flustered, making a big deal out of intercourse, when you've just seen some kid killed in an auto accident. It just doesn't seem that important.

Basically, however, we doctors are like most men. I suspect that in our work we may be subjected to more temptations and opportunities than the average man, but we usually resist. We're as aware of the rules of society as are other people. We have wives and children whom we love and we don't want to hurt them.

Most of us learn, sometimes by experience, that extramarital affairs cost a lot more than they're worth.

15

Doctors' Wives

What kind of woman does a doctor go home to; what sort of life does she have? There are thousands of different answers, since no two doctors' wives are alike, but they all enjoy certain benefits and share common burdens. There are pluses and minuses to the job.

Many people think that a doctor's wife has it made. Money, prestige, glamour—all these things belong to the girl lucky enough to capture a physician. Once she puts legal clamps on some budding internist, surgeon or pediatrician, a woman can sit back and relax. Her worries are over. So most women —particularly the mothers of marriageable females—think.

In some respects this is true, because, with very few exceptions, doctors earn a good living, are accepted members of most levels of society, and do live an interesting, even glamorous, life. Naturally, their wives share this life. It's not a bad deal.

However, as is the case with most "good deals," there are a few problems. Doctors' wives have jobs to do, some of which are difficult. They are also subjected to temptations other wives don't face. Many of them don't do their jobs or resist their temptations as well as they might.

One of the little—but important—assignments a doctor's wife gets, is that of answering the telephone. To do this job well, a doctor's wife has to learn to be a good liar.

On my afternoon off I never answer the telephone; I leave it to Joan. She's a very poor liar, for a doctor's wife, but she's all I have. When the caller asks for me I like to have her say, "I'm sorry, he's out. If you want to leave your number I'll have him call when he gets back." But if it turns out the call is from the hospital or from the office of one of the other doctors in town, she says, "Oh, just a minute. He's coming in the driveway right now." After an appropriate delay—ten seconds or so—I take the phone. Since I'm the only surgeon in town I feel obligated to take calls from other doctors even on my free afternoons, evenings or weekends.

If the caller is a patient it's another matter. He or she probably has some complaint another doctor can manage as well as I. On my time off I feel free to duck these calls; other doctors are available. So when the patient asks when I'll be home, Joan says, "I really can't say [which is the truth; I won't let her], it's his afternoon off. If you call the clinic I'm sure one of the other doctors will take care of you."

Now, I, and every other doctor I know, consider these lies justifiable. One of the most wearing aspects of life as a physician is the twenty-four-hour duty. You're never completely free from your obligation to your patients. I frequently curse Alexander Graham Bell for inventing the telephone. Doctors' wives have to learn to handle this obnoxious instrument with great care and respect.

As I've said, Joan isn't a very good liar. I'm sure that most of the time patients suspect she's lying. When she says, "He's not in," while I'm stretched out on the couch reading, her voice has a distinct quaver to it. I've heard other doctors' wives lie through their teeth with the authority that the Pope himself, speaking *ex cathedra*, couldn't project. They are true masters of telephone deceit.

But bad as Joan is at lying, her telephone technique is infinitely safer than that of some doctors' wives. These are the ones—and they're numerous—who seem to think that because they're married to doctors they have medical degrees themselves. They don't hesitate to treat, over the phone, cases that

I wouldn't touch without the benefit of lab work, X-rays and three consultations.

One of the worst offenders I've ever met is Bernice Flanagan. Her husband, Leo, is a G.P. who is extremely busy. When Leo is out on a house call or busy delivering a baby and the phone rings, Bernice is in her glory.

"I'm sorry, Dr. Flanagan isn't here. He may not be back for several hours. Is there anything I can help you with?"

"Gee, I don't know, Mrs. Flanagan. My little Sarah has a high temperature and a rash all over her. It started this morning and it's getting worse. Dr. Flanagan gave me some medicine for Jimmy last month, when he had the flu. I wonder if I can use that?"

"What color is it?"

"It's a red liquid."

"Probably Declomycin suspension," Bernice says. "Yes, you go ahead and give Sarah two teaspoonfuls now and then one four times a day. Give her a sponge bath and some aspirin. If she's not better in a day or two, call me back."

This sort of thing is really a form of Russian roulette. I'll occasionally treat a patient on the basis of phone information, but only if I'm very sure what he's got. Bernice will treat anything without the slightest trepidation.

Once she almost got Leo sued for malpractice. He was out playing golf when a woman called about a child.

"He's two years old," she said, "and he fell out of his high chair this morning. He didn't cut himself and he wasn't knocked out, but now he's crying and he threw up his lunch. Is that anything to worry about?"

"No," said Bernice. "He's probably just shaken up. Give him two baby aspirin. He should be fine."

Later that night the woman called back. Fortunately, this time she caught Leo at home and repeated her story. "He's vomited twice more, Dr. Flanagan. And he just lies there in his crib."

"Bring him to the hospital right away," Leo said. "I'll meet you there."

The baby had a skull fracture. The vomiting had been the

result of bleeding within the skull. Happily, the child survived.

Leo chewed Bernice out for that one, but the effect was short-lived. Within a week she was back on the phone, doctoring everything from meningitis to backache.

Some wives start practicing medicine over the phone, or at the bridge club, as a result of pressure from patients. When the doctor isn't in, the patient may ask his wife for advice, particularly if she was a nurse, and many doctors are married to nurses. She's making a big mistake when she starts giving medical advice, but some just can't resist it. It's sort of an ego trip for them. I'm very happy that Joan, who wasn't a nurse and knows nothing of medicine, doesn't give out advice.

Some doctors' wives get involved in the practice of medicine in other ways. I once knew an internist, Roger Hanley, whose wife managed his office. She wasn't a nurse, so she couldn't give shots, but she acted as a receptionist, bill collector and general aide-de-camp.

This was very bad for Roger's practice. Patients sometimes want to complain about their long wait for the doctor, ask about the way the insurance forms have been mishandled, question the charges the doctor has made. They have a right to make these complaints and ask these questions. But they don't want to confront the doctor with them; it might spoil the doctor–patient rapport. So in most offices the receptionist or aide or bookkeeper serves as a buffer. When the receptionist, aide or bookkeeper is the doctor's wife, it's almost as bad as facing the doctor himself. The patients don't dare complain; instead, they find another doctor.

Some wives—those who are easygoing and not intimidating —are able to manage this role successfully. I know one doctor's wife who does. But Josie Hanley couldn't. She was a strong, demanding, unbending person who looked as if she'd hit anyone who complained about anything. She thought her Roger could do no wrong. Roger finally had to fire her. It was either that or go broke. Their marriage survived the episode, but barely.

Bill Richards' wife, Elaine, has a characteristic common to many doctors' wives; she thinks that doctors are better than other people. (Many doctors also suffer from this delusion.) You can spot a wife suffering from this malady by listening to her speak about her husband. She will always refer to him as "the Doctor." "The doctor never eats ice cream," she will tell her bridge partner. "He says it's bad for the heart." "The doctor doesn't like to stay up late. He works awfully hard every day and he needs his rest." When I hear Elaine talking like this, I feel like taking her by the hand, leading her over to her husband and saying, "Elaine, meet Dr. Richards. He says you can call him Bill." But I don't do it. I just sit and squirm.

If Joan started calling me "the Doctor"—something I can't imagine in my wildest dreams that she'd ever do—I'd stop her immediately, probably by referring to her in conversations as "the Wife." But Bill never stops Elaine; he loves being referred to in a style usually reserved for the deity.

One of the sad songs that doctors' wives often sing is the one that goes, "My husband the doctor is never home. I have to take care of the house and raise the children all alone." They can usually count on a loud round of applause and gobs of sympathy after a chorus of this little number. They are implying, of course, that the doctor isn't home because he's out saving lives. The wife shares vicariously in the glory the doctor receives for being so self-sacrificing.

Now, I'm perfectly willing to admit that once in a while you'll find a doctor, usually a G.P., who has such a big practice that he does have trouble getting home. But most of the time this is not the case.

The wife who rarely sees her doctor husband had better look for another reason for his absence. I've known several doctors who didn't get home much, and the fact is that they just didn't want to go home. Their wives were, in their opinion, shrews. So they hung around the hospital coffee shop, went to medical meetings (of which, in a big city, it's possible to find at least one almost every night), and otherwise frittered away their time. When they really wanted to get home—when they had a golf date or a party to go to—they managed to be on time. Except in rare instances, and they're getting rarer every year, no doctor has to neglect wife and family for his practice. But doctors' wives, and doctors, keep pretending they do.

One of the reasons some wives like to take an active part in their husbands' practices is that they don't trust them. They think if they're left out of sight too long they'll be into some hanky-panky, which may or may not be true.

Helen Amborn, whose husband, Fred, is a surgeon in a small town in New York, has actually pioneered in the field of "keeping tabs on my husband the doctor." She has taken up surgery as sort of a hobby. Honestly, I know it's difficult to believe, but Helen, who is not a nurse, now assists Fred in the operating room. When he repairs a hernia, takes out an appendix or removes a gall bladder, there, across the table from him, is Helen. She cuts sutures, tugs on retractors, ties knots. She even, heaven help us, sews up an occasional patient. The patients seem to tolerate it very well, which only proves that the mechanics of surgery aren't all that difficult to learn. Fred and the O.R. nurses trained Helen in six weeks. On the other hand, after a year of facing Helen at the operating table as well as at the breakfast table, Fred seems to be looking a bit under the weather. If she were my wife I'd be tempted to nick her with the scalpel every now and then, deeper each time. She'd have to choose between leaving me alone to work at my profession or keeping ten fingers on her hands.

Money is another thing doctors' wives have in common. Most doctors enjoy a good income. Their wives get to spend it.

For some of them this becomes a matter of staying one up on the other doctors' wives. Leona drives a Cadillac, Mary buys a Jaguar; Alice does over her entire living room, Lucille puts in a swimming pool; Mona accompanies Al to the cardiology meeting in San Francisco, Helen insists on flying to the surgical conference in Peru with Dan. There is no end to the amount of money a doctor's wife can blow in an attempt to keep up with the other wives.

Not all the wives—not even most of them—get involved in this competition. Those that are most susceptible seem to be

those who never had any money till they married their doctor
husbands. When hubby walks in with three or four thousand
for a month's work, they get carried away. They can't spend
it fast enough.

Often they argue that they're spending it for their husbands'
sake. "If I don't dress nicely, if we don't have a beautiful
home, if the children don't go to private schools, people are
going to think Bob's not a very good doctor." Strangely
enough, some doctors buy this line. (And even more
strangely, there's a kernel of truth in it. Would you go to a
doctor who drove a broken-down car, lived in the slum section of town and had a wife who took in laundry? You would
not.)

Besides spending money "to keep the doctor looking
prosperous," there is another thing that doctors' wives everywhere do to help their husbands' practice; they dress up in
short skirts and do the hootchy-kootchy at the hospital auxiliary benefit show and dance.

Every year, without fail, there is a picture in at least one of
the newspapers we regularly read of a group of doctors' wives
dressed up as can-can girls. "The wives of our local doctors,"
the caption reads, "put on a most entertaining musical extrava-
ganza last evening at the Roger Smith Hotel. They raised
three thousand dollars which will be used to refurnish the
nurses' lounge on the third floor of the Holy Oak Hospital."

This sort of undertaking seems to me, and to Joan, as service
above and beyond the call of duty. There is little doubt, however, that there are doctors' wives who thrive on it. They
can't wait for spring to come around to see if they can again
meet the challenge and lose enough weight to squeeze back
into their tights. They love it.

It takes a courageous doctor's wife not to do anything for
the hospital auxiliary. Even Joan, who is extremely apa-
thetic when it comes to promoting my practice, puts in one
afternoon a month running the coffee shop at the hospital. She
feels an obligation to do something for the hospital, and this
is a job she can do alone. Like me, she hates committees.

I give her credit, however. That one job is absolutely all

she does that could conceivably be construed as boosterizing for my practice. She figures I have my job, she has hers—I don't try to persuade people to call her in to keep house or raise their kids; she doesn't try to talk people into coming to me to have their gall bladders out.

Some doctors' wives make a full-time career out of promoting their husbands' practices. Sometimes the approach is so blatant it's embarrassing. For example, at a cocktail party one evening I overheard a conversation between Susan Robbins and Marie, a lawyer's wife.

"Is your back still bothering you?" Susan asked.

"I'm afraid it is," Marie said. "I've tried heat, pills and even traction, but it just doesn't seem to get any better. Dr. Rhodes says he's never seen a more stubborn case."

"Isn't that too bad," Susan said. "Just last night at dinner the doctor mentioned a patient he had with a back problem like yours. He'd given her some new treatment—something I couldn't begin to understand—and in less than a week she was all better. In fact, she was out at the Country Club playing golf."

"Gee," said Marie, "that sounds wonderful. You don't think the doctor would be willing to see me, do you?"

"I'm sure he would," Susan answered. "Why don't you call his office? No reflection on Dr. Rhodes, of course; he's a wonderful doctor. Probably just unlucky with your case."

Ordinarily, patient solicitation by the wives isn't as obvious as this. Usually it's just a matter of working on the Red Cross bloodmobile drive, joining the Women's Club, never missing a society meeting at the church. Use your time well at these meetings, talk about the latest triumphs of your doctor husband, invite other doctors' patients in for coffee; it's amazing how much some doctors' wives will do to bring the crowds into their husbands' offices. And even more amazing, how well it works.

It isn't always the wife's idea. Jim Robbins would get sorer than the devil if his wife dropped out of the Women's Club. After all, hasn't he been eating those creamed chicken lunches every Tuesday at the Rotary Club meetings for ten years? And Stan Wilson. Do you think he'd be in church every

Sunday if he wasn't getting all the Methodists in town in his office as a result? Let Lois try dropping out of the altar society; "Do you want a trip to the moon," as Ralph Kramden would say. A lot of doctors do all kinds of things they hate in order to boost their practices; why shouldn't their wives do the same? So they reason, and their wives cooperate.

One problem with which a doctor's wife is repeatedly confronted is that of how much to say when someone's illness is under discussion.

"I understand Helen Simonsen is pregnant again," someone says during coffee after the Women's Club meeting. Lorraine Stein, the obstetrician's wife, is in the group. Everyone is just dying to know if Helen really is "P.G."

Lorraine knows. They know she knows. There's a great temptation for Lorraine, all eyes on her, to say, "She certainly is. Two months. And she'd like to have an abortion."

What a juicy morsel! Lorraine could be the center of attention for hours. She could also put a big dent in her husband's practice. If she's smart she pretends, as Lorraine does, that she hasn't even heard the comment; she turns the conversation to the movie playing at the Hollywood.

Sarah is playing bridge. Her husband, Peter, operated on Jim Louis two days earlier. Sarah's partner says, "I understand Jim Louis has cancer. I feel so sorry for Mary."

What should Sarah say? "Yes, isn't it sad"? That's what the ladies want—confirmation of the rumor.

Sarah should keep her mouth shut, say nothing, or if she feels she has to talk, say simply, "I don't know. Peter hasn't told me." Which is, in all probability, a lie, but certainly a justifiable one.

It's probably a lie because most doctors do tell their wives about the patients they're treating. I tell Joan almost everything of any interest that's going on in my practice. But I make exceptions.

Liz Ramey came to me one day looking absolutely distraught. Liz is forty, the wife of a local businessman, and she and Bob are good friends of ours. "Bill," she said, without any preliminaries, "I think I'm pregnant. I don't want any more children. If I'm pregnant, I want an abortion."

I'm not an obstetrician and I don't do abortions. They're illegal in Minnesota. Liz knew this. She came to me because we're friends and she felt she could trust me. It turned out, to her great delight, that she wasn't pregnant after all. It was just a matter of a delayed period—something that's apt to happen now and then as you get older.

I've never told Joan about Liz's visit. It isn't that I don't trust Joan; I've never known her to talk indiscreetly. It's just that I don't think Liz would want her to know. It might change the rapport between them.

Nor will I ever tell Joan about the time Bruce Leffler came to me because he'd acquired, on a business trip, three big contracts for his insurance company and a nice case of gonorrhea as well. It was a tough case to manage (there's a chapter on venereal disease elsewhere in this book), and I would have liked to talk it over with Joan but I didn't. If Joan knew Bruce had picked up a venereal disease her whole attitude toward Bruce would have been affected. That wouldn't have been fair to Bruce.

But patients with cancer, routine pregnancies, problem cases—I talk about these to Joan. She knows nothing of medicine, but she does have common sense, and doctors, like everyone else, have to have someone with whom they can carry on an uninhibited, open discussion. I'm fortunate in having a wife whom I can trust to keep her mouth shut.

Having taken a swipe at some doctors' wives, let me try to take the curse off by admitting that most doctors' wives are very nice, pleasant people. And they do have to put up with annoyances to which the wives of other men aren't subjected.

One summer, for example, we had the six kids finally settled in the station wagon, luggage on the roof, and were about to leave town for a week's vacation, when the phone rang. Joan said, "Shall I answer it?" I thought it over for a few seconds and said, "Go ahead."

It turned out to be another doctor in town who had just gotten in three people injured in a car accident. One patient had a ruptured spleen, a second had cut all the tendons in her left wrist, and the third had an open fracture of the tibia. I had to operate on all three. Joan was disappointed, of course, but she didn't say, as some women might have, "Oh, why don't you tell them to call someone else?" Instead, while I drove off to the hospital she unloaded the kids and went out and bought food for dinner. We postponed the trip for one more day.

Every doctor's wife has to put up with late meals, canceled trips to the theater, even—worst of all—an occasional interruption at a critical period in an hour of romance. It's part of the package when she marries a doctor. Most women know this and accept it. Those that don't usually wind up losing their doctor husbands—either legally in the divorce court or, less obviously, to the hospital meetings and house calls to which he gives an increasing portion of his time. Much better for all concerned if a doctor's wife learns to accept with grace the unavoidable irritations of medical practice.

On balance, the life of a doctor's wife is an attractive one.

16

How Doctors Get Along With Each Other

After a doctor has learned to get along with his partners, his wife and the nurses, he has to learn how to get along with the other doctors in his community. You learn very quickly, when you get into practice, that how bright you were in medical school doesn't count nearly as much as your bedside manner when it comes to building and holding a practice. The average patient doesn't know where his doctor went to medical school or whether he finished at the top or bottom of his class. Nor does the patient care. What he's looking for is a kind, compassionate understanding person; a nice guy. If you're a specialist, as I am, and count on other doctors to send patients to you, then it's imperative that you be nice not only to patients but to the doctor that sends them to you. As a result, a lot of butt-kissing goes on in the medical world.

Fortunately, I don't have to do much of it. Since I'm the only surgeon in town the local doctors have to either refer their cases to me or go to the trouble of calling a surgeon in from another city. As long as I do a good job, and behave decently, they refer patients to me.

One of the reasons I enjoy practicing in Litchfield is that with occasional exceptions, all we doctors get along reasonably well together.

I don't try to knife any other local doctor, and as far as I know, no one tries to knife me. Not because we don't have the opportunities.

A few years ago a salesman named Leo Francis used to visit our clinic regularly. Leo was fifty years old, had a paunch and was inclined to puff after he walked up one flight of stairs. He was also a mild hypochondriac.

One afternoon he stopped by my office to tell me about a business problem and when we'd finished our discussion he said, "By the way, Dr. Nolen, I've had a pain in my chest for the last few days."

"Bad?" I asked.

"Not really. Just sort of annoying."

"Where?" He pointed up high on the left side.

"Let me listen a minute," I said. Leo opened his shirt and I put my stethoscope on his chest.

"Sounds O.K., Leo. Probably just a little neuritis. Don't worry about it."

A week later, on my afternoon off, Leo stopped by again, and this time he mentioned the pain to George. George ordered an electrocardiogram, and sure enough, Leo was having a coronary. George stuck him in the hospital. He was there for six weeks.

George could have really made me look bad. He knew and I knew that Leo's coronary had started before I'd seen him. If I had ordered the E.K.G. I'd have made the diagnosis.

But George protected me. He implied to Leo that the coronary had started the day George saw him, that an E.K.G. a week earlier would have been normal, that Leo had had neuritis for a week, and then a heart attack. I was very grateful.

I've had innumerable opportunities to put the screws to other doctors. Since most of my patients come as referrals from other doctors, I occasionally see their patients after they've messed them up.

Like the child that Joe Menton sent me. This was a six-year-old boy that he'd had in the hospital for a week, treating him for pneumonia. The kid wasn't getting any better.

"Take a look at him, will you, Bill?" he said. "I'm beginning to think he might have something wrong in his belly."

I went in to see the boy and it was obvious that he was sicker than hell. His nostrils flared when he breathed and the kid lay rigidly in his bed. All I had to do was touch his belly and he screamed.

The chest X-ray undoubtedly showed pneumonia in the right lower lobe of the lung, but not enough to account for all his symptoms. The child's temperature was 103 degrees, and his white blood count was 24,000; 8,000 is normal.

"I'll tell you, Joe," I said. "I think we'd better open this kid up. I've got a feeling he has a ruptured appendix as well as pneumonia."

I was right. The boy's belly was full of pus. We took out his appendix and drained an abscess that had formed in the pelvis.

After the operation we met with the family in the hospital lounge and I did the talking. "Your boy had two diseases, Mrs. Rollins," I said. "He had the pneumonia that brought him to the hospital, and which Dr. Menton has been treating very well, but while he's been here he also got appendicitis. Because his pneumonia made him so sick it was impossible to tell what was going on immediately. He's going to be sick for a few days, but he's tough and I think he'll be all right."

What I'd told them was the truth, sort of. The boy did have both appendicitis and pneumonia. What I didn't tell them was that he had probably had appendicitis for at least three days. But after all, this was only probable, though highly probable, and there was no sense in suggesting that Joe had missed the diagnosis. It wouldn't do the family any good and would only hurt Joe. I knew he'd protect me if the roles were reversed and I'd missed some medical ailment.

But once out of their immediate circle, doctors aren't always so anxious to protect their confreres. In big cities, where there's an overabundance of specialists in one field or another, it's not uncommon for one doctor to disparage another if he gets the chance.

It's easy to do. I have a friend practicing vascular surgery in a large city. He runs into this all the time. There are a lot of vascular surgeons in this particular community and not an awful lot of patients who need their blood vessels operated on. There's a great deal of competition for the cases.

Often the G.P.'s who refer the cases don't know much about the technical aspects of the surgery. There are differences of opinions even among the vascular surgeons about how to treat various diseases.

Doug Richardson, the guy I'm referring to, told me about one case he did.

"I worked hard on this case, Bill," Doug said. "The patient had blown a hole in a popliteal aneurysm [the popliteal artery is behind the knee; an aneurysm is a balloon-like weak spot], and it was a mess. I worked three hours dissecting out the vessels and putting in a vein graft. But the leg was too far gone. I had to amputate it three days later. Larry Simpson had sent me the case and he was very sympathetic.

"Then you know what happened? At a cocktail party a few weeks later Larry got talking to Ralph Leiter [another vascular surgeon] and he told him about the case. 'You mean Doug actually put in a vein graft instead of using teflon?' Ralph said. And that was all he said. But Larry got the message. He sent his next vascular case to Ralph—the bastard."

When one doctor knocks another to a third it's bad; but it's much worse when one doctor knocks another to a patient. This goes on a lot in some cities. I have a friend who practices in such a place and he told me what it's like.

"I'd been treating this woman for phlebitis [a vein inflammation]," he said. "She had high blood pressure and a history of an old bleeding ulcer, so I decided not to anticoagulate her [give her medicine to "thin" her blood so it won't clot easily]. As luck would have it she threw an embolus to her lung. Her husband got antsy and asked me to have Tom Lewis see her in consultation. Tom's the worst prick in town but what could I do? I asked him in.

"You can imagine what the son of a bitch did. He made it very plain to the family that if he had had the case from the beginning he would have anticoagulated her immediately.

He only hoped it wasn't too late now. He made me look like an ignoramus. I'm goddam lucky I didn't get sued."

Actually it's this sort of thing, one doctor knocking another to a patient, that starts a lot of malpractice suits. Plant the idea in the patient's mind that maybe he hasn't had the best possible treatment and off he goes to the lawyer. Thank the Lord there aren't too many doctors who pull these tricks.

Doctors in private practice, by and large, tend to protect each other. We're out in communities where we have to deal with all sorts of patients, and families, often under less than optimum conditions. We know what it's like to be harassed, to be overworked, to be pressured into doing things hastily. So we try to be nice. We don't lie to protect each other, but we don't throw the truth around with complete abandon either. A professor I know was once asked by an intern if he was going to write a paper on a very interesting case which, unfortunately, had been messed up at the university hospital where he was chief. "No," the professor answered, "I'm not. We don't hide our mistakes, but we don't advertise them either." That's the way most of us react.

17

Malpractice

One of the reasons most of us go out of our way to protect our confreres is the fear of a malpractice suit.

I've never been sued for malpractice, but I've had some awfully narrow escapes.

The closest I've come was with Art Golden. Art was a patient of Stu Nielsen's. About six months after I moved to Litchfield, Stu asked me to take a look at Art. "He's got a tremendous incisional hernia, Bill," Stu said, "and he's been afraid to have it fixed. But it's getting bigger and more difficult to manage. Take a look at it and see if you think we can fix it."

Art came into my office a few days later. He seemed like a nice guy. He was fifty-six years old and in generally good health. He ran a dry-cleaning business in Litchfield.

He had one hell of a hernia. Stu had taken Art's gall bladder out ten years earlier and Art had developed an infection. The infection had destroyed the muscular layers of the abdomen, and when he finally healed he was left with a huge hernia: just skin and a thin layer of fat over the peritoneum, the inner lining of the abdomen. The hernia was about the size of a small watermelon. I wasn't anxious to repair it.

"Art," I said, "you've got quite a hernia. It's so big that I'm not sure I can find enough good tissue to fix it. Maybe you ought to stick with your girdle." Art had been wearing a girdle for five years.

"Doc, I don't want to," he said. "I'm on my feet at the shop all day and this hernia just about kills me. I want the thing fixed."

"O.K.," I said, "we'll give it a try."

A week later we operated on Art. We had to make a big hole in his belly, but we took our time, and after a couple of hours, we managed to bring together enough good tissue from the edges of the hernia to fix it. I used big, strong stitches, because there was a lot of strain on them. The case went reasonably well.

Postoperatively the wound drained a little fluid. This isn't unusual after a big hernia operation; there's often a big space in the fat where the hernia used to be and fluid seeps into this space. The drainage quit after a few days and the wound healed nicely. We sent Art home in ten days. His hernia was fixed, he was pleased, and so were Stu and I.

I didn't see Art about his hernia again. Stu checked it six weeks later and reported that it was well healed. Once in a while I'd meet Art when I stopped into the hotel for a cup of coffee, and three years later I operated on his wife Norma's elbow when she broke it. When I did see him he was always pleasant and he often told me how glad he was that he'd had his hernia fixed.

Six years after the operation Art had some trouble with his bowels. Nothing much, just a little constipation, but Stu, who was still his family doctor, thought he ought to have X-rays. When the first film was taken, lo and behold, down in the right lower portion of his abdomen, was a nice big metal clamp.

I nearly died when Stu showed me the film. We dug out some X-rays he'd taken before the hernia operation, just to make certain the clamp hadn't been left behind when Stu took out his gall bladder. No such luck. I was the guy who had left it in. It had gotten lost in that big hole we'd made in his belly.

By this time Art's constipation had cleared up, which meant that it was unrelated to the clamp. The clamp was actually not doing Art any harm. It was just an incidental finding, like the extra bone some people have in the wrist.

"What'll we do?" I asked Stu.

"I suppose we've got to tell him," Stu said, "and the sooner the better. Everyone in the hospital knows about it by now."

"I guess you're right," I answered. "But what'll we tell him? Should we offer to take the damn thing out for free? Once he knows he's got it in him he's going to start worrying about it, and so will we. There's a chance that a loop of bowel could get mixed up in it."

"I tell you what," Stu said. "He's got a small hernia on the other side. Let's tell him we'll fix that hernia for nothing and at the same time we'll reach in and get the clamp. That way he won't be going through an operation just for the clamp."

"Sounds fine to me," I said. "Let's hope he goes for it."

We called Art in, showed him the X-ray, and made our offer. Art studied the film awhile and then sat back. He was frowning.

"I could sue the two of you, couldn't I?" he asked.

This shook me, but I tried not to show it. "I guess you could, Art," I said.

"I'd win too, wouldn't I?"

"Probably," I answered. It was pointless to argue. He had us.

"All right," he said, standing up and grinning. "I'm tempted to make you two sweat, but I haven't got it in me. I'm too glad to be rid of that watermelon. Fix the other hernia, pick up the rest of your equipment and we'll call it square."

Stu and I had lucked out.

A few weeks later, when I went to a restaurant for a cup of coffee, a friend of mine, Bob Norcross, came up to me, gave me a wink and said, "I hear you're not much of a carpenter—you don't pick up your tools when you finish a job." Then he laughed and walked off. There aren't many secrets kept in a small town.

All doctors worry about malpractice suits—not consciously, of course, but the fear is always in the back of their minds. They never know when the blow is going to fall.

The reason we worry is that we're so awfully vulnerable. There are usually several different ways to manage any given illness. If something goes sour, if the patient gets a complication which results in disability or death, it's always possible to ask, "Wouldn't it have been better to use some other treatment?" We repeatedly ask ourselves this question. If a patient or his family asks it, and can convince a lawyer that the answer is yes, we've got a malpractice suit on our hands.

Here's an example of what I mean. About a year after I arrived in Litchfield, one of my partners, Paul Halstead, asked me to see a patient, Ralph Warner, with him.

Ralph was fifty-nine years old, a garage mechanic, husky and generally healthy. He had only one problem—he couldn't urinate. He had to get up two or three times a night, had trouble starting his stream, couldn't empty his bladder. This is the classic history of the man whose prostate has enlarged and is beginning to block the outlet of his bladder. It happens to a great many middle-aged men. Ralph's prostate was about three times the normal size.

"What do you think, Bill?" Paul asked.

"Mighty big prostate," I answered. "He'll have to have it out. How do you want to do it?"

"From above," Paul said, "I think it's too big for a T.U.R. I'll put him on the schedule for next Wednesday. Can you help me?"

"I'll be there."

What we'd been talking about was the operation we were going to perform on Ralph's prostate. There are several operations that can be used, but basically it's a matter of deciding whether to do the operation through the urethra—the T.U.R., or trans-urethral resection, which Paul had mentioned—or from above.

The T.U.R. doesn't require an incision—you put a metal tube into the urethral opening at the end of the penis and through it you shave off pieces of the prostate, enlarging the urinary passage. When he operates from above the surgeon opens the bladder, puts his finger into it, and enucleates the prostate. The T.U.R. is used most of the time; the open procedure is reserved for very large prostates.

Paul and I operated on Ralph. When we got into the bladder we found that the gland was more fibrous than we'd expected. Paul had a difficult time shelling it out, and when he finally had it removed we found that he'd torn the urethra a little bit below the gland. We sewed it up and got out.

Ralph had a stormy postoperative recovery. He bled a lot, as prostatectomy patients often do, and when he finally healed he had a stricture, a tight scar, where Paul had torn the urethra. We had to pass dilators up Ralph's urethra to stretch the scar. It was six months before we had him back to normal.

Or almost to normal. He still had one problem: he couldn't get an erection.

Now, this happens once in a while after a prostatectomy. Most times the reason is purely psychological—95 percent of impotence problems are—and that was, as far as we could tell, the explanation for Ralph's impotence.

But Ralph didn't believe it. He knew we'd been shoving hardware up his penis to widen the scar, and as far as he was concerned, this was what had messed him up. In the six months it had taken us to get him better he'd compared notes with patients who'd had the T.U.R. operation and most of them had been all better in six weeks. More important, all of them who'd been able to get it up before surgery could still get it up. Ralph blamed us for his problem—he thought we should have given him the other operation. He decided to sue.

In a group practice, like the one I'm in, when one partner gets sued we all get sued. We got together to talk the situation over.

"I'd fight it, Paul," I said. "We didn't do one thing that was unreasonable. So we got a tear in the urethra—so what? That's not the first time a urethra's been torn and it won't be the last. That's one of the risks of the operation."

"Yeah, but, Bill," Paul said, "let me ask you this. If you had it to do over again how would you do Ralph—with a T.U.R. or from above?"

"I wouldn't operate on the bastard at all," I said. "I'd send him to one of my enemies."

"I know, I know," Paul said. "So would I. But if you had to do him, how would you do it?"

"From below," I conceded.

"O.K.," Paul said, "we'd do him from below. We've got to admit it. We made a mistake in judgment. How's that going to sound in court?"

"Who's going to testify against us? There isn't a surgeon in the world who would second-guess us on this thing. Not on a matter of judgment."

"Maybe you're right," Paul said. "All right, we'll fight it if the insurance company agrees. I don't like it, but I suppose we should."

The insurance company didn't agree. They thought we might win the case but that it could be a tough fight. Juries are pretty free with insurance money, in any case, and when a patient could swear that he became impotent immediately after an operation on his prostate, they'd probably be mighty sympathetic. Our malpractice insurers settled out of court.

Now, in this case we really weren't guilty of malpractice. Admittedly, we might have made a different choice if we had it to do again, but the chances are Ralph would have wound up impotent either way. The problem was strictly psychological. By settling we took the easy way out.

The fear of malpractice suits can really hamper a surgeon. If he can't make decisions, based on experience and training, without fear that he'll be sued if something goes wrong, he can't function.

Generally speaking, according to the law, the surgeon isn't in any legal danger if what he has done is reasonable. In malpractice cases the one who is doing the suing has to prove that the doctor did not provide care of the quality that a patient could expect to obtain from the other doctors in the same community. If you're a G.P. you're expected to provide care of at least the same average quality as the other G.P.'s who practice in your area; if you're a surgeon you have to be as good as the other surgeons who operate in your hospital. All of which is perfectly reasonable.

Strangely enough, in the cases which really represent malpractice the guilty physician is rarely ever sued.

Take Jack Nadler, for example. Jack's a G.P. and a nice

enough guy. He's a wild dresser, a great golfer, and wonderful fun at a party. Everyone likes him. He has a big practice. Despite his other activities he makes a point of being readily available and people like that.

But if there is one aspect of general practice at which Jack isn't very good, it's surgery. He's a flashy operator and a fast surgeon, but he's careless. His patients have more complications than they should.

Still, Jack would never be guilty of malpractice if he stuck to the relatively uncomplicated operations like hemorrhoids, appendectomies and hernia repairs. He could get the average patient through these procedures. But Jack doesn't stick to the really simple stuff; he tackles cases he has no business handling. And sometimes he botches them.

Like Abe Riley. Abe runs a store in Litchfield. I play golf with him often, and Joan and I occasionally play bridge with him and his wife, Anne. Abe and his family have always gone to Jack for their medical care.

A few years ago Abe got yellow jaundice. Jack admitted him to the hospital, got some X-rays and blood studies, and decided Abe had gallstones. Not only did he have gallstones in his gall bladder, one or more of them had slipped into the common duct, the tubelike structure about the diameter of a pencil that runs from the gall bladder to the intestine. Abe had jaundice because a stone was blocking the flow of the bile and it was backing up into Abe's bloodstream.

If the patient is thin and the gall bladder isn't inflamed, removing the gall bladder can be relatively easy. On the other hand, if the gall bladder is infected or irritated by stones, the wall gets thick and the operation can be a bloody mess. And when there's a stone in the common bile duct the operation is always tricky. It's no operation for a guy who isn't fully trained and specializing in surgery. It was no operation for Jack Nadler to tackle.

One of the big problems the layman runs into is that of deciding what his family doctor can and cannot do. He has no way of evaluating his doctor's capabilities. To most people a doctor is a doctor is a doctor. If one does some surgery he's a surgeon. So they just take the word of the person who's caring for them.

Most of the time this works out all right. The G.P. who finds a patient with bowel cancer will refer the patient to a surgeon; the surgeon who sees a patient with a heart attack will call for an internist. The internist whose patient develops a bad back will ask an orthopedist to take over.

Unfortunately, some doctors don't recognize their limitations. They tackle things that are beyond their capabilities. They hate to admit that there's anything they can't treat. Jack is like this.

So instead of asking me to operate on Abe, Jack decided to do the operation himself. Abe didn't interfere: he figured if Jack said he could do it, why, it must be so. Jack arranged to have Brian O'Connor, another G.P., help him. I saw the case on the schedule, even stopped by Abe's room to say hello, but I didn't tell Abe that he was a damn fool to let Jack operate on him. I didn't dare. Not only would I have antagonized Jack so that he'd never send me another patient, I'd have been in trouble with every doctor on the staff. We all feel we have the right to decide what we can and cannot do. We feel we're each the best judge of our own capabilities.

Jack did the case and Jack screwed it up. He got Abe's gall bladder out without too much difficulty, and he even fished one stone out of the common duct, but he missed two others. They showed up on the X-rays Jack ordered two weeks later when he found that Abe wouldn't stop draining bile. Now Jack asked me to take a look at Abe.

After examining Abe I wanted to say, "Jack, you jackass, you've messed this whole case up," but I didn't. I had neither the guts nor the heart to say what I felt.

Instead I said, "Gee, Jack, that's a tough break. It looks as if there are still two stones in the duct. They must have come down from the liver after you operated. We'd better go back and get them." Both Jack and I knew I was lying—that those stones had been there when Jack operated on Abe—but I wanted to let Jack save face.

So we reoperated on Abe. Getting those stones out now was

twice as difficult as it would have been had they been removed at the first operation. But Abe was tough and he came through it all right. For an older, more decrepit patient a second operation could have been fatal.

Now, that case, to me, is a perfect example of malpractice. Abe had had two operations, with all the attendant risks, when he should have had one. It cost him an extra month of recuperation, to say nothing of the extra expense. All because Jack Nadler acted like a pompous ass and refused to admit that he wasn't God Almighty.

Abe didn't sue, of course. As far as he's concerned, Jack did a great job. He thinks Jack saved his life, that the two operations were completely necessary. In fact, he's even more grateful to Jack than he would have been if he'd gotten by with one operation. Jack saved him twice.

Half the secret—probably more than half the secret—to avoiding malpractice suits lies in learning how to talk to patients.

One approach all doctors use is that of maximizing, in talking to the patient's family, the risks and complications of an operation.

For example, when I took out Joe Ross's stomach I said to his wife the day before the operation, "Mrs. Ross, this is going to be a big operation. I think Joe will come through it all right, but I'm sure you know that with any major operation there are plenty of risks. Joe's ulcer may be stuck to his pancreas, and that could make it difficult to remove. There are big blood vessels going to the stomach, and sometimes they bleed. After the operation there's always the danger of infection, and sometimes it takes a while for the portion of stomach we leave in to start working again. Joe needs the operation—he's been bleeding from the ulcer and it hasn't gotten better on medical treatment—and, he should do just fine. But I want you to know there are risks."

"I appreciate your telling me, Dr. Nolen," she said. "I'm sure you'll do the best job possible."

Now, with this warning, if something did go sour in Joe's case Mrs. Ross would not be inclined to blame me.

With Joe, my approach was entirely different. Any patient who's going to have his stomach out knows it's a big operation. The surgeon doesn't have to play up the dangers to him. What Joe needed was reassurance so that he'd be relatively calm going into the operating room. So when I checked him the day before the operation, I said, "Joe, except for that ulcer you're in damn good shape. You ought to sail through this operation quite nicely. You may have some pain for the first day or two, but before you know it you'll be up and around eating. You're going to feel a lot better with that ulcer out."

I wasn't lying to either Joe or Mrs. Ross. It's just a matter of knowing what points to emphasize to each.

Accident cases are the worst malpractice threat. Any time I see a patient who has been hurt in an automobile accident I know there's going to be some suing going on, and I don't want to be one of those sued.

Which means that I don't always treat injured patients reasonably; I'm apt to overtreat them. Any patient that comes to me after an auto accident and complains of pain in the back or neck, gets X-rays of the spine. I know damn well that those X-rays aren't going to show anything, that the bones are all right, but I want X-ray proof of that fact. I don't want to find myself in the witness stand a year later listening to some lawyer say, "But, Doctor, do you mean to tell me that you didn't order any X-rays of my client's neck? Weren't you concerned, Doctor, that she might have a fracture?" That kind of question really gets to a jury and makes the doctor look like an idiot. So I feel obligated to get the X-rays, let the patient have an exposure to radiation that he doesn't really need, let him spend an extra thirty or forty bucks. That's what he wants, that's what he'll get. It's stupid, but this is the way we have to practice to protect ourselves.

One of the biggest complaints lawyers have against doctors is that they have a terrible time finding one doctor who will testify against another in a malpractice case. The lawyers complain that we doctors maintain a conspiracy of silence. It's not true, but I can see why they think it might be. Unless the case represents a four-plus violation of reasonable practice, we are reluctant to criticize another doctor. We all live in glass houses and we're very hesitant about throwing stones.

A few years ago a lawyer friend of mine, Ralph Thompson, came to see me one afternoon.

"Bill," he said, "I've got a problem. A woman, a Louise Swanson from Valparaiso, came to see me the other day. She's forty years old. About a year ago she began having pain in her back and she went to see a doctor in Valparaiso, a man named Black. He told her she needed to have her uterus out, and he operated on her. After the operation she had even more pain in her back, but he told her not to worry about it, that it would go away. It didn't. She went to another doctor, a man named Larson, and he got some X-rays and found that her original back pain was from a herniated disc in her spine. He also found that her right kidney wasn't working. They had to take it out, and when they did they found that Black had tied off the ureter when he took out the uterus—that's why the kidney wouldn't work. I've got a copy of the hospital record which shows that the uterus was normal. I think my client was a victim of malpractice, but Larson won't testify against Black. All he says is, 'These things happen.' What do you think?"

I knew Dr. Black. He had a bad reputation. He was too quick with the knife. He did a lot of operations that most surgeons considered worthless. But he was a smoothie and he had a big practice.

It was obvious that he had fouled up this case. He had made the wrong diagnosis, he had done the wrong operation, and he had done it poorly. His foul-ups had cost this woman her uterus and her right kidney without making her any better.

So did I agree to testify against Black? Did I agree to help this woman who had been an obvious victim of malpractice? Sorry, no.

"Ralph," I said, "off the record, I agree with you—your client has been mistreated. But I don't see how I can help you prove it.

"After all—what did Black do? First, he made the wrong diagnosis. Well, every doctor does at one time or another. I've taken out my share of normal appendices. You can't sue a man for that.

"Second, he took out an apparently normal uterus. That's no crime either. Even a uterus that looks normal can cause trouble if it bleeds.

"Third, he tied off the ureter. This is bad, I agree, but it's one of the risks of the operation. It shouldn't happen, but it sometimes does. I have to confess to having done it once myself in a case where a woman had a huge tumor of the uterus.

"So if we add it up, all we can say is Black made a lot of mistakes. I agree he screwed the case up completely and that he probably shouldn't have, but on each individual error he has a lot of company. I can't testify against him, and I doubt if any other doctor will. Sorry."

Ralph had to drop the case.

The cases where I've sweated most over the possibility of a malpractice suit are those where I get a complication, particularly one I should have avoided.

Thyroid operations commonly afford such situations. There's a nerve called the recurrent laryngeal on each side of the neck between the thyroid gland and the windpipe. These nerves are the size and color of white thread. They run to the two vocal cords. They are often difficult as the devil to see and they are easy to cut when you're removing an entire lobe of a thyroid gland.

To my knowledge, I've only cut one—which isn't too bad. As long as one vocal cord works the patient can talk and breathe all right, except for a slight hoarseness for a few weeks. But cut them both and the patient is in trouble. First, he can't speak, then after a few weeks when the vocal cords shrivel up, he'll have trouble breathing. It takes a complicated operation on the cords themselves to improve the situation, and no matter what you do the patient never quite gets back to normal.

I know a couple of surgeons who have cut both nerves. One was sued, the other wasn't. The fellow who was sued could probably have defended the case and won—there's hardly a surgeon in the world with any experience who hasn't either cut a nerve or had a near miss—but he chose not to and his insurance company agreed. He wasn't anxious to have the publicity; and, besides, he knew that the patient's disability was due to his error, unintentional or not. So he settled out of court.

There are doctors, generally hated by the rest of the medical profession, who make a career of testifying against other doctors. Most of them are full-time salaried physicians who work either for hospitals or big companies. They're in positions where they can avoid responsibility either because of the nature of their practice—they may give insurance physicals all day—or can dump all responsibility and liability onto their employers. Either way, they never need to worry about being sued themselves, are never inclined to say, "There but for the grace of God go I," and are perfectly willing to throw stones at other doctors—for a nice big fat fee.

The best way to get at these doctors is to let the jury know just what they're like. Stool pigeons are very unpopular. Fair is fair, but if a doctor is spending the bulk of his time running around testifying against other doctors he just has to be rotten, and probably not a very good doctor either. If he were any good he'd be too busy taking care of patients to spend all his time in court. The last time I saw one of these gentlemen—an internist from a big-city V.A. hospital who came out to a small town near here to testify against a local G.P. in behalf of a client who had no legitimate gripe—the lawyer got the "stool pigeon" message across and the jury didn't give the plaintiff a nickel.

There are some cases in which the plaintiff doesn't need a doctor to testify in his behalf. These are the so-called res ipsa loquitur, "the thing speaks for itself," cases. Like the case Art Golden had against me if he'd cared to press it. Show a jury an X-ray and point out a big clamp sitting in a patient's belly, and the jury doesn't need Dr. Mayo to tell them the doctor is at fault. Nor, if a surgeon fixes the hernia on some boy who was supposed to have his tonsils out, and takes two normal tonsils out of another child with a hernia—things like this do happen —does the jury need any medical expert to tell them somebody goofed.

I don't want to leave the impression that no respectable doctor will ever testify against another doctor, no matter how flagrant the malpractice. I don't want to be invited to testify in a malpractice suit, but if I'm asked and if there's a real case, I'd do it. Most doctors would.

I'd have testified in Jean Simmons' case if I'd had to. Jean, who lives in another town, came to me because she had no sensation in part of her hand and was having difficulty moving her thumb. A few months earlier she had cut her wrist falling through a window, and her local doctor had sewed it up. She had told him about the numbness and he had assured her it would get better. But six months had gone by and it hadn't improved. She wondered if it ever would. So did I. I reoperated on her and found that her doctor had sewn the lower end of the median nerve to the top end of a tendon, and vice versa. He had confused the two structures. I undid them and sewed them back where they belonged.

Now, if this woman had chosen to sue her doctor I'd have been willing to testify in her behalf. Not eager, but willing. Admittedly, the median nerve looks something like a tendon, but any doctor that can't tell them apart has no business operating on a wrist.

Jean chose not to sue. After I explained to her gently, of course, what had been done, she said, "Well, isn't that too bad. Dr. Garvey will feel just terrible—and he's such a nice doctor! He comes every time we call him, night or day, and I hate to think of hurting him. Maybe we can tell him it was something else." Dr. Garvey didn't get sued.

Which leads to one final comment. The doctors least likely to get sued for malpractice are those who have good rapport with their patients. Most patients are decent people; if they like a doctor, and if they know he's going all out for them, they're not apt to be after his neck if something goes wrong.

That's why in small towns, like Litchfield, we don't have many malpractice suits. Our patients are our friends, and we get along. In Los Angeles, in New York, in Chicago, my malpractice insurance rates would be several times higher than they are in Litchfield. The big-city doctor–patient relationship is often very impersonal. The patient thinks the doctor is gouging him and the doctor feels the patient is out to crucify him.

Too often they're both right.

18

Can Doctors Keep Doctors Honest?

Closely related to the problem of malpractice is the question of who ought to supervise medical work and make certain high standards are maintained.

As chief of surgery it's my job to make certain that anyone who operates in our hospital is capable of doing well any operation he undertakes. I know Jack Nadler should not be doing any major surgery, so why do I remain silent when I see his patients subjected to unnecessary surgical risks?

It probably sounds like a cop-out, but honestly it wouldn't do any good. We doctors reserve for ourselves the right to decide what is and is not within our range of competence. Even if everyone else on the staff agreed with me that Jack shouldn't do major surgery, no one would side with me if I were to try and prevent him from operating. He has an M.D., a license to practice medicine and surgery, and I have no right to interfere with that license unless I can prove gross negligence, which I can't. If I were to ax Jack Nadler, my confreres would ask themselves, Which one of us might be next?

Doctors make a show of policing themselves but in fact don't do much of a job of it. At a hospital where I once worked there was a surgeon on the staff who had become a real menace. He was going through a period of emotional instability, was drinking a lot, and every now and then he'd come into the operating room so hung over he could hardly keep his eyes open. His hands shook and mentally he was in a fog.

The other surgeons on the staff would sit in the dressing room and say things like, "Man, did you see Charlie today? He can't even open his eyes," or "Thank God, it's not my hernia Charlie's fixing"—but no one made a move to take away Charlie's surgical privileges. The head nurse in the operating room always made certain that Charlie had a capable intern or resident assigned to help him and Charlie would blunder through his operations. Neither the chief of surgery nor any other staff surgeon had the courage to confront Charlie and suspend his operating privileges.

A friend of mine, Sam Ryan, who is chief of surgery and the only surgeon in a small hospital in another state, told me of an experience he had—an experience that points up the defects in self-regulation by the medical profession. "At one time there was a doctor on our staff," Sam said, "a Dr. Mendez, who had gone to medical school in South America. I assume he graduated, but I don't know. He had managed to complete an internship in a small hospital in the United States [most small hospitals are so desperate for interns that they'll take anyone with an M.D. degree]. When he completed his internship he went into practice in a small town called Centerville. Centerville is one of the hundreds of towns in our country without a doctor and desperate for medical help. Dr. Mendez received a temporary permit to practice, even though he flunked the licensing exams, and, since there was no hospital in Centerville, we accepted him on our staff. There was no legal way we could keep him off.

"One Saturday afternoon he called me, since I was chief of surgery, to get my permission to do a Caesarean section on a patient. We require a consultation by a second physician before we permit anyone to do a Caesarean section.

"'I don't know a thing about obstetrics, Jose,' I told him. 'Why don't you call Lee Rice—he does a lot of obstetrics—and ask him to consult with you?' Jose agreed to call Lee.

"The next day I asked Lee how the Caesarean section went.

"'Sam,' he said, 'that woman didn't need a Caesarean section any more than you need one. Hell, she'd had six other kids and never had any difficulty delivering. I came over, examined her, and everything seemed fine. She just wasn't in very strong labor. I told Jose to wait awhile. An hour after I left, that baby popped right out. That guy knows nothing about obstetrics.'"

Nor did he know anything about appendicitis. Twice Sam had to take ruptured appendices out of patients whom Jose had been treating for "intestinal flu."

"His knowledge of medicine was as superficial as his knowledge of obstetrics and surgery. Harvey Victor, who practices in a small town near the one where Jose settled, said to me one morning, 'Sam, that Jose is an idiot. In the last week I've seen about twenty patients who went to his office with runny noses and muscle ache. He told them they had infectious mononucleosis and put them all on antibiotics. People around Centerville got to talking and when they discovered that he had made the same diagnosis on everyone who went to his office last week they began to wonder if he knew what he was talking about, so some of them came to me. Not one of them had infectious mononucleosis; all they had were colds. Apparently that was his "disease of the week."'"

Finally, much to the relief of everyone on the staff, Jose flunked his state medical examinations again and had to quit practice. Centerville was again without a doctor—but far better to be without any doctor at all than to be treated by an incompetent public menace who just happens to have an M.D.

My experiences with Jack and Charlie, and Sam's experience with Jose, make what I consider a most important point: doctors just cannot be relied upon to police themselves. We're too afraid of hurting the feelings of our confreres, of losing referrals from them, of being overcritical. We lean over backward in order not to judge our fellow doctors too harshly, and often we do this to such an extreme that it poses a threat to the well-being of patients. A surgeon practically has to become a mass murderer before his fellow surgeons will take away his surgical privileges.

Doctors claim that only doctors can and should judge the work of other doctors—a system known as peer review. This system, organized medicine protests, is the only reasonable way to ensure that medical practice will remain high-grade and economical.

The claim has some merit: it does take medical knowledge to judge the expertise of a doctor. But as the sole judges of their colleagues, doctors are a dismal failure. Not only are doctors unwilling to criticize the professional competence of their colleagues, they're also unwilling to knock their style of practice, even though it's obviously wasteful and expensive.

I've sat in on chart-review conferences, designed to make certain that no one is unnecessarily tying up a hospital bed. We pull out the chart of one of Tom Rice's patients, a woman who is still in the hospital three months after having her hip nailed.

"How come Emily Johnson is still in the hospital?" someone asks. "According to Tom's notes she's walking well on crutches. Couldn't she go home?"

"Oh, you know Tom," someone else answers. "He likes to wait till his patients are off crutches completely. Besides, Emily can pay for it. She's got good insurance coverage." Nothing more is said. We go on to the next chart.

Hardly ever does any doctor on the staff approach any other doctor and question his practice methods. It just isn't done. We're all one big happy congenial family.

What's needed to make doctors practice high-grade and economical medicine is the participation in peer review of intelligent laymen, who aren't worried about offending doctors. We need some hard-boiled businessman at our meeting, some guy who will say, "Hey, what gives? Why is it that every appendix case Mendez sends in is ruptured? Isn't that supposed to be pretty rare?" and "How come this patient of Dr. Rice's is still sitting around the hospital after three months? I thought you doctors were supposed to get hip patients out in about six weeks?" That sort of provocative questioning would shake up men like Jose and Tom Rice—and they need shaking up.

It would also take the pressure off us, their fellow doctors. We could go to Tom and Jose, and put the blame for the pressure on the businessman. Cowards that we are, some of us would welcome the chance to shake up Tom and Jose, but we haven't got the courage to do it ourselves.

It's a myth, perpetuated by the medical profession, that "only doctors can judge other doctors." Intelligent laymen, with technical help from doctors, could do it better. In fact, lay participation is an absolute necessity if we're ever going to have really effective cost and quality control in medicine.

I asked Sam what had happened to Jose after he left Centerville.

"That's sad, Bill," Sam said. "When Jose left town I thought I'd heard the last of him, but I was wrong. About six months later he settled in another town, Jonesville. This town had a hospital, and since their only doctor had recently moved to a warmer climate, the people of Jonesville were desperate for medical help. They welcomed Jose with open arms.

"It seemed odd to me that Jose should have passed his licensing exam, after failing on two previous occasions. At a chance meeting with a member of the licensing board I learned the reason why.

"Jose had taken the examination for the third time and, as usual, had flunked—his grade was four points below that established by the board as 'passing.'

"However, one of the other doctors who took the examination with Jose—I'll call him Dr. X—had some very influential friends among the medical hierarchy. Dr. X had also failed the examination by four points. His powerful friends raised hell with the examining board, contending that it was Dr. X's lack of command of the English language, and not a lack of medical knowledge, that had caused him to fail the examination. They wanted Dr. X to have a license.

"The board gave in to the pressure. They decided, arbitrarily, to lower the passing grade by four points. Dr. X got his license.

"Unfortunately, Jose heard what had happened; he knew he had had the same grade as Dr. X, and he demanded that he be licensed too. The board could hardly say No; his license was approved.

"So now Jose is back in action, practicing the 'healing' arts, completely unsupervised by anyone—physician or layman. God help his patients!"

Why are doctors like Jose allowed to practice—and here the word "practice" can be taken in the nonprofessional sense—in the United States?

Essentially it's a matter of supply and demand. We don't produce enough doctors to go around; small towns, state hospitals and veterans hospitals scrounge around to find men who can offer any sort of medical help. No one looks too closely at the man's credentials; they assume that anyone with an M.D., no matter where he got it, is better than no one. This is an understandable, if not always accurate, assumption.

Licensing of physicians varies from state to state. Loopholes are usually available to permit unqualified people to practice. Once he's out in practice, he can get away, literally, with murder. There are hundreds of Jose's around; heaven only knows how much harm they cause. One physician, who had an M.D. from a diploma mill in Havana, was apparently responsible for multiple deaths in a state hospital where he was employed as a ward physician. He had done some strange things, such as treating a choking patient by feeding him a boiled potato and a banana. Though numerous complaints had been lodged against him by nurses and aides—you don't need much medical education to suspect that administration of a boiled potato and a banana is rather a bizarre way to treat a choking victim—this particular doctor held his post for almost six years on a continually renewed "temporary" permit.

I hope I won't be accused of being hypercritical if I suggest that perhaps peer review and licensing procedures could stand some improvements.

19

Money

Money, unfortunately, is one factor that occasionally prevents doctors from doing their best for their patients.

It's really too bad, because money is something about which doctors should never have to worry. Even at the height (or depth) of the 1970 economic recession, when big-income business executives were ready to sell apples on Wall Street, the doctors were on easy street. Jobs paying thirty thousand dollars a year, for a forty-hour week, were advertised as usual in the *Journal of the American Medical Association;* and, again as usual, there were no takers. There just aren't enough M.D.'s to go around. Get that M.D. degree and you'll never have to worry about making a living. A very good one, at that.

But, as someone said, "Money is like sex—only too much is enough,"—and so, just like everyone else, doctors do spend a lot of time thinking about money.

People hate to spend money for medical care. This is perfectly understandable. Who wants to part with a thousand dollars for the privilege of spending a week in the hospital suffering through a gall bladder operation? No one. Much more fun to spend the thousand on new clothes or a trip to Florida.

So we doctors, who earn our living by providing medical care, are bound to be the target of resentment from our patients. We're selling a product—health—that patients have to

have and hate to pay for. Under the fee-for-service system
there is no way we can have both love and money.

I'm not immune to this feeling of resentment. Fortunately,
five of my children have had their teeth come in straight. But
Julius needs orthodontic treatment, braces and all that. I'm
glad the orthodontist is going to straighten Julius' teeth; but
I resent every one of the many checks I have to send him. I
wish orthodontic care were "free"; or at least that the charges
were hidden, as is the case with most of the things that we get
"free." If I didn't have to pay the orthodontist, I'd like him
better. I'm sure many of my patients feel the same toward me.

When I moved to Litchfield, saturated with surgical knowledge, I was completely naive about the business side of medical practice. I could take out a stomach, set a broken ankle,
diagnose appendicitis, but I didn't know a thing about
money. I was thirty-two years old and I'd done several hundred operations, but I'd never sent a patient a bill.

As a result of my inexperience I had a rude awakening when
I arrived in town. Since I was the only trained surgeon in the
community, the only man who had gone through a surgical
residency, I, quite naturally it seemed to me, expected that all
the doctors on the hospital staff would immediately refer all
their major surgical cases to me. Why call in a surgeon from
Minneapolis, sixty-five miles away, to take out a stomach when
I was right there in town and happy to go to work?

It didn't happen. My clinic partners, of course, referred most
of their major cases to me, though some of them persisted in
doing gall bladders, hysterectomies and other surgery of
about the same magnitude themselves, but the other doctors
on the staff, with one exception, continued to call on a surgeon from Minneapolis when they had major surgical cases.

I was surprised, and slightly chagrined, but then, I rational-
ized that they wanted to see how good a surgeon I was: the
proper piece of paper didn't mean a thing to them; they
wanted to see how well I operated.

So I was patient. I assisted my partners on hernias, gall
bladders, hysterectomies, and did an occasional bowel or
stomach case; I wasn't awfully busy, but it was still early. I

figured in three months, six at the most, I'd be doing all the big stuff.

The six months went by and still no business. Everyone was very friendly, but no one sent me any patients. I was getting restless. Then one afternoon, while I was playing golf, I got a break. Charlie Stapleton drove out to the Golf Club and caught me as I was coming in on the ninth fairway.

"Bill," he said, "I just got a woman in with an embolus in her femoral artery. It happened about two hours ago. I hate to bother you on your afternoon off but I'd appreciate it if you'd come over and see what has to be done."

"Sure, Charlie," I said. "I'll be right there."

An embolus in the femoral artery is a surgical emergency. The femoral artery is the major artery to the leg. When a clot, or embolus, plugs it up, the entire leg is deprived of its blood supply. Unless the embolus is removed in less than six hours the patient usually loses the leg.

The patient, a Mrs. Schneider, was no rose. She was seventy-six years old and she had chronic heart disease—most of these emboli break loose from clots that are found in diseased hearts. Her lungs weren't bad, but her kidney function was borderline. Her leg was already cool from lack of blood flow. She was a poor risk.

After I examined her I said, "Well, Charlie, we're damned if we do and damned if we don't. She's a lousy risk, but if we don't get that plug out she's sure going to lose her leg. Let's do her."

Everything went beautifully. Exposing the artery in the groin, clamping it above and below the clot, opening the vessel, fishing out the embolus and closing the incision in the artery—all this isn't awfully difficult. On the other hand, it's no soft touch either. There are lots of things that can go wrong. Nothing did. We saved Mrs. Schneider's leg.

Now, I felt certain, I'd be busy at last. Most of the patients I'd operated on in my first six months had done well, but maybe Charlie hadn't known this. Now they'd seen what I could do with a tough case. Surely they'd send me their elective major cases.

Not a bit of it. The next week Louis Broman, their Minneapolis surgeon, was out to do a thyroid and a stomach for them. They were still friendly to me, but no business came my way.

A month later, I got another case. Dick Hopkins got a perforated ulcer patient in at two in the morning and he called me. I sewed up the hole and the patient made a rapid recovery. But a week later, when one of Dick's patients needed her gall bladder removed, he called Louis Broman out from Minneapolis to do it.

I'd been in Litchfield almost a year now, and I was still spending a lot of time doing nothing. I finally decided, To hell with it, I'm going to get this straightened out. A few weeks later Brian O'Connor called at three in the morning and said, "Bill, would you mind coming over to see a patient for me? I think he's got a strangulated intestine." I got out of bed, went to the hospital and did the case. But when I was through I said, "Brian, I want to talk to you for a minute. Let's have a cup of coffee." We went back to the doctors' dressing room and sat down. "Brian," I said, "I'm goddam sick of only doing your emergencies. I'm good enough for you at three in the morning, but all the elective gravy you send to Louis Broman. If I'm going to do the emergencies, then I want a fair share of the elective stuff."

"All right, Bill," Brian said, "you've got a point. Let's have a little talk."

The root of the problem, the reason I hadn't gotten their referrals was, as I should have suspected if I hadn't been so naive, an economic one.

Sure, all the doctors who worked in the hospital were out to save lives and alleviate suffering, but they also had to earn a living. We were friends in the scientific medical world but competitors in the economic medical world.

I was a surgeon; fine. But I was also a member of the Litchfield Clinic. If Brian O'Connor sent me a patient who needed his stomach out, how was he to know that I wouldn't then treat the man's heart disease, or send him to one of my partners for such treatment? Brian wasn't afraid Louis Broman would try to steal his patients; he was way off in Minneapolis.

But he hadn't been too sure about me. I hadn't stolen any of the few cases he'd sent me, so he was willing to believe me when I assured him I'd bend over backward to get his patients back to him.

The second problem was also an economic one, but a bit trickier. When Louis Broman drove out from Minneapolis to take out a gall bladder he would see the patient just before surgery and then, usually, never again. Brian provided the preoperative care, the assistance at surgery and the postoperative care.

Naturally, Brian charged for what he did; Louis charged only for the operation. This usually amounted to a fifty–fifty division of the total fee. Louis would charge a hundred and fifty dollars for taking out a gall bladder; Brian charged a hundred and fifty dollars for his contribution to the case. It wasn't fee-splitting in the technical sense, because each of them billed the patient directly; but the result was the same.

What if Brian referred the gall bladder patient to me? I was right there in town; it would be only natural for me to provide the preoperative and postoperative care. I'd charge three hundred dollars and Brian would only get fifty or so for helping me on the case. He was better off financially if he had Louis come out.

This was a stickler for me. The College of Surgeons is most insistent that the surgeon provide the pre- and postoperative care. They say he's the only one with the knowledge to do so.

Frankly, I didn't agree. After all, for all the years before I'd moved to Litchfield these G.P.'s had been doing a lot of surgery themselves, as well as assisting and providing pre- and postoperative care on the major cases done by visiting surgeons. Why, just because I was in town, should they stop? It didn't seem reasonable to me.

"O.K., Brian," I said, "I'll go along. When I do the case you provide the pre- and postoperative care with one stipulation: if I think that it's the kind of case where I ought to give the patient regular personal attention after surgery, then I'll do it and charge for it."

"Fine with me," Brian said. "There have been plenty of

times I'd just as soon have had Louis take over on a case if he had been in town. And I'll let you know if there are any hitches in the postoperative period."

So, with the money problem resolved, I started getting the referrals. In fact, Louis Broman never operated in Litchfield again.

I learned very quickly that most of the doctors in town were interested in money—but no more interested than men in other professions or businesses. Despite the stories to the contrary, I've never known a doctor to deny medical care to anyone, regardless of whether or not the patient had a nickel. (Don't misread this. I'm not saying such doctors don't exist. They probably do. I just don't happen to know them.)

Personally, I rarely know when I see a patient what his or her financial situation is like. We have standard fees for most of the services we perform: five dollars for an office call, eight dollars for a house call, three hundred dollars for a cholecystectomy. When I take care of a patient I fill out a slip listing the patient's name, what I've done and my charges, and leave it on my desk. An office girl picks up the slips each day and takes care of the billings.

Most of the time that's the last I hear of the case. The insurance papers appear on my desk a day or two later and I sign them, but I don't bother reading them. Business matters I leave to others.

Naturally, we occasionally run into collection problems. We have a routine for handling them.

Once a month we clinic doctors meet for an hour with the girl who runs our business office. She reads off the names of all those patients who have owed us money for over six months and paid nothing on their bills. Then whichever one of us is concerned decides what to do. If the patient is Bernie Reynolds, who runs a sporting goods store here in town, I'd probably say, "Let it ride. Bernie had a tough break a few months ago; lost some uninsured merchandise in a warehouse fire. He'll pay up as soon as he gets back on his feet." And we go on.

The next name is Leroy Johnson. "Leroy has owed us three

hundred dollars since September," Gerrie, our office manager, says.

"He's my patient," Paul answers. "Can't understand why he hasn't paid. Better send him a letter, Gerrie."

Gerrie puts a little mark near Leroy's name. Tomorrow she'll mail Leroy a letter reminding him of his bill and asking that he stop in to discuss it. If he doesn't respond to this letter he'll get a second, still low-key, ten days later.

We move on. The next patient is Jim Fitzgerald, one of our local policemen. George is the doctor for Jim's family.

"Don't send Jim a letter yet," George says. "His wife is six months pregnant. Bring it up again if he hasn't paid in another three months." We never nudge a patient to pay his bill when he or one of his family is currently receiving treatment for an illness. We don't want them worrying about money problems on top of their medical ones.

Next we come to another one of Paul's patients, Sam Bateman.

"Not Sam, again," says Paul, after Gerrie has read his name. "I thought we sent him a letter just a few months ago."

"We did," says Gerrie. "He came in to see me and agreed to pay ten dollars a week. He kept at it for three weeks, and I haven't seen him since."

"How much does he owe us?"

"Nine hundred dollars."

"Well, he can certainly pay. He's making good money at Minnesota Mining and his wife is teaching. I'll call him myself. Put a note on my desk."

So it goes, for about half an hour. Some patients get our first two letters, others we excuse or delay. It depends on their circumstances.

"Now, for the third letters," Gerrie says. "We have ten patients."

These are the patients who haven't responded to either of the first two letters. The third letter is sent via registered mail and informs the patient that unless he contacts us within ten days, we'll turn his account over to a collection agency.

Most patients who receive letter number three come in to talk their money problem over with Gerrie.

"Charlie Brennan," Gerrie says.

"Goddam it!" Paul says. "Didn't he come in? I saw him yesterday driving a new Buick. I can't understand some people. Sure, send him number three."

Charlie Brennan is the typical sort of patient who bugs all doctors. Charlie owns a lot of commercial real estate in Litchfield. I don't know exactly what his income is, but it has to be high. He spends three months every winter in Phoenix and he has a nice home here in town. As Paul pointed out, he buys an expensive new car every year.

But he doesn't pay his doctor bills. He pays everyone else—he has to or they'll refuse him goods and services—but he refuses to pay us. He knows we won't turn him down if he comes in sick. He takes advantage of us.

So Charlie gets the third letter. We hope he'll pay up before we turn him over to the collector. (The collection agency keeps about half of whatever it collects.)

Most of the patients who don't respond to our third letters, and whom we have to turn over to the collector, are real dead beats. Some are poor—patients who work at menial jobs and earn just enough to buy another bottle of booze—but many, like Charlie Brennan, could easily pay us if they chose to.

Transients are always a bad risk. I went to the hospital one Sunday evening to see a patient, a Mrs. Hastings, who had cut her foot on a piece of glass while swimming in a lake near Litchfield. She was from Minneapolis and was just out visiting friends.

I introduced myself to her, looked at her foot and told her I'd have to put in some stitches.

"But, Doctor," she said, "are you a surgeon?" It often amazes nonresidents that any specialist could possibly live in a small town.

"Yes, I am, Mrs. Hastings," I answered.

"I didn't mean to question your credentials, Doctor," she said (though that was precisely what she was doing), "but we're used to first-class medical care. Our family doctor is an associate professor at the university."

"If you'd like, Mrs. Hastings, I'd be happy to let you drive to Minneapolis to your professor. I can simply bandage this foot up and leave it for him to sew." I hate to treat patients who act as if they're doing me a favor by letting me work on them.

"No, no, please go ahead," she said. "We plan to vacation here for two more days."

So I sewed up her foot—about a fifteen-minute job. I sent her a bill for fifteen dollars, about half what it would have cost in Minneapolis.

She never paid my bill. After we sent her the second letter we got a note from her saying that she considered fifteen dollars "far too much for fifteen minutes of work from an insulting doctor." What she really meant was, Forget it, Buster—I'm in Minneapolis and you'll never see me again.

We forgot it; it wasn't worth a fight.

Having said that most doctors aren't money-hungry, now I have to admit that a few are.

Take Steve Charrah. I see a patient of his every now and then. Louise Gardy goes to him regularly, but Steve was out of town the last time Louise got sick, so she came in to see me. Thumbing through her back record to bring myself up-to-date on Louise's recent illnesses, I ran across several of the slips Steve had put in on Louise. One read:

Call to hospital to see pt. with chest pain	$10.00
Chest X-ray interpretation	3.00
E.K.G. interpretation	5.00
TOTAL	$18.00

Another time he had sewed up a cut on Louise's arm. The entry read:

Hospital call	$10.00
Suturing, 2 stitches	15.00
TOTAL	$25.00

Now, these aren't big bills, they aren't going to drive Louise to the poorhouse, but they're bigger than I'd have put in on both instances. In the first case my total charge would have been ten dollars; I'd have considered reading the chest film and the E.K.G. part of the call. In the second my total charge would have been fifteen dollars; if I sew someone up I figure that was the purpose of the call and don't make a special charge for appearing at the hospital.

Still, Louise just loves Steve. "When will Dr. Charrah be back, Dr. Nolen?" she asked me. "He really understands my case."

All Steve's patients love him. He has a great bedside manner. When he talks to a patient he convinces him that he is the most important person in his life; and, for the moment, he is. Steve socks it to his patients on his charges, but I've yet to hear a single patient complain, and Steve has a very big practice.

Which brings us to the crux of the money situation in medical practice. We're selling a rather nebulous product, personal care. Pills and surgery are tangible things, admittedly, but how we deliver them is another matter, and a very important one. An injection given by a kind, compassionate doctor often does the patient more good than the same medication injected by a brusque, impersonal physician. Perhaps the compassionate doctor, one like Steve, who produces the better result, is entitled to a slightly greater fee for his mastery of the "art of medicine."

I don't know—any more than I know why I should charge a hundred and seventy-five dollars to take out an appendix, while a surgeon in New York City charges five hundred dollars for the same job. Or why I should charge three hundred dollars for removing a gall bladder, while some surgeons in Los Angeles charge a thousand dollars and other surgeons in New Hampshire charge two hundred dollars. Which of us is right?

There's no way to decide. Medical and surgical fees are a matter of tradition, not logic. Most doctors in most localities set them so that, by working the relatively long hours that are almost universally required of physicians because there aren't enough of us to go around, the doctor winds up with an income that puts him in roughly the top 5 percentile of his community. That's probably why a New York City doctor, if he can get patients to pay, charges more than I do. He's got to earn a lot more to keep up with the high New York City incomes than I do to keep up with the upper crust locally.

Maybe I should reduce my charges by 50 percent and cut my income in half. But I probably won't. I'm used to my standard of living and I'm reluctant to lower it. I have yet to meet anyone, in any business or profession, who has voluntarily reduced his income—unless he could see some advantage to himself in doing so. The fact remains that most doctors charge what they consider reasonable fees for their services. Just like everyone else, we want money because we have to buy homes, cars and life insurance; we have to educate our children; we want to take vacations.

It used to be common practice for doctors to raise their fees for wealthy patients and reduce them for poor patients. Unfortunately, while they found it easy enough to spot the rich, doctors often had difficulty in identifying the poor. Consequently fees were rarely lowered.

Now most private patients have insurance, and some doctors tend to put these people in the wealthy category. They figure that if their usual fee for an appendectomy is two hundred dollars and the patient has insurance that will pay the entire two hundred dollars, then they may as well charge him three hundred dollars. After all, he'll only have to dig up an extra hundred dollars; it'll still be like getting the operation for half price.

This is illogical and unfair. The patient is paying health insurance premiums just so he won't have to dig into his pocket when he becomes ill. The doctor has no right to bleed the patient a little more just because the patient has had foresight. A two-hundred-dollar appendectomy doesn't become one that's worth three hundred dollars just because an insurance company is paying part of the bill. The doctors that follow this policy are greedy—and responsible in part for the rising cost of medical insurance.

The obvious way for a patient to avoid overcharges is to ask the doctor about his fees. It has always amazed me how reluctant patients are to do this. I'll bet that I'm not asked about my charges more than once a year.

I know why; patients are embarrassed about bringing the subject up for discussion. They'd like to feel that money isn't a factor in their relationship with the doctor. Nor do they want to offend the doctor by suggesting that money is one of his considerations when he provides medical care.

The doctor doesn't bring the subject up for similar reasons. I can't bring myself to say, "Now, Mrs. Larson, let's talk about my fee. I'm going to charge you three hundred dollars for removing your gall bladder. Can you pay for it?" It's difficult for a doctor to initiate money talk without giving the impression he's money-mad. So the subject goes unmentioned till the bill arrives, and the patient has to figure out a way to pay it.

I'd like to be able to say that if I were a patient, I'd bring up the subject of money in dealing with my doctor—but I'd be lying. When my son was operated on by an orthopedist I wanted to know what, if anything, he would charge, but I didn't have the courage to ask. It would have embarrassed both of us.

But though I can't do it, I think patients should ask the doctor what his charges will be. It may offend some doctors—it probably will—but it's a risk worth taking. It's better for everyone to get the fee problem resolved in advance.

There's another advantage for the patient in asking about fees; he's apt to be charged less than he otherwise would. I know that is the way I respond. One afternoon I went to the hospital and put three stitches in a small cut in Timmy Dunne's scalp. It took me about five minutes while his father, Larry, watched. When I was done Larry said, "How much do I owe you, Doc?"

"Why don't I just bill you, Larry?" I said, trying to evade the issue.

"No sense in that, Doc," Larry said. "Might as well save some paper work. I'll give you a check."

"O.K.," I said. "Make it out for ten dollars."

If I had billed Larry I'd have charged him fifteen dollars, but face to face I didn't have the courage; he knew how quickly I had sewed up the cut. Larry saved five dollars by putting me on the spot.

In the realm of money we doctors are neither saints nor devils, we're just plain ordinary men.

Which brings me to my pigs.

One afternoon, two or three summers ago, Joan and I played in a two-ball foursome at the Golf Club. As partners we drew Nick Kopple and his wife, Bernice.

I knew Nick reasonably well; I played basketball with him at men's recreation on Monday nights, and I knew he was a farmer, but I didn't know what kind—cows, pigs or strictly crops. It turned out that along with growing wheat, corn and soybeans Nick had an egg business, and when we finished our round of golf he invited us to come out sometime and look around his farm. About a week later, on a Sunday afternoon, we drove out.

Nick's farm is just south of town, and he has a nice home and several other buildings in good condition. He took us through the chicken house, showed us how they collected and stored eggs, and then we went back to the kitchen. As we were sitting around drinking coffee I said, "Nick, what about those long low buildings out by your big barn. What are they for?"

"Pigs," he said.

"How come they're empty?"

"Right now," Nick said, "I'm pretty well committed to the egg business. I'd have to spread myself awfully thin, financially, to run a pig operation too."

"That's too bad," I said. "It's a shame to let those buildings stand empty." The talk turned to other matters and after about an hour we left.

As we were driving home I said to Joan, "You know, it's too bad about Nick's pigs. He seems like a hard-working ambitious guy. It's a shame he can't run a pig operation."

"Now, listen," Joan said, "I know exactly what you're going to say, so don't say it. You want to go into the pig business with

Nick. Don't do it. You don't know any more about pigs than you do about gorillas."

"It can't be too difficult to learn," I said. "Besides, Nick knows all about them. I'd just be putting up the money."

That evening I took out the *World Book* and read up on pigs. I found that they come in a variety of colors and shapes, that "a gilt" was a female that had never had any young, and that "to farrow" meant to give birth. I couldn't see what was so complicated about pigs.

The next day I called Nick and asked him if he'd be interested in having me back him in the pig business. He was delighted with the suggestion, and after we'd gotten together a couple of times we had a deal worked out. We'd buy twenty gilts and a boar; let the gilts get pregnant (a matter we could leave to the boar), and then, when the little pigs were born we'd raise them till they reached thirty pounds and sell them. These thirty-pound pigs are known as feeder pigs; farmers with lots of corn buy feeder pigs and feed them till they get to be two hundred and fifty pounds, at which point they sell them to be butchered. We'd keep out some of our female pigs for stock and in due time we'd have one hell of a lot of pigs, all producing babies. Nick would provide the knowledge and the labor, I'd buy the feed, we'd split the profits fifty–fifty. In a very short time we'd be wealthy.

So I sank five thousand bucks into the project. I figured that by the time my kids were ready for college our pig operation would be providing all the dough I'd need to educate them. I couldn't see how we'd miss.

Nick, like most young farmers, worked eight hours a day at another job to supplement his farm income; in Nick's case he worked "tower" shifts—three to eleven one week, eleven to seven the next, seven to three the third. He was a hard worker and so was his wife. He bought the pigs, fixed up the barn, and in a few months we had twenty female pigs all ready to go into labor.

I was enjoying every minute of it. Evenings, after leaving the office, I'd drive out to Nick's and look the pigs over. I'd make very sage comments on how fat they were and how healthy-looking. At cocktail parties I'd captivate my audience

with talk of Duroc sows, Yorkshire boars and the current price
of pork. I was a real spellbinder.

To make money raising feeder pigs, I had learned, it was
necessary to average seven pigs a litter. With fewer than
seven, expenses would exceed profits; with eight or more, depending on the market, the profits could be substantial. Since
some mother pigs gave birth to as many as twelve pigs at one
time, if you were fortunate you could make a lot of money.
We had bought very nice pigs, and whenever I counted my
piggies before they had hatched I based my profits on ten little
pigs per sow; this made for pleasant dreams.

It happened that just before our pigs were due to farrow
I had to leave town. Joan and I had made plans to go skiing
for a week, and though I wanted to postpone the trip, Joan
wouldn't hear of it.

"Those pigs will manage quite well without you," she said,
and then added rather nastily, "I always did." So we went.

I enjoyed my week of skiing, but constantly in the back of
my mind was concern over our pigs. On Friday night, as soon
as we got home, I called Nick.

"Nick," I said, "how'd it go? Have we got some little pigs?"

"Yeah," he said, "we've got forty."

"Forty?" I asked. "How many pigs farrowed? Four?"

"No," he answered, "all twenty."

I sat down. "For chrissake, Nick," I said, "what happened?
How come only two pigs to a litter?"

"We averaged nine a litter," he said. "But, goddammit, I was
working the eleven-to-seven shift last week and every one of
those pigs farrowed about two in the morning. By the time I
got home the mothers had rolled over and knocked off most
of their young."

I couldn't believe it. No one had ever warned me—I found
out later it was common—that the mother pig might inadvertently lie down and crush her offspring. I hadn't thought pigs
were brilliant, but neither had I ever dreamed they were that
dumb.

I was out a bundle, of course, and could hardly wait till
these pigs reached thirty pounds so we could sell them and I

could total up my losses. About three weeks later, when the damn things looked big enough to sell, I called Nick.

"What say, Nick," I said, "I just got another bill for a pile of pig feed. Aren't those babies big enough to get rid of yet?"

"I was just going to call you," Nick answered. "We can't sell them."

"Can't sell them?"—I was almost weeping—"Why?"

"They've all got hook nose."

"Hook nose?" I said. "What in the hell is that?"

"It's a disease pigs get. It's some kind of a virus. We can sell the pigs for slaughter when they're full-grown, but we can't sell them as feeder pigs. They'd bring the disease with them."

"Damn!" I said. "I suppose that means I'll be buying feed for those monsters for another six months."

"Looks that way," Nick said.

I decided I couldn't take it.

"Nick," I said, "I want out. I'll tell you what I'm going to do; I'm going to give you those forty hook-nosed pigs. They're all yours. You can shoot them or feed them—it's all the same to me. I'm going to take my licking and get out."

"Gee, Bill, thanks," Nick said. "That's nice of you."

Oddly enough, he meant it.

My motive in going so deeply into this painful episode in my life is simply this; it illustrates quite well what an idiot I am about investments, and in the investment line I'm a reasonably typical doctor.

Doctors are, to put it mildly, great suckers for "deals." I've got friends who have lost their shirts in such diverse investments as banana plantations, bowling alleys and Angus cattle. You name it, some doctor will buy it.

The reason is obvious. Most doctors earn a pretty good living. But their profession offers none of the tax dodges that businessmen and lawyers find in their occupations. To hold on to their money, doctors are always looking for the tax shelter that speculative ventures afford. Since they have neither the time nor the knowledge to appraise these ventures wisely, they wind up easy prey to speculators out to make a fast buck.

For smart men, most doctors are damn fools about money.

20

Itinerant Surgery

When I was having such a frustrating time building a practice, the one guy I never got sore at was Louis Broman, the fellow who'd drive out from Minneapolis to operate in Litchfield. He always did a good job for his patients, and if that was the way he chose to earn a living, so be it. We were competitors, but we respected each other.

Unfortunately, the medical hierarchy doesn't agree.

The American College of Surgeons, an organization to which the majority of trained (as opposed to untrained) surgeons belong, gets very upset if any of its members practice journeyman, or (as it's commonly called) itinerant, surgery. The College thinks this is a naughty thing to do.

Possibly you don't know what I mean by itinerant surgery, so I'll explain. In some small towns—Litchfield was one till I moved here—there are hospitals but no surgeons. Whatever operations are performed are done by the local G.P.'s. What the G.P.'s do depends on their training, their experience and their nerve. In some communities the only operations done are tonsillectomies and minor gynecological procedures. In others the G.P.'s will do appendectomies, hernias and hemorrhoids as well. And in a few, particularly where there are older G.P.'s who went into practice before specialization was so widespread, there's probably some G.P. surgeon who will take out a gall bladder, remove a uterus, and possibly even do some intestinal surgery.

In one hospital where I worked, the G.P. surgery ran the whole gamut from minor to major. One young G.P., educated in the era of specialization, did nothing other than tonsils. Another, a man with no training but tremendous nerve, would tackle anything that came in. I used to shudder when I'd see on the schedule that he was planning to do some difficult bowel case. I knew the patient was going to have to be very lucky to make it. But this doctor had no qualms. He figured he was as good as anyone else, and if the law recognized him as "a physician and surgeon," then why shouldn't he operate?

It was really frightening to watch him. He had no real knowledge of anatomy, nor did he have any concept of what good surgical technique was like. He'd learned by watching other G.P.'s and I'm certain he didn't understand what he had seen. It was as if I were to watch a pilot take off, fly and land a 747, and then, having seen it done once, call myself a pilot and try to fly. A little bad weather, a faulty motor or any other deviation from the normal and I wouldn't be able to handle it; I'd crack up.

And often, that's what happened to this doctor's patients. Anything but an easy, straightforward case and he was in trouble, to say nothing of his patient. He'd call me in after everything hit the fan and ask me to help him out. If was often touch and go.

Amazingly, he never felt the least bit guilty. He never blamed himself. It was always the patient's fault. "This guy sure had screwy anatomy," he'd say, or, "Man, what awful protoplasm. He just won't heal. Probably drinks too much." He never lost any sleep over his cases. He was too dumb.

In these towns with hospitals but no surgeons there are, of course, a lot of people who occasionally need operations. If the local G.P. finds a patient who needs his gall bladder removed, the G.P. has two choices: either send the patient to a surgeon who will operate on him in a big city hospital, or ask the surgeon to come out to the small-town hospital, operate on the patient, and then leave the aftercare to the G.P. The

American College of Surgeons says, "Send the patient away." A lot of the G.P.'s, and their patients, say, "Ask the surgeon to come out." If it's done properly I agree with the second approach.

The reason the College of Surgeons is against having the surgeon run out of town to operate is primarily because of the problem of aftercare. The College feels that the surgeon who does the operation ought to manage the patient through the postoperative period. They feel he's the only one who can do the job properly.

I say—and so do a lot of other doctors—nonsense. Most of the postoperative care in big city hospitals is administered by interns and residents. Hell, a star like Michael DeBakey is apt to leave for Europe an hour after he does some huge heart operation. Any of the big professors might do the same. The underlings provide the postoperative care. And no one says a word.

So why should anyone object if a G.P. with ten years' experience manages some patient through a one-week convalescence from gall bladder surgery? He'll spot a complication as quickly as, probably more quickly than, an intern or resident, and if he can't manage the complication himself, he can ask the general surgeon to return. As long as a general surgeon uses good sense—and by that I mean staying away from huge cases, like removal of a lung, where the G.P. hasn't the background or equipment to manage a major acute complication—there's no harm done by itinerant surgery.

In fact, there's a lot to be said for it. Surgery is a frightening event in an individual's life. Most people prefer to undergo such a traumatic experience on their home territory, with family and friends nearby. It's nice to wake up after an operation and recognize the nurse sitting at your bedside. It's reassuring.

Just as it's reassuring to have visiting you every day the doctor who has been taking care of you for years. You've probably got some sort of rapport with him or you wouldn't be going to him. You know he knows and understands you. He probably knows your whole family. You'd a lot rather have

him watching you than some intern or resident you met yesterday.

Finally, there's the matter of money. Most community hospitals charge less than big city hospitals. Rooms, medicine,
even nursing care are cheaper in a town like Litchfield than
in New York, Chicago or even Minneapolis. Partly this is because living expenses are generally less in small towns than in
big cities; and partly because community hospitals don't have,
or need, all the expensive sophisticated equipment of big city
hospitals. A patient who comes into the Litchfield hospital to
have his gall bladder out isn't shelling out an extra couple of
dollars a day for his room to help pay for the cobalt-therapy
machine in the basement. Nor is he paying an extra two dollars
a day for the interns' salaries. We have neither cobalt machines
nor interns.

Itinerant surgery should not be confused with "ghost surgery." The itinerant surgeon meets the patient before the operation—admittedly, not always long before the operation—and
usually talks with the patient and/or his family after the operation is over. The patient knows who performed the operation.

A ghost surgeon, as the label implies, flits into the operating
room after the patient has been put to sleep and leaves town
before he wakes up. The patient and family are led to believe
that the operation was performed by the doctor—usually a
G.P.—when actually all he did was to call the surgeon in. The
bill is sent by the G.P., who then splits the fee with the ghost
surgeon. The family never meets the ghost surgeon. As far as
they know, he doesn't even exist. Perhaps ghost surgery was
popular many years ago, but I can't believe any such practice
goes on anywhere now. I've certainly never heard of it. Anyone nuts enough to function in this fashion would be playing
Russian roulette with a bullet in every chamber. The anesthetist always writes the name of the operating surgeon on the
anesthesia sheet, and the operating-room nurses make notes
as well. If the patient got into trouble, the surgeon would be
sued for his shirt, and would stand an excellent chance of
losing his license. Any hospital that permitted this sort of prac-

tice would lose its accreditation immediately. Ghost surgery isn't only dishonest, it's impractical.

As you can probably guess from the tone of this preamble, I do some itinerant surgery. Not as much as some surgeons, who will fly a hundred miles or more to operate, but a little. I stay away from the really big cases, and don't go anywhere I can't reach in half an hour. Actually, I'm closer to the hospitals where I practice itinerant surgery than are many big-city surgeons from their home hospitals.

The first case I ever did outside of Litchfield was a gratifying one. I got a call about nine on a Friday night from a G.P. named Ted Greenfield, who ran his own private hospital in Cokato, a town twenty miles from Litchfield. Rather, it was his nurse, Pat, who called. "Dr. Nolen," she said, "could you come right away? We've got a real sick kid here and Dr. Greenfield needs help." I jumped into my car, and fifteen minutes later walked into the big white house that served as a hospital. An aide met me at the door and led me into the emergency room. Dr. Greenfield was standing at the head end of an old operating table on which lay a boy of about sixteen. Ted had a blood-soaked gauze sponge in his hand and was pressing on a cut in the boy's neck. He looked up when I walked in. "Hi, Bill," he said, "I need some help. This boy got kicked in the head at the football game tonight. He's breathing but otherwise he's completely out. I've started to do a tracheotomy on him but he's got a bull neck and I can't get to the trachea. See what you can do."

I put on the sterile rubber gloves Pat had laid out and picked up the knife. We stuck an extra pillow under the boy's shoulders to get his head back and his windpipe forward, and with Ted pulling the muscles aside I was able to get down to the trachea, make a cut and slip in the tracheotomy tube. We sucked out a lot of mucus and the boy breathed easier. He was still unconscious, but at least he wasn't in any danger of choking to death. With his airway under control we gave the boy a thorough examination. There was no evidence to suggest bleeding within the skull, and after about fifteen minutes he began to move around and moan. He was obviously improving.

"Just a bad concussion, I think," Ted said. "He ought to be all right. Let's go talk to his parents and then we'll have some coffee. Pat will call us if anything goes sour."

Ted's home was next door to the hospital—the two buildings were the only ones in the entire block—and when I walked into his house I got a very pleasant shock. The place was literally loaded with books and paintings. There was even a bookcase in the bathroom, the wall of which was papered with old *New Yorker* covers. Ted and his wife, Gudren, are two of the most interesting, cultured, sophisticated people I've ever met. It was a surprise to find them living in a farm town with a population of twelve hundred.

We sat down, had a highball instead of coffee, and Ted told me what his practice was like.

"I own the hospital," he told me. "I've had it for ten years. We've got fifteen beds, a nursery, an operating room and even a pharmacy; there's no druggist in town. I do everything. Deliver babies, take care of heart attacks and, like tonight, act as physician for the high school football team. I even examine eyes and prescribe glasses. There's no optometrist here. It's an interesting practice, as you can imagine. The only problem is that it ties me down so much. We get season tickets to the Guthrie Theatre, the symphony and even the Vikings; but when someone comes in in labor, or I've got a very sick patient, I have to skip. I've been looking for years for someone to come in with me, but I haven't had any luck. I can't find a doctor who wants to take the responsibility for running a hospital."

"You'll have to admit, it's a big order," I said. "The doctors graduating from medical school now are specialty-oriented. It's a tough job to find any G.P. at all, let alone one who's willing to prescribe glasses and dispense drugs."

"I know," Ted said. "I guess I'm one of a dying breed."

"But that's not your worry," he said, changing the subject. "I appreciated your coming down here tonight. I hate surgery and I stay away from it when I can. I do T and A's, D and C's, and other minor stuff I can handle alone. For the hernias, gall bladders, hysterectomies and the rest of it I get a surgeon out from Minneapolis. But you're a lot closer. Would you want to come down here once in a while?"

"Sure," I said, "I'd be happy to. Just give me a few days' notice on the elective stuff if you can." And for the next eight years, till Ted finally got sick of being on call twenty-four hours a day seven days a week and folded the hospital, I went to Cokato once or twice a week to operate.

We always had a ball. Ted is a great storyteller and he'd break me up with his jokes. He didn't have many instruments, so if we had more than one operation scheduled, Pat would have to resterilize the tools between cases. That meant a half hour for coffee and rolls each time. We'd sit around and talk—Ted was interested in and well read on everything from archeology to zoology. I enjoyed working with him.

The appearance of his O.R. was something that would make most surgeons shudder. The operating table must have been a hundred years old and the light was one of Edison's original models. We always had a horrible time getting the beam into focus on the incision.

His equipment was, to put it mildly, meager. Sometimes this got us into a bit of trouble. One day, for example, I was operating on a hip and I asked for a "driver." A driver is a metal rod that can be screwed onto the end of a three-flanged nail, and is used to pound the nail into the bone.

"Driver?" said Ted. "What's that?" I explained.

"Oh, come on, Willy," he said. "Don't get fancy with me. We haven't got any driver. Use this hammer. I bought it at the hardware store."

I thought he was kidding, but he wasn't. I took the hammer, just a plain ordinary one with a wooden handle, and drove the nail in.

It worked fine, but unfortunately, when I tried to attach a metal plate to the nail—something that had to be done to give the fracture solid fixation—I found that the hammer had messed up the threads in the end of the nail. I couldn't get the screw in to hold the plate.

"I'll have to put in a new nail," I said. "The threads on this one are shot. Give me an extractor."

Unfortunately, it turned out that Ted had no extractor either.

"Do you have any suggestions?" I asked him. "I can't get this goddam nail out without an extractor."

"Sure," he said, "leave it. Hell, that nail will hold well enough. I'll just keep Charlie in bed a couple of extra days."

There was nothing else I could do, so I left it. And, sure enough, it held.

After that experience, I tried to make certain, whenever I went to Cokato to operate, that all the necessary instruments were available. If Ted didn't have them I'd borrow them from the Litchfield Hospital and bring them along with me. I've never been hung up on fancy tools, but it's nice to have at least the bare essentials.

Despite the primitive nature of the operating room—the sink where we washed up was actually in the operating room itself, an arrangement that went out with spats (which, by the way, Ted still wore)—and the shortage of equipment, I never once had a complication that could be even remotely attributed to the facilities. A wound infection was a rare occurrence; the incidence was much lower than in any of the big hospitals.

The reason our results were so good was simple; there were very few people moving in and out of the operating room. The bigger and busier the hospital the heavier the stream of traffic in and out of the room. Nurses, aides, doctors and the patients themselves are all potential carriers of germs. If thirty people pass through an operating room in a day the chance of bringing in infection is ten times what it would be if only three people had been there.

There's another plus, from the hospital administrator's point of view, in having an itinerant surgeon come in rather than sending patients away: that word again—money. Even if the only operations done are tonsillectomies, D and C's and repair of lacerations, it's necessary to keep an operating room supplied and nurses on the payroll to staff it. If the O.R. isn't busy it loses money for the hospital. If it's a booming busy place it can be a big moneymaker. So it's to the interest of the administrator—the hospital board—and all the taxpayers in the community to keep the O.R. and all the other facilities (lab, X-ray department, physiotherapy) busy. It's the rare administrator who doesn't welcome the itinerant surgeon.

In 1968 the Cokato hospital closed its doors. Ted got tired of running the place all by himself. He would have stayed in Cokato and continued to practice if he could have persuaded the city fathers to buy the hospital from him, but they wouldn't. So at the age of sixty he chucked it. He sold his home and the hospital to someone who turned it into a home for the mentally retarded, and Ted, who had always had a particular interest in psychiatry, took a job with a state hospital—forty hours a week, no nights or weekends. He loves it.

Personally, I miss the trips to Cokato. I still do some surgery out of town, in a community twenty-five miles from Litchfield, but it's not quite the same. I ask for a "driver" now and I get it —I don't have Ted yelling at me because I'm wasting the silk sutures he bought at Woolworth's—and I can't find anyone who will argue with me about the merits of Norman Mailer's last book while we take out a gall bladder. I guess the one-man hospital is a thing of the past. There are no Renaissance men left in medicine.

21

Fee-Splitting

Anyone who thinks that the College of Surgeons gets uptight about itinerant surgery ought to see that organization respond when fee-splitting is mentioned. It's like waving a red flag at a bull. I agree that fee-splitting can be very bad news, but I don't think the problem is as serious as the publicity it gets suggests.

In the simplest form of fee-splitting the internist refers the patient to the surgeon for, we'll say, removal of his stomach. The surgeon operates, charges the patient five hundred dollars, and returns part of the fee to the internist. The internist's cut may vary anywhere from 10 to 50 percent of the total bill, depending on how many fee-splitting surgeons are around and how tough the competition for patients is.

Usually fee-splitting isn't done in quite so flagrant a style. A slightly more sophisticated approach is that in which the surgeon asks the internist to help him supervise the postoperative management of the case, even though the surgeon could easily handle it himself. The internist drops in to see the patient for each of the seven or eight postoperative days and puts in a fifteen-dollar charge for each visit. The surgeon then reduces his customary fee by the amount the internist charges.

In a hospital where there are no interns or residents the internist (or G.P. or pediatrician—I'm using "internist" just to keep it simple) can scrub in, assist at the operation and charge an assistant's fee—which comes out of the surgeon's pocket. Actually, most internists don't like this system, because they don't like to be in the operating room for the two or three hours it may take to do the surgery. They can earn more money in the same time seeing patients in their offices.

Billing for these procedures can be done either directly, each doctor sending a separate bill, or indirectly, the surgeon charging the total fee to the patient, and the internist charging the surgeon for his contribution to the case. How it's done depends on who is paying. If the patient pays out of his own pocket, the doctors may charge separately. If the patient has insurance, billing may be done differently. Some insurance companies will only pay one doctor. If this is the situation the surgeon will submit the total bill and the internist will charge the surgeon.

The American College of Surgeons has made rule after rule in a zealous attempt to stamp out fee-splitting. Every time they close one loophole, another opens up. Some rules are simply ignored.

There's a rule, for example, that the referring doctor shall not assist the surgeon at an operation. I pay no attention to that one. What am I supposed to do—tell Carlo Germain that he can't help me take the gall bladder out of his patient Mrs. Peterson? That I'm going to have his competitor, George Engel, help me instead? That would be the last time I'd ever get a case from Carlo Germain. I always ask the referring doctor to help me; and, of course, he charges for his services.

Fee-splitting tends to be a bigger problem in the metropolitan hospitals, where there are more surgeons than are really needed, than in small towns where the surgeons have plenty to do. A guy who is sitting around a coffee shop waiting for a case and wondering where he's going to get the money to pay his office nurse's salary, may figure, if he's offered a chance to split the fee on a gastrectomy, What the hell—two hundred and fifty is a lot more than nothing, and say Yes. The surgeon who is operating every day, who is up to his ears in cases, wouldn't consider kicking back even 10 percent to get another patient. He has more patients than he wants already.

There's another reason—I think a more important one than

the overabundance of surgeons—why fee-splitting persists despite repeated attempts to do away with it. Surgeons are highly paid for what they do, and G.P.'s, internists and other nonoperating doctors sometimes resent it. They think they should get a bigger bite out of the patient's dollar. They have a point.

Take a case I had recently. The phone rang at seven thirty in the morning, just as I was getting the last pancake off the griddle. It was Tom Brogan. "Bill," he said, "before you go to the operating room stop up on third floor and take a look at this eighty-year-old man I've got in. His name is Julius Cutler. His son called me at two this morning because he had been vomiting for three hours. I think he may have some gangrenous intestine in his belly."

At a quarter to eight I stopped in and briefly examined Julius. He had a very tender, distended abdomen. I glanced at the X-rays. They showed a block in the small intestine. The blood studies were those that we usually see after a patient has been vomiting. I said to Tom, "I'm sure you're right. He probably has some intestine twisted around an adhesion from his old appendectomy. We'd better open him up. I'll get this hernia done and we'll put him on the schedule before the gall bladder."

An hour later I opened up Julius' abdomen, untwisted the bowel, cut out the piece that was gangrenous, and spliced the bowel back together again. The case took me one hour and ten minutes.

I charged Julius three hundred dollars for my services, a fee which the family was happy to pay. Tom, who had come over to the hospital at three in the morning, examined Julius, ordered and interpreted the X-rays and laboratory work, started the intravenous fluid and passed the rubber tube into Julius' stomach to control vomiting—Tom, who had worked with Julius for four hours—charged twenty-five dollars for his services. The family complained when they got his bill. They thought he had overcharged them.

Not just individuals, but insurance companies and the government as well, are willing to reward surgeons liberally for what they do, but resent paying comparable fees for nonsurgical services.

The G.P. who gets up at midnight, makes a house call, takes a little boy to the hospital, waits around for the lab work and finally makes a diagnosis of appendicitis is lucky if he can collect fifteen dollars for his time and trouble. The surgeon who comes in, takes out the appendix and is back in bed within the hour gets two hundred dollars. Even though I'm a surgeon I'm inclined to think we get a better shake than some of our medical confreres.

I can almost hear the protestations of any surgeons who read this: "Think of the years of training we went through"; "Consider the responsibility we accept"; "Remember, we're charging not just for that hour in the operating room, but for the postoperative care as well."

I know all that as well as the next guy. I struggled through the training, I've sweated out tough cases, I've managed patients through a difficult postoperative period—I've done all those things, and often. I still say it: We get paid pretty well. And I can understand why the medical men sometimes think they deserve a piece of the action.

Everyone makes too big a deal out of fee-splitting. Not just the College of Surgeons—they have to make a lot of noise since it's their job to police us surgeons—but all doctors and even the public in general. "Fee-splitter" seems to be about the worst label you can hang on a doctor.

Let's be realistic: what doctor is going to send a patient to a surgeon if he thinks that surgeon is going to hurt the patient? No doctor would do that. Physicians put just as much of a premium on life and health as does anyone else. Perhaps more. No doctor is going to say to himself, I think I'll send my friend Charlie to Bill to have his gall bladder removed, even though Bill may kill him, because I want the two hundred bucks that Bill kicks back. No one is that money-hungry.

Admittedly, an internist might choose to send his friend Charlie to Bill, rather than Ralph, if both surgeons are, in his opinion, of equal skill and Bill will kick back two hundred dollars. He'll reason that everything else being equal, his patient won't suffer because the referral is made on that basis. That's the way the world is and all the rules that can be dreamed up aren't going to change things.

If we ever arrive at a time when every surgeon is fully occupied doing his thing, when all doctors can collect a reasonable fee for the work they do, then fee-splitting will disappear. Till that time it will be as impossible to stamp out as prostitution.

Which brings me to one last comment. I know of some surgeons with big "fat cat" practices who raise indignant voices at the surgical society meetings if they hear that some young doctor, just starting out, is letting the referring G.P. help him on cases. Yet these same men always send very lush Christmas gifts to the doctors who have been referring to them for years. "That's different," they say when the subject is brought up. "It's a matter of degree."

Every time I hear them use this argument I'm reminded of that old chestnut, usually attributed to George Bernard Shaw. At a dinner party one evening he was talking to a "society woman." He asked her, in the course of the conversation, if she would consider going to bed with him for a million dollars. She laughed and acknowledged that she probably would.

"How about two bucks?" he then asked. At this she got up on her high horse and said, "What do you think I am—a prostitute?"

"Madam," he answered, "we have already established that fact. We are now merely quibbling over price."

22

The Town–Gown Battle

Those of us who are out in private practice, actually taking care of patients and responsible to them as private individuals, have an esprit de corps rather like that which front-line troops have in a war. We know what it's like to get up at night and rush to the hospital to take care of a kid whose skull has been fractured in an automobile accident, what it's like to listen a dozen times a day to women with backaches or dizziness, and how wearing it is to sweat out a coronary on a man who is not only a patient but a close friend. We know what it's like to stand alone and fight for our patients under less than ideal conditions. We understand and protect each other.

We private practitioners, the "town" doctors as we've been labeled, are also united in our resentment and distrust of the "white tower" boys, the academic "gown" segment of the medical world, the doctors who work full time at the university hospitals or the "name" clinics. We often get the feeling that protected by the aura of the institution in which they work, they sit back and take pot shots at those of us in private practice. We think that they don't have any real understanding of the problems we face and we resent their critical attitude. The "town–gown" conflict is a real and often bitter part of medical life.

Here's the sort of distasteful incident that keeps the battle going. One afternoon I was sitting in my office reading a journal and waiting for my nurse to bring in the next patient when a woman walked by, glared at me, continued on, hesitated, then turned back and stopped at my open door. I could see she was on the verge of tears.

"Dr. Nolen," she said, "could I talk to you for a few minutes?"

"Sure," I said, "come on in."

I recognized her now. Her name was Mrs. Wroe. Her son, Jimmy, a husky seventeen-year-old boy, had been killed in an automobile accident about three months earlier. She sat down, wiped her eyes and started talking.

"Dr. Nolen," she said, "for the last two months I've been lying awake at night trying to get up the courage to talk to you. You may as well know that I've been cursing you at the same time. Dr. Nolen—why didn't you operate on Jimmy when he was hurt? If you had he'd be alive today. I blame you for Jimmy's death."

As you can imagine, this statement shook me. I had felt badly about Jimmy's death—both as a doctor and as a parent—but I hadn't felt in the least responsible. Nor had I suspected that Mrs. Wroe blamed me. There was no reason why she should have.

I kept my voice calm as I asked her, "Why do you think I could have saved Jimmy, Mrs. Wroe?"

"Because," she answered, "Dr. Miller at the White Tower hospital told me so. Right after Jimmy died he said, 'It's too bad your local doctor didn't operate on Jimmy's leg. If he had done it right away Jimmy wouldn't have died.'"

I was furious. If I could have gotten my hands on Dr. Miller I'd have certainly been responsible for one death—his. But I hadn't any idea who Dr. Miller was and it was highly unlikely I'd ever be able to trace him. He was probably floating around on some other division at White Tower now, knocking other guys like me who are out in practice.

I spent the next half hour explaining to Mrs. Wroe, in great detail and in terms she could understand, what had happened to her son.

Jimmy had been brought to our hospital by ambulance at

one o'clock in the morning, after the car in which he and his
girl friend had been riding skidded on an icy highway and
struck a telephone pole. Jimmy had been thrown from the car
and had hit his head on the ground. When I saw him at the
hospital he had, along with several lacerations of his face and
arms, a fractured pelvis and a broken leg. He had also sustained a severe concussion, and though conscious, he was not
fully alert.

After quickly calming his girl friend, who had only been
shaken up, I turned my attention to Jimmy. I sewed up his
lacerations and got X-rays of his head, pelvis and leg. There
was no skull fracture, but the pelvis and leg X-rays confirmed
my clinical impression: he had some mean fractures. The
pelvic break could be treated adequately with bed rest, but the
leg would probably need open surgery. However, because I
was concerned about Jimmy's head injury, I didn't want to
risk operating on him right away. I put the leg in a cast, which
didn't require any anesthesia, and had the nurses put Jimmy
to bed. I wanted to follow his course for a few hours.

I was glad I did. The next morning, when I examined him,
the pupil of one eye was bigger than the other and the reflexes
on one side were hyperactive—both signs that there might be
bleeding in the skull. I took Mrs. Wroe aside, explained to her
that Jimmy might need brain surgery, and since there was no
neurosurgeon in our town I suggested a transfer to a bigger
hospital. Mrs. Wroe was concerned about money and thought
care might be less expensive at White Tower, so that's where
I sent Jimmy.

The last thing I was worried about at the time was Jimmy's
leg. He wasn't going to die of that injury. It could be operated
on successfully anytime in the next week or so. But the head
needed attention and promptly. Brain hemorrhages can be
rapidly fatal.

The rest of the story I got several weeks later, when the
White Tower doctors finally got around to writing to me. After
Jimmy's arrival they had done angiograms (X-rays of the
blood vessels in the brain). Their studies confirmed what I'd
suspected—Jimmy had a blood clot within his skull—and a

neurosurgeon operated on him. At the same time, while he was asleep, the orthopedist fixed the fracture of his leg.

Jimmy didn't make it. The injury to his brain had been too severe. He died six hours after the operation.

It was at that time, when breaking the news to Mrs. Wroe, that Dr. Miller had put the blame on me. It was his comment that I could have saved Jimmy that had been responsible for the two months of anguish Mrs. Wroe had suffered.

After going over the case with Mrs. Wroe, all I said was, "Dr. Miller just didn't understand. The broken leg had nothing to do with Jimmy's death. It was the head injury. And I'm certain that the doctors at White Tower did all that could be done to save Jimmy. He was in excellent hands. It was just that the brain damage was too severe."

When I finished talking to her Mrs. Wroe said, "Thank you, Dr. Nolen. I miss Jimmy, but I could hardly live with the idea that he could have been saved. I can accept his death better now. And I'm sorry I cursed you. I didn't understand."

As a member of the "town" (private practitioner) rather than the "gown" (full-time, salaried, academic) segment of medicine, I cite this example to show one of the characteristics of the academic institutions that we doctors in practice resent: the tendency to blame us when things go wrong with the patients we send them. They sit in their ivory towers, surrounded by all the latest in laboratory equipment, with interns, residents and super specialists of all varieties at their side, and knock those of us who are out in the community hospitals taking care of 98 percent of the ailments of 98 percent of the people. We resent their attitude.

Most of the time the knocks they give us aren't deserved. I don't know who Dr. Miller is, as I said, but I'd guess he's either some super specialist who knows nothing except how to take care of bones, or a resident still wet behind the ears. I didn't deserve the crack he took at me from his position of security in the White Tower, and to take it he had to be either vicious or stupid. I hope it was the latter.

Even though I resent the arrogance of some of the white

tower doctors I can see how they come by it. They're in a position where they can't lose.

Take the case of Louis Langerin. Louis came to our clinic one day complaining of a skin rash. "I've had it for two weeks, Doc," he said, "and it's beginning to bug me. I thought it would go away by itself so I haven't done anything to it. But it's getting worse. It itches like the devil."

George, who saw him, thought it was an allergic reaction, possibly to a new soap Louis's wife had started using, so he gave him the appropriate ointment. When the rash was no better after a week, George switched to a different cream. Still no improvement. So he switched to a third.

All hell broke loose. Louis's rash, which had been confined mostly to his arms and legs, spread to his body and his genitalia. He was itching and scratching so he could hardly walk.

Now George shipped him off, with a copy of his history, to a dermatologist at a white tower. The dermatologist looked over the list of medications George had tried, stopped them all and put Louis on the one thing George hadn't used—cortisone. Within three days Louis was all better. Naturally, he thought the dermatologist was a brilliant man and that George was an idiot; a conclusion the dermatologist did nothing to discourage.

The truth was something else. Louis's problem was an allergy to something, probably the soap. George had followed the wise course in sticking to medications which were not as high-powered as cortisone. Unfortunately, Louis reacted to them. By the time he got to the dermatologist Louis had had all the medicines which the dermatologist would have used if he'd seen Louis earlier. So he used cortisone, which worked.

The point is that the only patients we doctors ship off to the big centers are the ones who get into trouble or don't respond to routine treatments. So the man in the white tower can do no wrong; if the patient dies or gets worse it's the fault of the guy who sent the patient in; if the patient gets better the white tower doctor gets all the credit. It's a very nice spot to be in.

Anyone who doesn't think the gown doctors look down upon the town doctors ought to attend a "grand rounds" ses-

sion at a white tower someday and become acquainted with
the L.M.D. syndrome.

The L.M.D., as all medical school graduates know, is the
Local Medical Doctor, and at grand rounds the impression
one gets is that all L.M.D.'s are first cousins of Denny Dim-
wit. They never do anything right.

At grand rounds, interns or senior medical students "present" cases to the assembled big daddies of the white tower
staff. The intern stands up in front of this audience and begins
by saying something like: "Mr. Renando is a thirty-nine-year-
old white male who was referred to the White Tower because
of persistent rectal bleeding. The L.M.D. who had been taking
care of Mr. Renando was unable to determine the cause of
the bleeding." At this point a smirk is clearly visible not only
on the face of the intern but on the faces of some of the faculty
and medical students assembled in the hall. The intern then
goes on to explain in detail all the silly things that the L.M.D.
did, to no avail. Following which, he reports on all the clever
studies that have been done by the wise doctors with the
sophisticated equipment at the White Tower. And then the
big daddies discuss the case for another fifteen minutes, dropping pearl after pearl for the medical students to gather up.
Then on to the next case on which some other poor unfortunate L.M.D. has struck out.

If all this sounds just a little bit bitter, let me assure you, it is.
I'm one of the town guys, mostly, and I resent the knocks that
the white tower boys take at us. Throw them out into a community hospital, away from the computers and all their
subspecialist buddies, and they wouldn't be worth the powder
to blow them to hell. They need ten special tests and three
helpers to diagnose appendicitis.

But bitterness aside, it's worth pointing out that the disparaging attitude the white-tower doctors take toward practicing
physicians, the L.M.D.'s, is responsible in no small part for the
maldistribution of doctors in this country today. Who teaches
medical students? The white-tower doctors. Where do they
teach them? At the white-tower hospital. What do they
teach the students, by implication at least? That all the doctors

who aren't full time at white tower are fatheads. It's no wonder that the big cities are loaded with surgeons and internists
who have little to do but sit around twiddling their thumbs.
These people won't cut the umbilical cord that ties them to
the white tower. They don't want to be labeled "L.M.D.'s."
So the communities that need doctors can't attract them. And,
of course, since most medical schools have few or no G.P.'s on
the teaching staff, students are not tempted to go into general
practice, even though they know that G.P.'s, not super
specialists, are what our country needs most.

Nowhere is the town–gown conflict more obvious than in
the struggle for control of the "teaching" hospitals.

Twenty years ago—even ten years ago—much of the teaching in hospitals associated with medical schools was done by
doctors in private practice, who would spend a few hours each
week working with medical students. Most of them taught for
nothing; they welcomed the stimulation that came from as-
sociating with and being questioned by medical students.

The system helped the students too. Doctors who work full
time in one hospital get into a rut. They develop philosophies
of treatment that never vary; they teach students only one
way to manage patients—their way. The doctors in private
practice who donated time to the teaching hospital often came
from different training centers where they'd been exposed to
other ideas. The student under their tutelage would find that
there was more than one way to practice medicine. He could
then choose from a variety of systems the techniques he preferred.

In the last ten years this cross-fertilization has all but dis-
appeared. At the teaching hospital in Minneapolis with which
I was affiliated till my appointment was canceled in 1971, the
trend has been obvious. Ten years ago a dozen or so doctors
from private practice would always come to the surgical conferences and discuss and criticize the management of cases;
now the only ones who attend the conferences are the full-
time salaried doctors, all of whom have been trained at that
hospital. They are all nice fellows, but they're an inbred group.
And the doctors they train will think as they do—or else.

It isn't just in Minneapolis that this has occurred, it's happening everywhere. The full-time salaried doctors don't want the private practitioners around. They freeze them out as completely as they can. They want to run things their way.

This aspect of the town–gown battle affects not only the quality of instruction given medical students but the quality of care available at private hospitals. If the academic doctors and the private doctors would cooperate, private hospitals could be used to provide part of the training of interns and residents. They could spend part of their residency years at private hospitals, working under the direction of private practitioners. This would be good for the man in training and good for the private hospital. The only ones for whom it would not be good are the full-time salaried men at the medical school hospital whose power might be slightly diffused.

So, though cooperative ventures sometimes can be arranged, often there is friction and the programs never realize their full potential. The program may even fade away and die, a victim of the town–gown battle.

Doctors out in practice occasionally get a chance to knock the professors.

One case comes particularly to mind. Charlie Stapleton caught me on rounds one day and said, "Bill, I've got a patient in who I think needs surgery. He bled heavily three months ago and went to the Black Clinic. They sent him through the usual mill—consultants, X-rays, lab work, the whole business—and finally decided he had bled from a hiatus hernia. He's bleeding again and I guess we'd better fix it."

A hiatus hernia, a condition in which part of the stomach slides up into the chest, is a very common finding. About one out of every ten adults has it to some degree. But of all the hiatus hernias that exist in this world only about one in a hundred causes any trouble. And bleeding from a hiatus hernia is usually not massive.

I looked the patient over and then called Charlie. "Charlie," I said, "I agree Mr. Lang needs surgery, but before we do him let's get another set of stomach X-rays. He's bleeding awfully heavy for a man with nothing but a hiatus hernia."

Our radiologist X-rayed Mr. Lang and, sure enough, along with the hiatus hernia was a cancer, high up in the stomach where it could be missed if the radiologist was having an off day. Apparently just that had happened at the Black Clinic, because when we sent for their films the malignancy could be seen—through the retrospectroscope, of course, which gives everyone 20/20 vision.

We operated on Mr. Lang and were able to get the tumor out. Since it all happened over five years ago, and Mr. Lang is still healthy, I assume we cured him. But that isn't my point in telling you about the case.

My point is that when we told Mr. Lang that he had a tumor of the stomach, he asked, "Why didn't the doctors at the Black Clinic find it?"

We could have said, "Because their radiologist wasn't on the ball," or, "Because even the Black Clinic makes mistakes once in a while," but we didn't. Instead we said, "These things sometimes don't show up on X-ray when they're awfully small. We were lucky to find it." We could have knocked the Black Clinic, but we didn't. We held our tongues. We practitioners, out in the "town," know how awfully vulnerable we are. We treat the gown doctors the way we'd like to be treated by them.

Nothing in this world is absolute and I'd be the last guy to say that all the white tower boys are baddies and all the working stiffs good guys. There are bastards in private practice who knock any and every one they can and doctors on the full-time staffs at the white-tower hospitals or big clinics who bend over backward to protect the doctor who sends them a screwed-up case.

Like Steve Michalik. Steve is a big heavy fellow who works for a furniture company. Carlo referred Steve to me because he was having almost constant trouble with his bowels, pain, constipation, and even some bleeding. He had a disease called diverticulitis, inflammation in some little pouches, diverticuli, that had developed in his large intestine.

Most cases of diverticulitis can be treated medically, but once in a while it's necessary to operate. Steve hadn't done well on medicines and diet. He wanted an operation and I agreed that he needed one. We put him on the schedule at a time when he wasn't having any symptoms. I expected his bowel to be relatively free of inflammation.

This was important because I planned to remove the section of diseased bowel and sew the two ends together. It's safe to do this if the bowel isn't acutely inflamed. But if it is inflamed, then the wise surgeon does the operation in three stages: first a colostomy—bringing the upper bowel out on the abdominal wall to put the lower bowel at rest; three weeks later an operation to remove the diseased bowel; six weeks after that an operation to close the colostomy and restore the continuity of the bowel. I didn't want to put Steve through three operations. I wanted to do it all in one stage.

When I got Steve's abdomen opened and started to free the bowel I found, to my dismay, that there was more inflammation than I had expected. It wasn't awfully bad, but it wasn't good either. It became a matter of judgment as to whether it was safe to do the operation in one stage. I chose to try it.

It was a mistake. On the fifth postoperative day when I changed Steve's dressing, there was stool along the drain that ran from inside the abdomen to the skin. Steve had developed a leak at the point where I had sewed the two ends of the bowel together.

"What's that, Doc?" Steve asked me. "It smells like shit."

"It is, Steve," I said, "it is. Your bowel's leaking a little, but I expect it will stop in a few days." I didn't really expect it, but I hoped it would. Sometimes small leaks will seal themselves.

Steve's didn't. Every day when I changed the dressing there was more and more stool. "Christ, Doc," Steve said, "I'm not going to the can at all any more. Everything's coming out of here."

"I know it, Steve," I said. "I'm afraid I'm going to have to take you back to the operating room and do a colostomy to give that bowel a chance to heal. I hate to do it, but you're not going to get any better this way."

So I took Steve back and did the colostomy. Unfortunately, too late. The small intestine had gotten caught up in the inflammation along the leaky bowel, and three days after I did the colostomy the small intestine sprang a leak. I had to take Steve back to the operating room a third time to try to repair it.

Now Steve was in real trouble. Three weeks had gone by since his original operation and in those three weeks he'd been losing weight and strength. With his bowel leaking we couldn't get any nutrition into him. And the infection in his abdomen caused him to run a fever, which burned up a lot of calories. When his small intestine developed another leak, just five days after I'd fixed the first one, I knew Steve and I were in the soup.

One of the bad traits many doctors have is an inability to admit that they need help. Doctors hang on to patients a lot longer than they should. Sometimes it's disastrous for the patient.

I had probably hung on to Steve too long already. I was so involved in his problem and felt so responsible for it that I was losing my ability to make unemotional, proper judgments, but I finally realized what was happening. When I couldn't make up my mind whether or not to reoperate on Steve I swallowed my pride, called a surgeon at a white-tower hospital and transferred Steve to his care. This surgeon, Stanley Whitehead, spent two weeks getting Steve into shape, reoperated on him, and after a stormy postoperative course, finally got Steve well.

Stanley could have murdered me. A raised eyebrow, a snide comment, any sort of criticism, and he would have turned Steve against me. I knew I had botched the case; Stanley knew it—and I'm sure Steve suspected it. It wouldn't have taken much to confirm his suspicions.

When Steve came to my office for a checkup several weeks after Stanley had discharged him, I knew Stanley hadn't let me down. "Doc, I don't know how to thank you," Steve said. "Dr. Whitehead told me you did a fine job on my bowel. He said I'm cured for good of my diverticulitis. He told me not many guys could have gotten me through all those complications."

Dr. Whitehead could have added, "Nor would many surgeons have gotten you into all that trouble." Thank the Lord that most of the white tower doctors, Whitehead among them, are compassionate guys. It's too bad that the few know-it-alls can create so much trouble, misery and ill will.

There's an economic side to the town–gown conflict. Many of the doctors who are full-time staff members at the big clinics or white-tower hospitals are on salaries. This has two effects: one good, one bad.

The good effect is that these doctors don't have to worry about how many patients they see in a day, how many laboratory studies they order in a week, how many operations they perform in a month. If they see six hundred patients in a month their income is the same as when they see three hundred. So they can take their time and practice leisurely, thoughtful medicine (within limits, of course; if a doctor is too unproductive, i.e., lazy, even the white-tower hospital won't be able to afford him).

The negative effect of a salary is the same thing seen from another point of view. The doctor doesn't have to attract patients. Therefore he doesn't have to be nice, considerate, warm. As a consequence the most common gripe those of us in private practice hear from the patients who return from a trip to a white tower is, "I suppose I got good care, but I didn't like it. I felt as if nobody really cared about me. I was just a number. It's more like a factory than a hospital." White-tower doctors are often strong on the science of medicine but weak on the art.

They, on the other hand, feel that the "fee for service" system encourages us town doctors to do tests, give shots, perform operations just for the money. They think that we're more concerned with a buck than with the patient's welfare. And they're sure that we don't read the medical literature, go to seminars and meetings, keep up with medical progress, because we don't have to. They think we're con artists who know how to butter up patients but don't know how to treat them intelligently. All of which we, of course, deny.

Competition between doctors is natural and in some respects, if you'll excuse the word, healthy. If a surgeon tries to operate better than his competitor, and an internist tries to read electrocardiograms better than anyone else, medical standards go up. But the town–gown competition is bitter and bad for everyone. White-tower doctors, with all their facilities, can make a significant contribution to medical care; so can the practitioners out in private practice. Each has something special to contribute to the patient.

Unfortunately, as long as we resent and battle each other instead of working together, we're not going to do as much for our patients as we could.

23

The Writing Game: Doctor Style

Some doctors, particularly those in the academic world, prefer to be rewarded for what they do with fame rather than money. They accept incomes which may be lower than what they could earn in private practice—though still far above what the average man earns—in exchange for the opportunities to do research and/or write papers. And they do write! Academic medical men are second only to the members of the teaching profession in their desire to be published.

Which explains why doctors are slowly drowning in a flood of literature. There are hundreds of medical journals published every month, many of which are mailed out free and unsolicited to every doctor in the country. None of us have time to wade through them all. But the drug companies need to reach the doctors with their messages. They pay plenty to advertise in these magazines and have no trouble finding doctors to fill the editorial pages with their literary gems.

The articles that appear in the scientific journals, such as *Archives of Otolaryngology, Journal of Bone and Joint Surgery* and *Annals of Internal Medicine,* are written for the most part by doctors in academic medicine. If you want to move from instructor to assistant professor to associate professor, and on up the ladder, you have to have a bibliography.

The "publish or perish" philosophy applies to the medical aca-
demics just as rigidly as it does to others in university positions.

Since the length of the bibliography is as important, often
more important, than the individual quality of the articles, a
lot of garbage gets into print. Anyone who does ten appendectomies can get an article out of it. The pattern is always the
same.

The idea, and I use the word loosely, usually comes from
the top.

The professor of surgery, making rounds with his entourage,
looks in on a patient recovering from appendicitis. A light
flashes and he says to an associate professor, "Charlie, we
ought to write a paper on the effect of penicillin on appendicitis. Get someone onto it." They move on to the next bed. The
professor has set the wheels in motion.

After rounds are over, Charlie goes back to his office and
sends for Dave, an assistant professor battling hard to make
associate. "Dave," Charlie says, "you've always been interested in appendicitis. [Dave eagerly agrees, though if the
truth were known, nothing bores him more than appendicitis.]
The old man [all professors of surgery are known, affection-
ately, as the old man] is wondering what effect penicillin has
on our postoperative patients. Why don't you think up some
study we can do to find out about it?"

"Sure thing, Charlie," Dave says. "I'll get right at it." Dave
scampers back to his office and draws up an outline for the
projected study. Basically all he needs are the charts of ten
patients who had appendicitis and were given penicillin after
their operation and ten patients with appendicitis who didn't
get penicillin. From these charts he can get all the data he
needs to make several graphs (graphs are very important in a
"scientific" paper). One graph will show the temperature
curve in group A, a second will show the curve in group B. He
can also draw a graph showing the incidence of wound infection, a graph comparing the length of hospital stay in the two
groups and even a graph showing how quickly the members
of each group got out of bed. There is virtually no end to the

graphs and tables a diligent man can derive from a handful
of charts. When Dave is through with his outline he has ideas
for at least four graphs and six tables full of data. Now he calls
in George, the chief resident.

"George," Dave begins, "I've been thinking." This is not literally true, but it sounds good; George, of course, knows it
means the old man has had another "brilliant" idea. "We see a
lot of appendicitis around here. Some of our patients get
penicillin and some don't. I think it would be interesting to
find out what effect the penicillin has, don't you?"

George nods in agreement. There is no other possible choice
if he wants a staff appointment later. Dave pulls out his outline,
he and George go over it, and George leaves for the ward.

The first intern George bumps into gets the assignment. "Go
down to the chart room, Louis, and pull out the records on the
last ten appys we did who got penicillin, and the last ten who
didn't. We're going to do a little study."

"Jeez, George," Louis says, "I've got a cast to change, some
stitches to take out, and three new patients to examine. Can't
someone else do it?" Louis doesn't give a damn about the
study. As soon as this internship ends he's going into
psychiatry.

"Get your ass down there," George says, and Louis does.
(Interns have no rights.)

Two hours later Louis finally finishes battling with the
record-room clerks—hospital records are always misfiled—and
he trudges back to George's office. He dumps the charts on
George's desk, muttering as he does, "Shove them up your
ass." (George, of course, is not in the office at the time.) Louis
then gets on with his real work.

From this point things seesaw back and forth. Resident
George digs out the data and makes up the charts. Assistant
Professor Dave reviews the material and writes the article.
Associate Professor Charlie reviews it and sends it back with
suggestions for revision. George and Dave revise it together.
Charlie re-reviews it and passes it on to the Professor.

Now, you may ask, is all this revision necessary for such a
simple paper? Let me assure you it is. It is difficult as hell to

stretch an idea that is worth, at most, a brief paragraph into three or four pages. Oscar Wilde once said, "If I had more time I'd have written a shorter letter." But Oscar Wilde was a writer. These gentlemen are not.

One of the important functions of the revision is to work in a lot of references. A three-page article, well done, can include references to as many as thirty other articles already cluttering up the literature. This gives the paper an aura of respectability.

And it's the wise author who includes among his references as many previous publications of the Professor's as possible. He uses statements such as, "Penicillin has been shown to be of little use against the entercoccus organism (1,2,3)." The "(1,2,3)" refers to the bibliography which accompanies the article and lists all previous works by the Chief.

The final or next to final revision done, the sacred papers are now passed on to the Professor. The Professor makes several more suggestions. If he couldn't make suggestions, particularly unnecessary ones, he wouldn't be a professor. The Professor's favorite suggestion is that the one paper be divided into three. For example, "The Effect of Penicillin on the Temperature of Postoperative Appendectomy Patients," "The Relationship of Penicillin Therapy to Postoperative Complications in Acute Appendicitis," and perhaps a little personal editorial by the Professor, "Are We Misusing Penicillin in Appendicitis Cases?" (The Professor will be able to dine out on these twenty cases for the next six months. And better three articles for the bibliography than one.) Finally the revising and subdividing are over. It now becomes necessary to decide which article will go to what magazine. There are a few medical (I use the word in a general sense to include surgery and the other specialties) journals which consistently publish articles of reasonable merit. *The New England Journal of Medicine* is one; the *Annals of Surgery* is another. You don't send some piece of nonsense to them because they won't publish it.

But there are dozens of other magazines with pages to be

filled each month. It's to them that you send your worthless offerings.

The Chief generally decides what magazine each article is best suited to, and from the list of available markets he chooses the appropriate three. He signs the cover letter, which virtually assures the acceptance of the article. The editorial board members all know the Professor's name and don't dare say No. After all, he sits on editorial boards himself and accepts the garbage they send him.

But before the articles are mailed, one critical decision remains to be made: Who gets the by-line? Or rather, in what order shall the by-line be arranged, because almost without exception, credits for medical articles go to more than one author. Often as many as six or eight people will get a by-line on a two-page article.

The place of honor is the first position, of course, and supposedly the guy whose idea it was or the one who did the most work goes first. (This does not, of course, apply in the case of an intern. If his name goes on at all it's somewhere in the middle. He doesn't need the credit as badly as the others.) The Professor tucks his name in last, a ploy known as "doing the humble bit."

The other names go on in order of seniority. But everyone —with the possible exception of the file clerk who found the charts (probably the most difficult part of the entire project) —gets his name on as an author. That's the way bibliographies are made.

Now, if this sounds like a far-out example, let me assure you it is not. (Having thought of the idea, I now have our record librarian digging out the records on our last twenty appendectomy patients.) Patients with gall bladder disease, men with coronaries, women with bunions—they all get analyzed sixteen ways from Sunday. And it all indiscriminately gets published. One medical writer for the lay press wrote to me complaining that every month the stack of medical publications that landed on his desk was over three feet high. He was drowning, along with us doctors, in a flood of nonsense.

One of the sorry side effects of this superabundance of trivia is that the occasional grain of wheat gets overlooked among the bushels of chaff (how about that for a metaphor!). Some guy may have a bright idea from which many of us could benefit, but we never get to see it. It's at the eighteen-inch depth in the pile, and we only get the top twelve inches read each month.

But at least this kind of writing is innocuous. It doesn't hurt anyone to have the literature cluttered up with worthless articles like "Carcinoma of the Infra Papillary Duodenum," a report of a single case (*Surgery*, February 1956), by Richard Flandreau, M.D., and William A. Nolen, M.D. The few people who read it won't be damaged by it.

But there's another kind of medical writing that actually hurts people. That's the stuff, published in the general-circulation magazines and newspapers, that gives false hope to all the patients, and potential patients, who read it. Headlines, such as "New Discovery Makes Cancer of Uterus Curable," "Heart Transplant Successful," "Amputated Arm Sewed Back on Boy," that imply the medical profession can cure diseases and solve problems that are still beyond them. Part of the responsibility for such misleading articles lies with the medical writer who's looking for a sensational headline. But most of the blame should be attributed to the physician who makes his pronouncement before he has sufficient evidence that the procedure is really worthwhile. Because an arm does not turn black ten minutes after it's sewed back on does not mean that the operation is a success. It's more than likely that a year later the arm will still be hanging, immobile, without sensation, completely useless, from the elbow of the man to whom it has been "restored." When it's amputated and replaced with a useful artificial limb no one's going to splash across the front page a headline saying "Restored Limb Amputated!" Nor, when the patient with the heart transplant dies, does that news make the front page; it's tucked away in the obituary column. The misled public remains in the dark. These announcements, made either in prematurely published articles or, worse, in newspapers or over television, put us practicing doctors on the spot.

One afternoon, shortly after some limb restorer made the headlines, I had to go to the hospital to see the result of one of the farm accidents that occur in large numbers in rural areas. A fourteen-year-old boy, helping his father on the farm, had gotten his left arm chopped off by the blade of a corn picker. The father had his son, Greg, in the back seat, the remnants of the arm, crushed and contaminated with manure, dangling by a few shreds of skin.

I knew the farmer, a fellow named Chad Robinson. He was a nice guy with six kids scrambling to make a living on a hundred and twenty acres south of Litchfield. The children of most farmers have to work after school and all summer if the family's going to subsist. Chad's family was no exception.

I took one look at Greg's arm and called Chad aside. "He's going to lose that arm, Chad. There's no circulation left. All that's holding it on is a few shreds of skin. I'm sorry."

"Jeez, Doc," Chad said, almost in tears. "Can't you fix it? Greg's left-handed."

"There's no way, Chad," I said. "That arm will be black in a few hours. He might get an infection that would kill him."

"But goddammit, Doc, just last week there was a piece in the paper about a guy whose arm was completely cut off and they sewed it back."

"I know, Chad," I said, "but that was different. It was a clean cut and they had the patient in the operating room fifteen minutes after the accident. Greg's arm is all crushed and dirty, and it's at least an hour since he was hurt. It just can't be done."

Chad was wiping his eyes with his sleeve now. His wife had her arm around him consoling him.

"I knew I should never have let him work that picker," Chad said. "He's just too young." He looked up at me. "All right, Doc," he said, "you know what you're doing. Go ahead."

I took the arm off and Greg did well. But I hear through the grapevine—in small towns, word gets around—that Chad still believes the university doctors might have saved Greg's arm. The little bit of incomplete information that Chad got from the newspaper headlines has messed up my relationship with him.

I had the same kind of experience the week after some jackass published an article in the Sunday paper which implied that the tonsils were a bulwark not only against infections but even against cancer. I hate to do tonsillectomies, as I've mentioned elsewhere, but it so happened that I'd done one case about three days before this item hit the press. On Monday I got a call from the mother of the child I'd operated on. It took me fifteen minutes to explain to her that Johnny, whose tonsils were nothing but two lumps of infected tissue, really had needed the operation. And I still think she feels that by taking out his tonsils, I've doomed Johnny to a premature death from some horrendous disease. I'd like to shoot the man responsible for that article.

The medical writing I've referred to here is either utter nonsense or material that is spouted impetuously to the press by some researcher who gets carried away by his own transient triumph. But some medical articles which are the end result of "scholarly" research are even more damaging and dangerous than these. These articles give an undeserved aura of respectability to a treatment or procedure that after a year or two or three, proves to be not only worthless but often dangerous. It's difficult to understand how some of these kooky ideas last even as long as they do; and more difficult still to comprehend how doctors, who are, by and large, reasonably intelligent and well-educated men, can accept as gospel what any reasonable person ought to immediately recognize as hot air. But now and then, we do. Read about two recent examples, in the next chapter, and weep.

24

Two Medical Screw-Ups

The men who devote a lot of time to research are, generally, dedicated to their work. Anyone who can go into a dog laboratory every day has to be dedicated. Row on row of kennels, each of which contains some innocent mutt whose insides have been manipulated by a surgeon so that the dog is doomed to a lingering death—anyone who can stand that atmosphere year after year has to be dedicated to his work. (Yes, I know we have to experiment on animals so that we can help humans. No, I'm not a member of the S.P.C.A. No, I'm not being critical; it's just that I haven't got the stomach for this sort of thing.)

To these men, these doctors who spend much of their lives in laboratories, we all owe a great debt. They are the ones who have made the medical discoveries that permit us to lead the long, healthy lives we now enjoy. Without men devoted to research we would still be dying of lung, kidney and heart diseases which have long since been conquered. There is much left to do, but much has been done.

There is, however, one trap into which doctors engaged in research fall with some frequency: that of deciding prematurely that what they want to be true is true. They formulate some theory that sounds interesting, and which if true, will be of great value to medicine, and then set out to prove it is true. In the university hospitals it's sort of a joke—which, like most jokes, has an element of truth to it—that when the professor sends his interns and residents into the dog lab to investigate one of his new ideas, it's their job to prove he's correct. The assistant resident who comes out of the dog lab with a pile of data proving that the professor's theory is all wet is not apt to become chief resident.

It's easy, approaching research with this attitude, to "prove" that almost anything is true. If one or two dogs die, who shouldn't have died if the professor's theory was correct, forget about them. You can always attribute their deaths to "unrelated causes" and throw them out of the series. The objective in some research programs seems to be solely to prove that the professor is a brilliant man.

All of which, if not admirable, is perfectly understandable. Research physicians are human. A lot of them earn less doing research than they could earn in private practice. They're giving up money in the hope that they'll achieve fame. (They may deny this, but it's true; anyone who needs substantiation from another source might read *The Double Helix*, by Nobel Prize-winner James Watson; it tells about the competition for fame among physicists.) Imagine how they must feel if after ten or twenty years in a dog lab, they haven't made one single substantial contribution to medicine? Most men will do almost anything to avoid that situation, so—not always consciously—they deceive the public and themselves.

In medicine, as in all of science, the man who does it first gets the acclaim; does anyone know the name of the second man to fly the Atlantic? This leads occasionally to premature attempts to translate work in the dog lab to human beings. The sad, somewhat lethal venture into heart transplantation is an excellent example of this sort of thing, as was the nauseating controversy between Michael DeBakey and Denton Cooley that got so much publicity when they began squabbling over who had the right to the artificial heart. This childish behavior among grown men would be humorous if it weren't for the fact that the end result for some innocent men and women is an unnecessarily early death.

Doctors have gotten a big bump on themselves. Like most

other men, and I'm no exception, they enjoy seeing their names in print; but since they traffic in human lives, this desire for fame and publicity ("Barnard dances with Gina Lollobrigida") can lead them into a very dangerous practice. They announce their medical triumphs not in a conservative style in the medical journals, where the results can be criticized, reexamined, evaluated and confirmed or denied according to merit by their peers, but in the lay press, where, exposed only to an uncritical public, they can be ballyhooed. After all, who reads the *Journal of Thoracic Surgery?* Five thousand doctors, tops. Seventeen million people read the *Reader's Digest.*

It's time the practice was stopped. The question is, How? Pleading with the researchers hasn't done the trick—it has been tried. What is needed is a more drastic measure: full publicity for the rotten failures that have been advertised as "triumphs" in the lay press to give their promoters a brief moment in the spotlight. Maybe seeing their work exposed for just what it is, rather than what they proclaimed it would be, will encourage the self-restraint and good judgment that seem to be so obviously lacking now. Call it blackmail if you like. Herewith are reports not of two triumphs but of two miserable medical-surgical flops of the last twenty years.

1. *The gastric freeze*

Patients with duodenal ulcers are not difficult to find. It's estimated that at some time in his life one out of every ten Americans harbors an ulcer. Most of the victims are men, but when women get ulcers, they have bad ones.

The disease is easy to treat but difficult to cure. About 90 percent of the cases will respond to medical measures—diet, antacids, sedatives—but many of these will have recurrent symptoms once treatment is discontinued. Some patients have flare-ups of their ulcers, chiefly in the spring or fall, year after year after year.

The 10 percent of ulcer patients who fail to respond to medical measures require surgery. The standard operation is gastrectomy (removal of part of the stomach) with or without vagotomy, i.e., a cutting of the nerves that run down from the brain to the stomach and stimulate acid secretion. The operation for ulcer is a major one, carrying with it a mortality rate somewhere between 2 and 10 percent, and some of those that survive the operation are plagued afterward with a variety of digestive complaints. There is no completely satisfactory cure for duodenal ulcer.

Which makes the disease a prime target of the medical and surgical researchers. There are literally dozens of operations discussed in the surgical textbooks and journals. None, over the long run, has proved to be a significant improvement over the standard gastrectomy, removal of the lower two-thirds of the stomach, devised by Bilroth, a German surgeon, in 1885.

In 1960 a group of surgeon-investigators got the bright idea that they might be able to "cure" duodenal ulcers by freezing the stomach. At that time general hypothermia (cooling of the patient to temperatures several degrees below normal) was sometimes used to help patients through major surgical procedures, particularly operations on the brain, heart or liver. The theory was that metabolism slowed down at lower temperatures, and that, with its metabolism slowed, the body could better withstand a reduction of blood flow and oxygen supply to its organs. The theory had proven true in practice. When body temperatures were lowered from a normal 98.6° F. (or 37° C.) to 86° F. (or 30° C.), there were improved survival rates in many instances.

In studying the effects of hypothermia it had been learned that under general hypothermia, acid secretion in the stomach also slowed down. Instead of pouring out several quarts of acid in a twenty-four-hour period the cooled stomach would secrete little or no acid. And where the normal gastric secretion was also rich in digestive enzymes the cooled secretion was not.

A reduction in the flow of acid and digestive enzymes is nice, but it's the sort of thing that can be accomplished with medication or surgery. Besides, it would be impossible to cool down the entire body of a duodenal-ulcer patient for the prolonged period of time it would take to cure his ulcer.

But the investigators asked themselves, Instead of cooling the entire body, what if we were to cool only the stomach? and what if we not only cooled it but froze it? Mightn't this, even if done for only a few hours, not simply reduce gastric secretion but eliminate it entirely?

It was an idea worth looking into and they did. Balloons were constructed which the patient could swallow and through which the doctor could circulate cold solutions—absolute alcohol was one of the favorites. With the patient on a warming blanket, to prevent a decline in general body temperature, it was possible to literally freeze the entire wall of the stomach. Working with dogs, it was shown that after a two-hour exposure to the cold solution the normally pliable stomach could be cracked like an eggshell. It was that solid.

Moreover, the stomach secretions did cease flowing. The stomach produced no acid while frozen and, even better, continued to produce no acid for weeks after the freezing. After the experimental trials* in animals the technique was applied to humans and it worked.

A breakthrough! According to what has recently become standard medical practice the report was issued not only to the *Journal of the American Medical Association* (May 12, 1962) but to the *Reader's Digest* ("They're Freezing Ulcers to Death," January 1963). Thousands of ulcer victims from all over the country ran to their doctors asking to have their stomachs frozen.

Many of these doctors were—if you'll excuse the expression —caught with their pants down. The technique hadn't been well publicized in medical circles, and if they hadn't read the *Digest*, they might not even have heard of it. Their patients knew more about the gastric freeze than they did.

* One of the tricks used to demonstrate the effectiveness of the freeze was to put a tube into the nose of a frog to supply it with oxygen, and lower the frog into the stomach of a live dog. From the ordinary stomach at normal temperatures the frog could be pulled out six hours later, completely digested. From the frozen dog's stomach the frog would emerge still hopping and healthy. A revolting but impressive piece of showmanship.

Moreover, the more conservative and wiser heads in the medical profession were cautious. They'd seen fads in ulcer treatment come and go and this new method hadn't stood even the briefest test of time. Nor was this just another pill, relatively innocuous, that could be experimented with at will. Freezing a patient's stomach might, they reasoned, prove to be a dangerous thing to do. As one old and experienced surgeon said to me, "Look, Bill, what happens when you get frostbite of the ear? The ear falls off. Why the hell should the stomach be any different?"

But under the stress of patients' pressure, many doctors succumbed. Machines for gastric freezing were manufactured and demonstrated at medical and surgical meetings; hospitals all over the country established facilities where doctors, surgeons and medical men could admit their ulcer patients and freeze their stomachs.

It wasn't long before the fears of the skeptics were confirmed. Six months after having their stomachs frozen, it was learned, most of the victims had their ulcers back. The hardy ones who would sit still for a re-freezing were even more bitterly disappointed. The second time around, most ulcers came back even more quickly.

Nor was this all the bad news. Some patients, shortly after the freeze, would shed part of the lining of their stomachs and bleed. The bleeding often required transfusions and, on occasion, made emergency surgery necessary. A few patients' frozen stomachs became perforated. An occasional patient died.

It took a while for the news to get around—remember, "breakthroughs" always make the front page, failures show up in the obituary columns—but eventually it did. The gastric freezers closed up shop and the doctors returned to the old stand-bys—pills, diet and surgery.

The entire episode, from the first "freeze" to the last, took about five years. If you'd like a "gastric freeze" machine for your very own you can pick one up for a song.

2. The internal-mammary-artery ligation

This procedure was publicized a few years back as a "new, simple, safe surgical cure for coronary heart disease." Hundreds of thousands of people in the United States die of that disease every year, so you can imagine how popular this simple, safe cure was at the time (1957, to be exact).

The principle was a simple one. There are two arteries, the internal mammaries, that run side by side down the inside of the front of the chest wall, one on either side of the sternum (the breastbone, in lay language). About halfway down the chest, over the heart, the arteries divide in two. One branch, the pericardio-phrenic, heads inward to the pericardium, the sac in which the heart lies. The other continues down to terminate in the abdomen.

A Philadelphia surgeon came up with the idea that if he were to tie off the branch of the internal mammary artery that ran to the abdomen, perhaps all the blood that once flowed through it would be diverted down the remaining branch to the sac around the heart. This increased flow to the pericardium might, via connections between the pericardial vessels and the heart vessels proper, increase the blood supply to the heart. This could cure patients of angina, the heart pain that victims of coronary artery disease have.

It didn't seem, to most surgeons, a completely logical assumption; after all, tying off one artery to an organ anywhere else had never noticeably increased blood flow to that organ via other arteries. Still, it was worth looking into.

The studies which were done to confirm this hypothesis were equivocal, to say the least. Injections into the internal mammary artery of dogs showed, according to one surgeon's study, more dye reaching the heart after the abdominal branch of the internal mammary was tied off than it did with both branches open. But not everyone agreed with his findings. Moreover, the studies were open to criticism because of anatomic variations which made the research situation in the dog not a parallel of the human condition. In essence, you could believe what you wanted to believe on the basis of the laboratory work.

The Philadelphia surgeon was, naturally, a believer in his own brilliant theory. He was quick to move his activities from the laboratory into the operating room. Since there were thousands of victims of coronary artery disease, and the operation was a relatively simple one, he had no difficulty finding patients.

His reported results were fantastic, to put it mildly. Almost all his patients improved. Again, unfortunately, it was possible only to measure the subjective response—did the patient have his pain as often? Was it as severe? Could he walk farther or work longer now than before the pain recurred? The answers were almost always favorable.

But pain is a nebulous thing, and patients with coronary artery disease live in a constant state of fear and hope. They want so badly to be free of their disease that simply suggesting to them that they will benefit from an operation is often enough to make them feel better. The surgical literature of the last fifty years is replete with reports of operations designed to "cure" coronary artery disease, including one in which talcum powder was sprinkled on the heart to stimulate the growth of new vessels. All these operations supposedly "cured" some patients; all have subsequently been relegated to a deserved obscurity.

The favorable reports that were quickly published in the journals made converts of many doctors. The operation was a simple one—it could, if necessary, be performed under local anesthesia—and there was no difficulty persuading patients, frightened of their disease and sick of constant pill-taking, that "it's worth a try." Doctors all over the country—G.P.'s, as well as surgeons—quickly embraced the internal mammary ligation. Prices ranged from a hundred dollars to a thousand dollars a crack.

Eventually, of course, the skeptics had their day. Double-blind studies were done and patients with sham operations—operations in which only the skin was cut—had results every bit as good as those with the real operations. Patients who had

had the operation died just as quickly as those who had not had it. The operation, after its brief moment in the sun, was relegated to its limbo. No one ever does it any more.

Lest I be branded a traitor to my profession—a not unlikely possibility—let me say here and now that I am all in favor of *judicious* medical and surgical research. If there are to be advances in medicine, new treatments must be tried. There is always the possibility that some of them will fail, that a few patients will be hurt, but it is a risk that must be run.

The key word is "judicious." New modalities of treatment should be introduced under controlled and limited circumstances by well-prepared, ethical investigators, and the results should be evaluated by men who have the background and training to make a considered value judgment on the merits of the procedure. "Breakthroughs" should not be announced in the lay press to victims of diseases who will grasp at any straw.

Dwell for a moment on the man with the frozen ulcer who died of hemorrhage when the lining of his stomach peeled off; reflect on the poor guy who went out jogging after his internal-mammary-artery ligation and precipitated a coronary. These people are seriously ill or dead, damn it, and they shouldn't be. They were sold a bill of goods by medical hucksters.

I chose these two examples not only because they are so demonstrably asinine, but because the diseases with which they dealt are so widespread that it would be difficult to underestimate the number of victims the perpetrators of these farces may have gulled. Certainly there were thousands.

But they weren't the only two examples I could have chosen. Far from it. In the interest of brevity I left out the story of the many worthless operations done to "cure" asthma; the frightening story of the drug that was supposed to lower blood cholesterol but, instead, caused cataracts; and the continuing serial devoted to antibiotic combinations that are of no value except to the man who sells them. Nor did I mention the "cancer cures" that periodically turn up in the press to raise, and then dash, the hopes of innumerable victims. One could easily write a book on recent medical flops. There are many of them.

So beware. The next time you read of some miraculous medical innovation, some "cure" for a previously incurable disease, some wonderful "breakthrough," think twice before you believe it and then don't. It may be just the brainchild of some publicity-minded doctor blowing his own horn.

25

Choosing a Doctor

There are, of course, a great many fine doctors in this world. And most doctors are decent men. But sometimes it seems to the layman, when he's looking for a doctor, that all he can find are the bad apples.

Partly, at least, that's because when it comes to picking a doctor, most lay people behave like damn fools. Given a choice between a nincompoop with a smooth bedside manner and a genius with a rotten personality, the layman will almost invariably choose the nincompoop. The imbeciles who practice medicine always have huge practices.

George Engel is a classic example. The other doctors on the staff agree unanimously that the reason George's patients spend so long a time in the hospital is that they have to get over what they've got while George is treating them for something else. He is positively the worst diagnostician I've ever seen. He repeatedly sends me patients with liver disease under the mistaken impression that they have gallstones; and I've seen half a dozen of his patients with appendicitis, three or four days after he has treated them for "intestinal flu." He is, to put it bluntly, stupid.

Yet his office is always packed. He has so many patients that new arrivals in the community can't even get on his waiting list. No one is more admired by the public than George. "Best damn doctor in town" is a phrase commonly applied to him.

On the other hand, Larry Ferriter, who is undoubtedly the most knowledgeable guy around, has a very small practice. Many of his patients are the wives and children of other doctors. They send their families to him and go to him themselves, because they know that even though Larry can't make small talk and is apt to be brusque, almost belligerent, when answering questions, he's a very smart guy. When he makes a diagnosis it's almost invariably the correct one, and when he prescribes a medicine it's the one that will cure the patient. Larry is a doctor's doctor.

George is damn near a millionaire, while Larry's income is well below the average for a physician. That's the way things go in the medical profession.

Fortunately for the general public, even a guy like George is not a public menace. The competition for places in medical school is so tight that even the worst candidates admitted and graduated aren't awfully bad. George remembers that the most important section of the Hippocratic oath is the part that says, "Do no harm." People are tough, and as long as George doesn't interfere too much with nature most of his patients eventually get better by themselves. Invariably they'll give George credit for doing a fine job.

I have to concede that in some ways George does do a better job than Larry Ferriter. Take what he did for Rosalie Sanders, for example.

Rosalie went to Larry Ferriter when she developed back trouble, shortly after her daughter married a real bum, a kid who was a high school dropout and who was constantly in trouble with the law. Larry gave her his usual thorough examination—X-rays and all the rest of it—and could find nothing physical to explain the back pain. He recognized the possibility that her physical symptoms were emotional in origin, explained all this to Rosalie and sent her on her way.

A few weeks later Rosalie went to see George Engel. "Dr. Ferriter says my sore back comes from 'nerves,'" she said, "but I can't believe it. It hurts all the time, and I know I'm not imagining it."

George is not strong on emotional diseases. He assumes that

there's a physical explanation for everything. He admitted Rosalie to the hospital, gave her treatments with diathermy and traction, and ordered muscle relaxants for her. He treated Rosalie as if she had a serious derangement of her spine, even though there wasn't one bit of evidence to support the diagnosis.

Rosalie loved it. She had family and friends visiting her every day, sympathizing with her, consoling her. The two weeks in the hospital were just what she needed.

She got over her back trouble. Now whenever it flares up she goes in to see George, and he gives her a heat treatment or an injection or a pill, and she gets better again. Rosalie thinks the sun rises and sets on George. For Larry Ferriter she hasn't got one kind word. After all, he couldn't cure her back trouble.

For Rosalie, George was the right kind of doctor. Sixty percent of all the patients who go to a doctor have no physical ailments; many of these people need only a listener who will sympathize with them. A guy like George is just the right sort of doctor for these patients. Larry Ferriter isn't.

Another reason George does so well and Larry doesn't is that George has taken a leaf from the chiropractor's book. He uses the "laying on of hands" as one of his therapeutic techniques.

Chiropractic is fundamentally a lot of nonsense. I'm sure that all the chiropractors and their patients are going to think I say this because I'm an M.D. and I don't want anyone stealing patients from me. That's not so. If my patients want to go to the chiropractor, and a lot of them do, that's their privilege. I won't refer patients to a chiropractor, but I don't disown them because they've gone to one.

But the fact is that all this pulling and tugging on the neck and the back doesn't do a thing for constipation, migraine headaches, asthma, sinus trouble or most of the other ailments the chiropractor claims he can treat. There's no possible way manipulations can modify these diseases. Most chiropractors probably know this.

What they also know is what we M.D.'s know: most complaints, particularly the ones they treat, are, if not completely psychosomatic in origin, at least partly so. And if they're not great scientists, they aren't bad amateur psychiatrists—and good businessmen as well.

A patient comes to me with low back pain, a tension headache, trouble with his bowels, and what do I do? Not much. Take an X-ray possibly, give him a pill, tell him if he's not better to call me back in a few days. His complaints bore me and I show it. He leaves my office dissatisfied.

So he goes to a chiropractor. The chiropractor isn't bored with his complaints. He listens to him carefully, pokes and prods at the sore spots, takes X-rays of all the bones and joints, shows the patient the X-rays and points out where the problem is in the spine. (Show me the layman who can tell a normal spine X-ray from an abnormal one and I'll show you a very smart man; most M.D.'s have a terrible time spotting abnormalities in spine films.) He then says, "Charlie, it will take three weeks, but if you come in faithfully every Monday, Wednesday and Friday for a treatment I can cure you."

Charlie is delighted. He climbs up on the table and the chiropractor pulls, tugs and pounds away for ten minutes. When he's through, Charlie knows he's really had a treatment. He leaves the chiropractor's office a happy man.

For the X-rays, the pounding and an occasional treatment with some strange apparatus with flashing lights, Charlie has to pay plenty; but he doesn't resent it as much as he resented the five dollars he threw away at the M.D.'s office. The chiropractor did something for him; the M.D. didn't.

It's no wonder that a lot of people—not only the dopes but intelligent men and women—go to chiropractors. If I had a backache, and if I weren't an M.D., I might go to one myself.

There are some very strange criteria used by laymen in selecting a doctor. A lawyer friend of mine, a very intelligent guy, explained to me once why he had chosen George Engel as his family's doctor. "George will come to the house any hour of the day or night," he said. "That's what I look for in a doctor." "Even if when he gets there he doesn't know what he's doing?" I wanted to ask; but I didn't. We doctors don't ask those questions about our confreres.

A woman who is a good friend of Joan's once explained to

her why George is their family physician. "When my mother died," she said, "George came to the funeral. Not many doctors would have done that." True enough, but is funeral attendance a characteristic one should look for in a physician? Frankly, I'd be very nervous if I found my family doctor was a funeral buff.

What I'm saying, in essence, is that it's not brains or experience or formal training that brings a man patients. It's his bedside manner. In building a practice, knowledge of the science of medicine is much less important than mastery of the art.

How about specialists? Surely they, who rely primarily on referrals from other doctors, don't have to worry about the art of medicine. Surely they can be boors as long as they're very wise.

Not so. Admittedly, the specialist has to do a decent job if he's going to get referrals, but it's still the art and not the science that helps him build a practice.

Practically speaking, there's very little difference in the quality of the work done by one specialist as opposed to another. I'm sure, for example, that of the hundred or so orthopedic surgeons I have to choose from when I have a patient who needs a difficult bone operation, any or all of them will do a good job. One of the merits of the specialty training system in this country is that no one gets through it unless he is at least competent.

I'm not saying that of all these orthopedists one might not be a little better than another at performing a certain procedure. What I am saying is that they are all good; and I'm also confessing that neither I, nor any other doctor—including the orthopedists themselves—has any way of identifying the man who is the very best. It would be an impossible assignment.

Let me digress here for a moment and show you why. Suppose we tried to compare two orthopedic surgeons by looking over the records of the last hundred patients on whom each had done a hip operation. We find that 10 percent of Surgeon A's patients died after the operation, but only 5 percent of

Surgeon B's patients didn't make it. We might conclude Surgeon B is twice as good as Surgeon A.

The conclusion is not justified. Perhaps the average age of Surgeon A's patients was ninety, while that of Surgeon B's was only seventy. This would explain the difference in mortality. Or perhaps all of Surgeon A's patients had heart disease, while those of Surgeon B had healthy hearts. Or perhaps Surgeon A is a professor of surgery, famous for his ability to do hip operations; as a consequence, only the most complicated cases are referred to him.

The point is, it's difficult if not impossible to tell which specialist, if any, is "the best."

So how do doctors choose the specialists to whom they refer patients? Basically, the way the public chooses—according to the way the man has mastered the art of medicine.

The orthopedist to whom I refer my cases, for example, is a doctor who invariably phones me right after he sees my patient for the first time. "Bill," he said of a recent referral, "Mr. Simon has a very bad ankle. I agree with you; he needs a fusion. If you have no objection I'm going to admit him and put him on the schedule for next week."

"Fine, Ray, go ahead. Let me know how it goes."

Ray does. The next week, as soon as he has finished operating, he picks up the phone again, calls me and tells me all I want to know about the operation. Sometimes, when I'm busy, he may even tell me more than I want to know. But the point is, he keeps me well informed.

He also writes. When he first sees the patient, then right after the operation and at the time he discharges Mr. Simon he follows up his phone calls with a letter. Then there's no confusion about what has been said. I know what's going on.

This is invaluable to me. When Mr. Simon's relatives, who live in Litchfield, call and ask me how their daddy or their uncle or their brother is doing, I can give them the information. They appreciate it.

There are few things worse than having a patient's nephew call and ask, "Is it true that my uncle died this morning after his operation?" and not knowing what to say. I've had consultants put me in exactly that position. I hear about the demise of a patient via the local grapevine rather than from his doctor. It is, to say the least, embarrassing. I don't use those consultants any more.

Nor do I use those consultants, and there are many, who don't write for weeks after they've discharged a patient. The patient comes to my office for a postoperative examination three weeks after the consultant discharged him from the hospital. I haven't heard from the consultant. I don't know what he has done to my patient or what I'm expected to look for. So I have to get on the phone, track down the consultant and get the information. I might do that once, never twice.

At least as important as the way the consultant treats me is the way he treats the patient. I've had patients, all well after superb care by a consultant, come back to me and say, "You know, Dr. Nolen, I'm sure Dr. Hastings is a good doctor, but I don't like him. He never explained anything to me. In fact [and this is a very common complaint] he didn't even come to see me for three days after the operation. One of his partners was in charge. I didn't like that."

Now, I don't mind if a consultant doesn't see my patients every day. I don't see my own postoperative patients every day. I take time off too.

But I tell my patients when I'm not going to be around. I explain that one of my partners will be in to see them. The consultant should do the same.

It's the consultant's job not only to treat my patient but to do it in such a way that he or she likes him. If he can't manage it, I find a consultant who can.

How should a man or woman go about the job of choosing a doctor? If I moved to another city I'd ask a fellow surgeon whose judgment I trusted to recommend a general practitioner, a pediatrician, an internist—whatever type of doctor it was that I needed. I'd figure that he would know who was best—or more important, who was the worst—so I'd probably wind up with a pretty good doctor.

But the layman can't do that. He won't have the starting

point I'd have—the knowledge that at least this surgeon is a capable person. He'll have to work through other laymen.

In selecting a doctor you might just ask a friend whose judgment you trust for the name of his doctor. If the friend is alive and healthy, it would seem that the doctor is doing his job. And if the friend likes the doctor, his personality must be O.K. It's not a perfect system; you could wind up with a dope, but it's the easiest, and the one most people choose.

If you want to get more scientific about it, then you can work through the County Medical Society secretary (you can find his number in the phone book or get it from the hospital); he won't recommend one specific person, but at least the list he gives you won't include any real charlatans.

Personally, if I were a layman in a big city, I'd go to a hospital emergency room and ask the intern or resident on duty to recommend someone to me. The interns and residents are in a good position to evaluate the men on the hospital staff, and they can give you good advice. That way you'll also be sure to get a doctor who has staff privileges at the hospital where, if it becomes necessary, you'd like to be treated.

There's no simple, safe formula you can follow in choosing a doctor; but then, neither is there any simple formula for choosing a lawyer, hairdresser or mechanic. You ask around and you take your chances. I'm at the mercy of the mechanic who tells me I need a $300 "valve job"—whatever that is—on the motor of my car. He's at my mercy when I tell him he needs a $300 operation on his gall bladder. I hope and trust the mechanic is bright and honest; he has to put the same faith in me.

I'd say the chances of finding a responsible, honest, intelligent physician are at least as good—probably better—than the chances of finding the same qualities in a mechanic or lawyer.

I'm also certain that the mechanics and lawyers will disagree.

III

26

Doctors and Patients—
The Science of Medicine

George Bernard Shaw didn't like doctors. He said (I paraphrase), "I find it very difficult to trust a man who knows where my spleen is." He also said, "I find it difficult to believe a man who tells me that my gall bladder should be removed when he stands to earn three hundred dollars by performing the operation." George Bernard Shaw was a very smart man. I can sympathize with his point of view.

The work we doctors do is mysterious and awe-inspiring to the average layman—even to the above-average layman. We're the people who have the knowledge that allows us to prescribe pills or perform operations that will cure illnesses, make the sick well, save lives. Not having had the training in anatomy, pharmacology, bacteriology—the sciences doctors learn in medical school—the layman can't, unless we explain things, even begin to understand what we're doing or why. People have to either accept us almost entirely on faith when they literally put their lives in our hands or, like Shaw, stay away from us.

Since most people choose to rely on us doctors to keep them alive and healthy, they would like to believe we're omniscient, that we can do no wrong. Even though they know it's irrational to turn us into gods, they do it. They feel safer, believing that the man who is going to pick up the knife and cut out the cancer cannot err.

It must be wonderful to have that much faith in a doctor; it's an experience I envy the layman. Knowing doctors as I do, understanding the problems they're trying to solve, I'm a very poor patient. Most doctors are terrible patients, because we know so well just how fallible doctors are.

After twelve years of practice, after guiding patients through some four thousand operations, I've come to the conclusion that it's bad for patients to have either the blind trust in a doctor that most patients have or the complete lack of trust that Shaw expressed so well. It's best for patients to accept their doctors as men who have a special knowledge, acquired through years of education and training, who work with dedication and compassion to cure illnesses. They aren't omniscient—they do make errors—they're susceptible to all the frailties that afflict the human race. Doctors have a difficult job, but one that's rewarding, emotionally as well as financially. They—most of them—deserve the respect and gratitude usually given to anyone who helps make life more enjoyable. But they don't deserve adulation; in fact, doctors would be better off without it. They aren't gods, damn it, and they can't live up to godlike standards. Don't expect them to.

Unfortunately, and unwisely, some doctors encourage the worship that patients offer them. When a patient says, "Oh, Dr. Jones, how can I ever thank you for what you've done for me—you've performed a miracle," Dr. Jones believes her. He loves this adulation and he encourages all of his patients to worship him. There are too many Joneses in our profession. They make life difficult for the rest of us.

One of the reasons why patients are often forced to accept their doctors on faith is that they don't take the time to explain what they are doing and why. The doctor adopts the attitude, and I'm as guilty as most doctors, that patients couldn't understand even if he did explain; and besides, he's too busy. If a doctor spends ten minutes explaining diagnosis and treatment to every patient he sees, he'll never get out of the office or the hospital. It's easier to treat the patient like a child—"Here, take this medicine, it's good for you"—and run. The doctor–patient relationship, which we doctors speak of as if it were sacred, is in most instances virtually a parent–child relationship. The doctor, of course, is the parent.

Actually, most of the work we do is neither difficult nor mysterious. A little girl comes in with an earache. I look at the eardrum, see that it's red and order the appropriate antibiotic: penicillin, if the child isn't allergic to it, something else if she is. Naturally, I have to know what a normal eardrum looks like before I can judge this particular eardrum, and I have to know something about antibiotics and bacteria so that I can choose appropriate treatment, but since I possess this knowledge, I can diagnose and treat the patient quickly and easily.

Upper respiratory infections, ingrown toenails, broken fingers—the sort of problems we see day in and day out—aren't really much of a challenge. We don't have to be geniuses to manage our patients properly. The average man or woman could learn in six months how to recognize and treat most of the problems we doctors see in an average day.

There is some skill involved in taking a medical history. Asking the proper questions is not difficult; evaluating the answers can be.

It's amazing how many patients lie to doctors. They want help: they know the doctor needs an accurate history if he's to make the correct diagnosis, but they refuse to be honest. They don't like to admit some of the things they've been doing. For example, the answer to the question, "Do you drink alcoholic beverages?" always needs interpreting. If the patient answers Yes, I learned at Bellevue never to ask, "How much?" because you could never get an answer you could rely on. Instead I ask, "Do you drink two quarts a day?" Then the patient can act very righteous and reply, "Of course not; I hardly ever drink more than a quart." If asked "How much?" he'd probably admit to "an occasional highball," another standard answer.

Along with this reluctance to admit to things they're ashamed of, there's also a reluctance to confess to symptoms that the patient thinks may mean serious disease. Patients may deny that they have passed blood with a bowel movement or in their urine because they think these are signs of cancer—as they may be. The doctor taking a history must make certain that the patient, out of fear, is not deceiving him.

When the disease is not obvious, then we're tested a bit more. We have to play detective and look for clues in trying to find the culprit. Like all good detectives, we follow routines so that we don't overlook anything. Once in a while we have to play a hunch, but not often. Just as the Sam Spades have been replaced by the method men of the modern police department, so has the intuitive doctor who made diagnoses on the basis of experience and guesswork been replaced by the scientist of the 1970's.

The most important step in arriving at a diagnosis is the taking of a good history. Most doctors, if they had to choose between talking to a patient and examining him, would prefer to talk to him. Ask the right questions and most of the time you'll be able to figure out what the patient has. Doctors follow a routine they all learn in medical school. It goes: (1) chief complaint, (2) present illness, (3) past history, (4) family history, (5) social history, (6) system review.

Here, for example, is the history I recorded when a patient came to me complaining of abdominal pain:

Name Helen Anderson, *Age* 46

Chief complaint "I've been having pains in my stomach." [The chief complaint is usually recorded in the patient's own words.]

Present illness Mrs. Anderson states that she was well until three months ago, at which time she first noticed pain in her abdomen. The pain came on about half an hour after she had eaten a meal which, she thinks, consisted of pork chops and mashed potatoes with ice cream for dessert. The pain was located in the right upper quadrant of her abdomen, just beneath her ribs, and radiated into her back. She describes the pain as sharp and steady.

She became nauseated, but did not vomit. The pain went away, without treatment, after about an hour.

Since that time Mrs. Anderson has had similar attacks of pain once or twice a week, usually after eating. She thinks the attacks are most apt to occur when she has eaten greasy food.

Mrs. Anderson denies that she has ever had dark urine or light-colored stools. The whites of her eyes have never turned yellow.

Past history Appendix removed in 1934. Hospitalized with pneumonia in 1957. No other hospitalization except for the birth of her children. No history of heart, lung or kidney disease. Denies any history of other illnesses.

Family history Husband 48, and two children, ages 18 and 21, alive and well. One sister, living and well. Father died of heart trouble at 73. Mother living and well, age 71. No family history of tuberculosis, diabetes or cancer.

Social history Drinks an occasional beer—not more than two glasses a week. Smokes one pack of cigarettes daily. Does not take any medications.

System review

Head: Occasional headaches, relieved by aspirin.

Eyes, ears, nose, throat: Wears glasses for reading, no hearing problem, no nosebleeds, no difficulty swallowing.

Cardiorespiratory: No pains in chest or shortness of breath, occasional dry cough which she attributes to cigarette smoking, no ankle swelling.

Gastrointestinal: Good appetite, weight stable at 160 lbs., no vomiting, no change in bowel habits, no blood in stool.

Genitourinary: Menstrual periods last 3–5 days, regular 28–30 days; no bleeding between periods, no burning when she urinates, no blood in urine.

Musculoskeletal: No problems with use of extremities.

Neurological: No dizziness, no numbness.

The questions I asked Mrs. Anderson, in investigating the "present illness," are determined by the information she volunteers initially in her "chief complaint." As soon as she tells me her problem is "pain in the stomach," I immediately begin to think of all the things I know which can cause abdominal pain—the ordinary diseases being gallstones or an ulcer in the stomach or simple indigestion. As I get more information about the pain—what produces it, where it's located, whether it's steady or intermittent—I mentally begin to narrow the possibilities. This pain sounds more like that caused by gallstones than the pain produced by an ulcer. So now I ask about dark urine, light stools, and yellow eyes—the signs of jaundice that may or may not be associated with gallstones.

If Mrs. Anderson's pain had been in her chest my questions would have been directed along lines that would enable me to distinguish between heart disease, lung disorders or simple neuritis.

In obtaining the past history, family history, social history and particularly the system review, the questions I ask—and most doctors ask the same ones—are comprehensive. They protect me from making a premature diagnosis and missing symptoms of an illness other than gallstones which may really be producing her pain, or another disease—sometimes important, sometimes insignificant—which she may have in addition to gallstones and which I will have to take under consideration when I treat her. For example, if Mrs. Anderson tells me in response to one of my routine questions, "Yes, now that you mention it I have been awfully short of breath lately," it could mean that she is in early heart failure, a condition that should be treated first if she is to eventually have her gall bladder removed.

The physical examination on Mrs. Anderson reads as follows:

Temp. 98.6°. *Pulse* 76/min. *Respiration* 18/min. *Blood pressure* 136/84.

General Well-developed, slightly obese white female who does not appear acutely or chronically ill. She looks to be about her stated age.

Skin No cyanosis [blue color], no icterus [yellow color], no evidence of dehydration.

Head Full head of hair, normocephalic [head appears normal].

Eyes Pupils round, regular and equal, react to light. Sclerae [whites] not icteric.

Ears Canals clear, drums normal.

Nose Clear airway bilaterally.

Mouth Tongue protrudes in midline, tonsils atrophic [shrunken], teeth in good repair.

Neck Supple. Thyroid not enlarged, no enlarged glands in neck.

Chest Lungs clear to auscultation [listening with stethoscope].

Heart Normal rhythm, no murmurs.

Breasts Nipples everted, no masses palpable [can't be felt].

Abdomen Well-healed scar in right lower quadrant (from appendectomy), not distended—some tenderness to palpation in right upper quadrant; liver not palpable; no palpable organs or masses.

Genitalia Normal female genitalia, cervix smooth, uterus not enlarged.

Rectal No hemorrhoids, no palpable masses.

Extremities Moves all extremities, no pitting edema [swelling] of ankles, no varicosities, radial pulses [pulse in wrist] normal, dorsalis pedis and posterior tibial pulses [pulses in foot] palpable bilaterally.

Neurological No loss of sensation or motion, deep tendon reflexes [knee jerks] equal and active bilaterally.

Diagnosis: (1) Gall bladder disease.
             (2) R.O. [rule out] duodenal or gastric
                  ulcer.
             (3) Obesity.

The physical examination, like the history, is guided to some extent by the presumptive diagnosis I've made. Since I suspect gall bladder disease, I spend extra time looking for signs of it—yellow eyes, tenderness in the abdomen. As usual with gallstones, there isn't much physical evidence of the disease.

But again, as with the history, I don't skip any essential part of the physical examination. I might find, incidentally, a breast lump, a cancer, which, though not producing symptoms, is more of a threat to Mrs. Anderson than her gallstones. Or I might discover a cancer of the uterus that hasn't yet shown any symptoms. So I check everything.

If Mrs. Anderson had different complaints, something that suggested a nerve disorder, I'd have done a more thorough neurological examination. I would have pricked her with pins, had her balance on one foot, done a variety of other tests. I didn't do these things because I have no reason to suspect nerve disease; but I did check her tendon reflexes—the knee jerk—and the response of the pupils of her eyes to light so that I wouldn't miss any serious neurological disorder.

Thoroughness is the key to good medicine. The rectal examination, for example, is simple to do but often isn't done. The patient doesn't like to have the examination and the doctor doesn't like to do it, so unless the patient's complaint is "blood in the stool," or "pain in the rectum," the exam is often skipped. And rectal diseases are missed, not to be discovered till it's difficult or impossible to cure them.

The negatives—no shortness of breath, no blood in the stool —are recorded because they're evidence that Mrs. Anderson probably doesn't have certain serious ailments, and by recording the answers, we prove that we've asked the questions. The Hospital Accreditation Commission frowns on history and physical examinations that read simply: "Eyes, negative; cardiorespiratory system, negative; social history, not significant." In the face of such records, they wonder if the doctor has really asked all the questions he should. (As a matter of fact, I expect that if and when some specialist in internal medicine reads this he's going to say, "Dr. Nolen certainly doesn't do a thorough examination—why didn't he ask Mrs. Anderson whether she ever had ringing in the ears? And he should have looked further into her headaches." Some diagnosticians may cover more in their routine exams; but for a surgeon, I do a fairly extensive job.)

Next come the routine laboratory tests, examination of the urine and the blood. Serious kidney disease may not produce symptoms, but it will be detected by an examination easily done in the doctor's office. And anemia, particularly if it has come on gradually, may not produce symptoms. So these examinations are part of any reasonably complete physical examination.

Now, since I'm convinced by the history and physical examination that Mrs. Anderson's symptoms are probably due to gallstones, I list this as my number one diagnosis. My number two bet, a long shot, would be an ulcer. A third diagnosis, in addition to her primary symptom-producing disease, is obesity. Sometimes, in cases where the history and physical aren't very conclusive, the doctor may list five possible causes, in order of diminishing probability. He then sets out to narrow down the list till he emerges with the right answer.

In Mrs. Anderson's case, it's a simple matter to prove or disprove the accuracy of my diagnosis. I order X-ray studies of her gall bladder; she takes pills which contain a dye that will be absorbed into her bloodstream, passed through her liver, mixed with bile and stored briefly in her gall bladder. She takes the pills in the evening; in the morning X-rays will show the dye in her gall bladder. If there are no stones the gall bladder will be full of dye. If there are stones they will show up as dark, round circles lying in the dye. If her gall bladder doesn't show up at all, that will mean it isn't working properly and is diseased. The X-rays will tell me if I'm right or wrong in my diagnosis. If I'm right I proceed to treatment; if wrong I'll do other studies—specifically, X-ray studies of the stomach—to see if my second diagnosis, ulcer, is the culprit. If I'm wrong again—hardly likely, I'm not that bad a diagnostician—I'll do more and more studies till I find the explanation for the pain. If things really get desperate, I may even call in another doctor to help me. Treatment, for the most part, comes right out of a book: surgery, antibiotics, radiation, pills to help the heart, the lung, the bowel. With every year that passes we're adding more techniques and drugs to our armamentarium; we have better, more efficient ways to treat, and prevent, diseases. The most difficult assignment the doctor has is that of keeping up with what's going on. Treating the patient, or finding some specialist who can do it for him, is ordinarily not difficult.

Really, this is all there is to the science of medicine. It's just a big game of cops and robbers. There are clever cops and dumb cops, stupid robbers and brilliant robbers. The dumb cops don't always catch the crooks as early as they should; the brilliant criminals sometimes escape entirely. But generally, with all the sophisticated equipment now available, the cop-doctor ought to find the robber-disease with relative ease most of the time. And execute him with one of the many weapons at his command.

I've written in detail on diagnosis and treatment to prove a point. The science of medicine is not so difficult that the layman can't understand it. We doctors aren't geniuses, nor are we magicians, and there's no reason to hold us in awe. We do our jobs as other men do theirs.

How well we perform as doctors depends not so much on our mastery of the science of medicine—we're expected to be good at that—but on our knowledge of the art. It's in this realm —applying our technical knowledge not to diseases but to people—that we most often fail.

27

Doctors and Patients—
The Art of Medicine

The art of medicine, the way in which a doctor manages his relationships with his patients, is the secret to success in practice—success not only in acquiring and holding on to patients but in treating their illnesses. If a doctor can establish a relationship of warmth and trust, he has taken a big stride in the direction of curing his patients' illnesses.

Unfortunately, when a doctor goes into practice he isn't usually very good at the art of medicine. His education and experience have taught him very little about relating to patients.

Consider his education: up through high school the would-be physician lives a reasonably normal life, but once he gets to college things change. Many students, probably most, enjoy their years in college. They study, but they don't study to the exclusion of everything else. They engage in sports, get involved in dramatics, work on the newspaper, play in the band, raise a little hell. They want good marks, but they aren't obsessed with the need for straight A's. They can get jobs or get into law school without leading the class.

The premed is in a different situation. He has to get not good marks but great marks if he's going to be accepted in a medical school. As I said before, there are only about twelve

thousand freshman medical students accepted each year, and
there are some forty-five thousand applications for those positions. The premed has to work very hard to be one of the
select group.

So the college experience for the vast majority of premeds
isn't very pleasant. He spends most of his time worrying about
grades. The social experiences that should be an important
part of his college development are kept to a minimum.

When he graduates, he probably lacks the breadth of education that four years in college should have given him. When
other students are studying Shakespeare and philosophy, he's
fooling around with a Bunsen burner in chemistry lab or picking apart a rabbit in the zoology department. He has to take so
many science courses that he hasn't got time for the humani-
ties. The graduate who enters medical school is probably not
the "well-rounded individual" that admissions offices admire
in theory and reject in practice.

In medical school things go from bad to worse. For four
years he studies nothing but the human body—its anatomy,
physiology and disease. He takes no courses in the liberal arts
or the social sciences. Medical school graduates are medical
scientists, not humanists.

Now, depending on what field of medical practice he in-
tends to enter, the student spends one to five years in a hospital. Here he learns to apply to patients the knowledge he
acquired in medical school.

A hospital is a little world unto itself. Everyone in the hospital is either sick or working to cure sickness. In the years he
spends in a hospital the doctor learns to relate to other people
only in a restricted sense; he is the healer, they need his
ministrations. He acquires the habit of thinking of people only
as patients; he never sees them well, at their jobs, with their
families. He develops a distorted view of what the world is
really like.

So when he does leave the hospital, when he goes out to
practice in some town or city, he's not well prepared to do so.
He knows enough about the science of medicine—after all

those years of training he should—but he knows little about the art. He hasn't had time for that.

He has to learn it. He has to learn, from the position of power and prestige that society automatically allocates to the physician, how to relate to his fellow professionals, his family, his community. Most important of all, he has to learn to relate to his patients not only as patients but as people.

It's a difficult transition. I know, because I've been through it. When I began practice, I could remove a stomach, fix a broken hip, take out an appendix; but I had never sent a bill to a patient, had never made a house call, had never competed with another doctor for patients, had never lived in a community where I had to concern myself with things like the schools, the taxes, the local politics. I had never before lived among my patients as a friend, a neighbor, a man raising a family and earning a living. I had a lot to learn about the art of medicine.

I was fortunate, when I entered practice, that I went into a group. I was able to observe my partners as they practiced and see how they developed rapport with their patients. I picked up a lot of useful information fast—faster than I could have if, like many doctors, I had gone into practice alone.

For example, I noticed early on that whenever Paul Hauser saw a patient he almost always sat down and took the patient's blood pressure. It didn't take me long to realize that it wasn't so much that Paul was interested in the patient's blood pressure as that in the process of taking it Paul could put his hands on the patient's arm—touch him. This physical contact helped to establish a closer relationship with the patient.

It also gave the patient a chance to sit for a minute or two, to calm down, before he told Paul his troubles. And it made the patient feel that Paul wasn't rushing him; if he could take time for a blood-pressure reading, he had time to spare. Patients like to feel that the doctor isn't trying to escape them.

But just because Paul took the patient's blood pressure didn't mean he would spend the next half hour with the patient. He didn't. He saw his patients and treated them just as quickly as anyone else. But Paul's patients thought they were getting more time because he didn't seem to be rushing them. Another doctor could give them the same amount of time and the patient would complain, "He hasn't got time for me—I should go to someone else." Paul's patients are the most loyal I've ever seen. If he takes a month's vacation and they become ill while he's gone, they wait for him if they possibly can. No one ever quits Paul Hauser.

Steve Charrah had his own way of making the patient feel welcome. After he finished treating the patient for whatever it was he had come for, he always asked, "Now, is there anything else I can do for you today?" Sometimes he'd wait with this question till the patient had her coat on and was halfway out the door so that she would find it awkward coming back in. But it still had the desired effect; she felt as if Steve were willing to spend the rest of the afternoon listening to her complaints. She'd leave happy and loyal to Steve.

In the hospital one of the techniques I noticed George Engel use with regularity was that of always sitting down when he visited his patients. He might sit in a chair or on the edge of the bed, but George always sat. This gave the patient the impression that George was settling in for a long conversation; in fact, he rarely spends more than two minutes with any patient. But again, they never feel he's giving them the brush-off. They would if he did as many doctors do: run in, stand at the foot of the bed and run out. Most hospital patients don't need doctors' visits longer than two minutes, but they hate to think that's all the time they get for their five or ten dollars. (The doctor spends more of his time going over their charts, lab reports and X-rays; but the patient isn't always aware of this.)

Now let me confess that though I'm aware of the techniques that Paul and Steve and George use, I don't use any of them. If I used them they wouldn't work because I'm not Paul, Steve or George. I don't like to take blood-pressure readings, I figure my nurse can do it as well as I and I don't want to waste time on the job; I can't ask a patient, "Is there anything else?" because I'm sure my whole attitude would make her realize that I didn't want to hear any more; I don't sit when I'm making hospital rounds, because I just wouldn't be able to. I run up and down the corridors—that's my style.

Still, seeing how Paul, Steve and George worked made me realize the importance of building rapport with my patients —of letting them know I cared about them as people—and that, really, is what the art of medicine is all about. It would have been phony of me to try to use techniques which come naturally to other doctors but not to me, so I refused to use them. Instead I've tried to let patients know I care in other ways, ways that are natural to me.

I'll give one example. As a surgeon, most of my patients are, naturally, patients on whom I'm going to operate or have operated. I know, from listening to them complain about other doctors who have operated on them, that the one thing they seem to resent most is not knowing what is going to be or has been done to them. Some surgeons—many surgeons—get very haughty if a patient even dares to question them. They act like little tin gods. I've never thought this was fair. I know very well that if I were going to have my insides reorganized, I'd certainly insist on knowing how it was going to be done. It's my body, damn it, and I have a right to any information as to how it's going to be rearranged.

So I always explain operations to patients before surgery, and if I had to modify my approach because of what I found I go over it all again afterward. Usually I draw a picture of the stomach, gall bladder or bowel and explain how I'm going to take something out and how I'll hook things together afterward. Often I sketch the operation on a napkin at the patient's bedside and I leave the drawing with him or her so it can be shown to other members of the family.

Patients appreciate these explanations and drawings. I offer them these things because I think it's their right to have them and my job to provide them, just as I don't think it's my job to take a patient's blood pressure. This, and, I suppose, other things I do, help make up for my defects as a doctor—I'm in and out of postoperative patients' rooms so fast, if the case is going smoothly, that if they blink they don't see me—and I've been able to build and hold a good surgical practice (primarily, of course, because I'm a very good surgeon; but I think drawing pictures helps).

Patients tend to drift to doctors whose personalities suit them.

Ray Walters, for example, is a four-plus alarmist. To hear Ray talk you'd think every patient he sees is on the brink of death. His coronary patients have the "worst heart attacks I've ever seen"; the woman with the flu is "on the verge of pneumonia"; the kid with the broken wrist has "the most smashed-up bone you can imagine." None of his patients have mild or moderate illnesses.

He has an excellent practice. There are patients who like to feel that they are suffering from a classic illness, the worst of its kind. Everyone has heard women brag that "Dr. Walters [or Smith or Jones] told me he had never seen as many stones as there were in my gall bladder"; and I'd like to have a nickel for every patient who has said, "My doctor told me that my appendix is the worst he had ever seen"—I could retire. Every doctor exaggerates a little, but Ray Walters does it all the time. His patients love it.

Ray is sincere. He is a born pessimist. He believes that all of his patients with heart attacks will die, that all his patients with colds will soon have pneumonia. He is thrilled whenever a patient survives—and since they aren't very sick, most do. His natural alarmist attitude brings him a big practice.

The patients who go to Carlo Germain are the ones who really want to spend a lot of time with the doctor. Steve Charrah's patients *think* they've had a lot of time; Carlo's really get it. He is, to put it mildly, very slow. I can see ten patients with serious ailments in the time it takes Carlo to diagnose and treat a cold. He is incapable of rushing.

Fine, that's his way of doing things. His patients spend hours in his waiting rooms—he rarely gets home till late in the evening and hardly ever on Saturday or Sunday—but it doesn't seem to bother him. It's his way of practicing medicine.

His patients are very loyal. Some patients prefer a doctor who keeps them waiting for hours. They mistrust the man they can get to see immediately; "Why isn't he busier?" they

ask themselves. And when they do get to see Carlo they get all
the time with him that they could possibly want. They love
him.

Some doctors never learn how to treat patients—chiefly
because they don't care about them. To them the practice of
medicine is simply a way to make a living. They get no
particular kick out of helping people.

These doctors are usually found in specialties where the
doctor–patient relationship is of relatively little importance.
If they don't go into such specialties immediately, they eventually do; they learn, after a few months of treating patients,
that they don't like the work and that patients don't like them
—so they can't build a practice.

Even in specialties such doctors sometimes have difficulty.
I sent a woman to a radiologist for a series of treatments for
a cancer, and after her visit she came back to my office and
said, "Dr. Nolen, I want you to refer me to someone else. That
doctor is positively rude. He wouldn't answer any of my questions and wasn't even civil. He ordered me to go here and
there without offering any explanation as to why I was supposed to go. When I had difficulty understanding some of his
instructions he looked at me as if I were an imbecile. I'm not
used to being treated in that fashion, and I don't intend to
be." This wasn't the first complaint I'd had about this radiologist. Even in a relatively impersonal specialty he can't manage
patient contact. I don't send my patients to him any more.

As I've learned over the years, the one thing essential to the
successful practice of the art of medicine is to be yourself.
Don't be a phony. Try never to lose sight of the fact, and it's
easy to do, that a patient comes to you at a difficult, worri-
some, trying moment in his life. What is routine to the doctor
—appendicitis, pregnancy, heart trouble—is not routine to the
patient. It's his appendix, her baby, his heart; the patient is
deeply concerned about his or her problem and expects you
to be. And you should be. Treat the patient as you'd want
to be treated if the roles were reversed. It's the only fair way to
do the job. The doctor who won't should get out of medicine.

28

The Dying Patient

Of all the jobs I have to do as a physician the most difficult by far is that of caring for the dying. It drains me physically and emotionally to face patients who are losing the battle for life.

At one time, for more than a month, I had three patients in the hospital who were all dying lingering deaths. There were days in that period when I could hardly bring myself to go to the hospital.

Lena Overton was one of the patients. Lena was a cheerful, gentle, soft-spoken woman of fifty-eight when she first came to see me. Her husband had died in a farm accident a few years earlier and she was living with an unmarried son. He ran the family farm and Lena kept house for him.

"How are you, Lena?" I asked when she came into my office. "I haven't seen you for a long time. Not since I took that cyst off your back a couple of years ago."

"I've been fine, Dr. Nolen," she said. "Haven't had any problems. Not till the last few weeks, that is."

"What's been bothering you?" I asked.

"I'm sort of embarrassed to talk about it," Lena said, "but I guess I have to. There's been some bleeding. Down between my legs. Not much, but some. Enough so I have to wear a pad once in a while. My periods stopped almost ten years ago, so I can't understand what it could be."

"We'll find out, Lena," I said. "Don't you worry. Miss Barney will help you get undressed and I'll examine you. We'll fix you up." I left the room while my office nurse helped Lena get onto the examining table.

It didn't take long to find the cause of Lena's bleeding; she had an ugly sore about two inches in circumference on her labia. It looked like a cancer. Fortunately, I was reasonably certain that I could cut out the entire growth.

But then I examined Lena's groin; it's to the glands in this area that a tumor of the labia will first spread. And here we weren't so lucky. The glands in the groin were hard. They weren't painful; she hadn't even been aware that they were enlarged. But there was no doubt; they were loaded with tumor. I wasn't at all certain I'd be able to get them out.

After Lena had dressed I sat down and talked to her. "Lena," I said, "I have bad news. You've got a growth. In all probability it's cancer. I'll want to run some other tests, but then you'll need an operation. I'll have to remove the growth itself, and I'll have to also remove some swollen glands in your groin. I think they have tumor in them."

"I kind of thought you'd find something bad," Lena said. "When will I have to go to the hospital?"

"The sooner the better. Today, if you can arrange it."

"Oh, I couldn't go in today, Dr. Nolen," she said. "I'll have to get someone to cook and clean for Roy. Today's Thursday; how about Monday?"

"O.K., Lena," I said. "I'll arrange it." There was no sense pushing her. I was pretty sure I wouldn't be able to cure her anyway.

The next week I operated on Lena. I was able to remove the original tumor, but when I tried to get the glands out of the groin I found I couldn't. They were wrapped around the femoral artery (the main artery to the leg), and to get them I'd have had to amputate Lena's buttock, thigh and leg. I wasn't ready to do that, particularly when the chance of curing her, even then, was remote. I decided to use radiation.

Lena was cheery after the operation, her wounds healed nicely and in a week she was ready to go home. I explained the need for X-ray treatment and arranged an appointment with the radiologist.

The X-ray treatments burned Lena's skin. For a month after the treatments were completed Lena came to my office three times a week. I peeled off the dead skin and put dressings on the raw areas. The sessions were painful ones for Lena but she never complained. Finally, she was healed.

I didn't see Lena again for six months. This time, when she returned, she was limping badly.

"I'm a real pest, Dr. Nolen," she said. "Now my leg is bothering me."

I examined her leg. It was swollen almost twice the normal size and obviously full of fluid. I checked her groin. The glands were not only easily felt, but they were bigger than they had been originally. They were blocking the veins in Lena's leg.

"Sorry, Lena," I said. "It looks like we'll have to put you back in the hospital. The glands in your groin are blocking up your blood vessels."

"All right, Dr. Nolen," she said. "Whatever you say." This time she went in immediately. She was pale and weak and she knew she couldn't take care of her son even if she stayed home.

After a few days in bed in the hospital Lena was reasonably comfortable. The swelling went out of her leg, and after I transfused her with three pints of blood she began to feel more like herself. "I'm much better now, Doctor," she said, "thanks to you." I cringed. I knew it wouldn't last.

Lena felt so good in a week that she insisted I let her go home. "Come on, Dr. Nolen," she said, "no sense in me staying here. Hospital beds are for sick people."

"All right, Lena," I said, "but take it easy. Get off your feet every chance you get, and be sure to come in and see me in a week."

A week later she was still in good spirits. Her blood level had dropped a little, but not enough to make her feel weak. And her leg was only slightly swollen.

But the next week it was obvious she was in trouble again. She was dragging her leg when she came to my office and was so weak that she could hardly talk without running out of breath. "I guess I'd better go back into the hospital, Dr. Nolen," she said. "I'm afraid I'm not as strong as I thought I was." She smiled at me.

Now, along with the swelling and weakness, Lena had pain. "I can't seem to get comfortable, Dr. Nolen," she said. "It's sore up here in my groin. Just like a boil." The tumor in the glands had begun to erode through the skin. It wasn't only painful, it was foul-smelling.

"I'll order you something for the pain, Lena. You be sure to ask for it whenever you hurt." I started Lena on codeine, but within a week it wasn't controlling her. I moved on to Demerol.

Every day now became a nightmare. There was nothing I could do to cure Lena. Surgery, radiation, drugs—the tumor was too extensive for any of them. I had her moved into a private room so the smell of the rotting tumor wouldn't upset any other patient. My visits always followed the same pattern.

"How are you today, Lena?"

"Not too bad, Doctor."

"Are you having much pain?"

"Some, but I can stand it."

"Does the pain medicine help?"

"Not like it used to."

"I'll increase the dose, Lena. I don't want you to be uncomfortable."

Lena's flesh was almost visibly melting away. She developed pressure sores on her buttocks and her back, even though the nurses turned her frequently. She ate almost nothing. I was giving her morphine now, increasing the dose constantly, and this constipated her. She required enemas every few days.

For the first few days of this, her final hospital admission, Lena talked occasionally of going home. After two weeks she didn't mention it again. It was as clear to her as it was to me that she was going to die.

It took her six weeks; she had been a very strong woman.

It was agony all the way, but fortunately, for most of the last week she was in a coma. One morning, at six o'clock, the nurse stopped in to take her temperature and found her dead. When she called and told me, I was relieved. It had been a long, hard, impossible fight. I was happy for Lena, and for myself, that it was finally over.

The other two dying patients I had in the hospital at the same time as Lena were a twenty-three-year-old boy whose cancer, which had started in a small mole on his back, had now spread all through the organs of his body; and a fifty-three-year-old woman, with seven children, dying of cancer of the rectum. The boy took three weeks to die; the woman, five. I'm not going to describe the cases in detail. I hate to even think about them.

There's a certain point, in dealing with critically ill patients, when it becomes apparent to any reasonable doctor that the game is over and you've lost. The patient is beyond the reach of anything you can offer him or her. There is nothing that can be done to prevent an inevitable death.

Some doctors are quicker than others to recognize and accept the fact that that time has been reached. Some fight losing battles long after it's reasonable to do so.

I don't blame them. I do it myself. It's so damn hard to quit.

For example, I gave anti-cancer drugs to the twenty-three-year-old boy with tumor all through his body right up till the day he died. I knew it wasn't doing him any good, but I couldn't bear to tell his young wife that we had nothing to offer. I could rationalize and justify the treatment to myself—after all the drug I was using was an anti-cancer drug; even if the chances were one in a million or one in a hundred million that it would help, I had to use it. At least it didn't hurt him.

In retrospect, I know I shouldn't have done it. The drug cost was twenty dollars a day, and his family didn't have twenty dollars a day to waste. It wasn't reasonable to use the medicine. But at the time, neither I nor the family thought much about what was "reasonable."

With Lena I had used some restraint. When she stopped eating I didn't give her intravenous fluids—something many doctors (I'm included) often do. I might have been able to keep Lena alive for another few days, perhaps even a week, if I had. But to what purpose?

With Lena I avoided another trap I—and other surgeons—occasionally fall into. We get knife-happy. We take our scalpels and try to cut out all the cancer in the patient's body long after it's reasonable to think we can do it.

At one point I was tempted. The only cancer that I could identify with certainly in Lena's body was in the groin and up along the blood vessels in Lena's pelvis. By cutting off the buttock and entire left lower extremity of Lena's body I might have been able to get around it all. I seriously considered trying.

Thank the Lord I had the sense to discuss the case with another surgeon—one who didn't know Lena, who didn't have to watch her suffer, who wasn't emotionally involved.

"Don't be crazy, Bill," he said. "Even if you can get around it all and keep her alive, you haven't got a snowball's chance in hell of curing her. That tumor is all over the other side by now. You know that as well as I do." I took his advice and didn't put Lena through a horrendous, mutilating, futile operation.

Sometimes I have to fight to stop people from going crazy, from doing wild, irresponsible, expensive things when a member of the family becomes hopelessly ill. They refuse to accept the knowledge that nothing can be done, that their husband or daughter or father is afflicted with a disease beyond the reach of any therapy.

Like Gus Schneider. His son, Steve, broke his back in an auto accident. His spinal cord was cut completely in two, leaving Steve, at seventeen, paralyzed from the waist down.

I took care of Steve at the time of the accident, and though I knew it was hopeless I had a neurosurgeon see him in consultation. He confirmed my diagnosis and we broke the news to Gus.

He absolutely refused to accept it. He couldn't believe that his son, Steve, who had been a fine athlete, would never be able to walk again. We showed him the X-rays, explained in detail what had happened and why the case was hopeless; not a word registered. Gus had closed his mind.

As soon as Steve's condition was stable, so that it was safe for him to travel, Gus asked me to transfer him to a famous clinic.

"Gus," I said, "I'll be glad to arrange it for you. I know how you feel. But I have to tell you you're wasting your time and your money. No one can cure Steve. We can offer him reha-bilitation—we can get him up in a wheelchair and, maybe later, on braces or crutches, but no one is going to get him to move those legs again." I might as well have been talking to the wall.

Gus took Steve to the clinic. They tested him, took X-rays, repeated all the studies we had done and came up with the same answer: nothing to be done. Gus brought Steve home.

But not for long. Within a month, this time without talking to me, Gus took Steve to another clinic, one run by a group of crackpots on the lunatic fringe of medicine. There, of course, they didn't discourage Gus. They gave him some "special" foods to feed Steve and some medicines to take, and told him to bring Steve back in six months. They charged him two thou-sand dollars for his four-day stay.

Fortunately, three months later Gus came to his senses. I was able to get across to him the message that these charlatans were simply preying on him, that they were bleeding him just because he couldn't accept the misfortune that had struck down his son. When I finally got through to him we got Steve on physiotherapy and he became completely self-sufficient; he learned to accept his misfortune and live with it.

You don't have to be stupid to behave as Gus did. Gus, in fact, is an intelligent man. Anyone who gets into a spot that seems hopeless will grasp at straws. More than once, I've seen parents—people with good, solid, common sense—run them-selves into bankruptcy pursuing will-o'-the-wisp "cures" for a child with an inevitably fatal disease. They travel all over the country—to naturopaths, hydropaths, faith healers—who prom-ise cures long after the medical doctors have had to admit defeat. It's beyond me how these bastards can sell false hope to desperate people at fantastic prices and still sleep at night.

Sometimes when I'm unable to talk someone out of a futile attempt to avoid the inevitable, I ask the minister or priest to talk to the family. If they have a close relationship, if the rapport is good, the clergyman can sometimes get through to the family when I can't. It's an individual thing, dependent entirely on the ability of the clergyman and the faith of the family.

One question that I'm often asked by the families of patients who have cancer is, "How long has he got—how many months [or days or weeks] will he live?"

I hate that question. I never know how to answer it. Quite simply, I can't tell. I've often had cases in which a cancer of one form or another had spread beyond the point where I could remove it. Some of these patients have died in six weeks; some have lived six months; others, not many but a few, have lived several years. Any doctor who has been in practice very long knows that it's a hazardous business to predict how long a patient will live. We're wrong too often.

My approach, after being burned several times, is to say simply, "I don't know." Then I add, "Take each day as it comes. There's no sense in anticipating trouble. Encourage your father [or husband or wife] to live as normally as possible. When and if problems arise we'll handle them at the time." Then I get the patient out of the hospital, back to his home, his family and his job as quickly as possible.

Sometimes, unfortunately, the patient is back in the hospital for the last time in a few weeks; but there are occasions when months or years go by and the patient continues to lead a comfortable, productive life. Taking a positive attitude—not worrying in advance about what may happen and when—helps to make these long interludes happy ones.

When the dying patient is elderly, and by that I mean physiologically old—senile, bedridden, disoriented—then an approaching death is much easier to accept. In fact, I'll frequently have a son or a daughter tell me, "Dr. Nolen, if you aren't going to be able to save my father, then just keep him comfortable. We hope you won't do anything to simply pro-

long his life." Then I can discontinue the intravenous fluids
and the antibiotics without a qualm.

Discontinuing the intravenous feedings and antibiotics,
taking away the supports we use to prop up a life, is one thing;
doing something to shorten a life is quite another. I have no
hesitation about the first; the second is beyond me.

I've been tempted, and not infrequently. There were days
when I would have liked to end Lena's misery. I hated to see
her suffer. An overdose of morphine and she'd have gone to
sleep for good.

I couldn't do it. I couldn't take that responsibility. Not because I thought there was any chance at all that she'd get well
—I knew that was out of the question—but because the idea of
taking a life is completely repugnant to me. Euthanasia is
something for which I have no stomach.

I couldn't have hastened Lena's death—I'm avoiding the
world "kill"—even if she had asked me to do so. But she never
did—and that has been my experience with hopeless patients
through twelve years of practice.

I have never had a patient ask me to put him out of his misery. No matter how bad life is, I have yet to find anyone who
wants me to hurry his departure from it. I've had elderly patients refuse an operation, saying, "I've lived long enough, let
me go," but that isn't the same thing. Resigning oneself to
fate is not the same as seeking death. No one I've ever cared
for has actually sought death, at least not openly.

I suppose some psychiatrist would say that my attitude toward the dying patient is a reflection of my own attitude toward death. I'm afraid of it, so I don't want to deal with it.
He'd be perfectly right; but I don't think that makes me
strange. I think my attitude is shared by most people. I know
it's shared by most doctors.

Actually, I think it's the best attitude for a doctor to have.
If I'm ill I certainly don't want a doctor taking care of me who
looks upon death as a big buddy. I want some guy who will
fight with every weapon he has to keep me alive, who will
struggle against death as long as there's any reasonable chance

to win the battle, who will outfox death if it can possibly be done.

But I also want a doctor who, when he sees he has lost the battle, will surrender gracefully and let me die, hopefully with dignity.

I think that's what most doctors try to offer their patients.

29

How Patients Look to Doctors

One of the problems in the doctor–patient relationship—in all human relationships, for that matter—is that people have difficulty seeing things from the other fellow's point of view. We doctors know what it is about patients that bothers us, but we can't understand why patients don't think we're perfect, or, I should say, wouldn't understand it if our blemishes weren't so well publicized in the lay press. Articles on our refusal to make house calls, the excessive fees we charge and our malpractice cases make good copy.

But no one seems to be interested in telling the story from the doctor's point of view. Let's try it, for a change.

There are certain types of patients who won't win any popularity contests run by doctors. We grit our teeth, provide their medical care and do the best job we can for them, but they are no joy to work with.

Gerald Fleischer is a classic example of one of these types—patients who want you to help them cheat the insurance company.

Gerald works in one of the local department stores. He came to me one afternoon complaining of a pain in his groin. I had him drop his pants and cough while I checked him for a hernia. Gerald had a hernia.

"When did you notice this, Gerald?" I asked.

"Friday night," he said. "We were going fishing and I was

trying to lift the canoe on top of the car when I felt something pop and the pain started. Tell you what, though, you'd better say I noticed it Friday afternoon when I was shoving crates around in the basement. That way workmen's compensation will pay for it."

I've decided, after twelve years in practice, that no one—and I include even bank presidents who do nothing more strenuous than lift their feet onto a desk—ever develops a hernia except at work. This sort of cheating bugs us doctors, but even worse is the guy who wants you to alter your records for him.

I once had an insurance man ask me to do this so he could put the screws to his own company. Bitsy Laurenson was his name and he came to me with a wrist that he had fractured when he slipped on the ice. He was covered by his company policy and I put him in the hospital, reduced the fracture and put his arm in a cast. It was a bad fracture and I kept him in the hospital a few days to be certain the bones didn't slip out of position.

While Bitsy was in the hospital his wife, Jean, came to me for a complete physical, including chest X-ray, electrocardiogram and Pap smear. His son Tommy also came in for a lengthy pre-college physical. I couldn't understand the sudden interest the Laurensons had taken in their health.

A few weeks later, after I'd sent out the bills, I got the picture. Bitsy came to me with the statement, sat down in the office and said, "Say, Doc, about this bill. I noticed you charged me a hundred dollars for my fracture, and you charged me fifty dollars for Jean's exam and fifteen for Tommy's."

"Well, Jean wanted all these tests, you know, Bitsy," I said. "They're expensive."

"Oh, I'm not complaining," he said. "I think you're very reasonable. Only I've got a suggestion. Why don't you raise the charge on my fracture to a hundred and sixty-five dollars —a hundred dollars is awfully low anyway—and forget about charging me for Jean and Tom? That way my company will pick up the whole tab."

"But, dammit, Bitsy," I said, "you'll be cheating your own company."

"Now, that's not exactly fair, Doc," he said. "After all, I've been paying premiums for years. I'm entitled to a little care. Besides, they've got plenty of dough."

A more subtle way of chiseling on the insurance company, and one with which many doctors cooperate, is to admit to the hospital for X-rays or minor surgery a patient who could just as well be treated in the office.

Here's an example. Mrs. Grottemy comes to me complaining of vague abdominal pains. I examine her and decide that she needs to have X-rays of her stomach, intestine and gall bladder. I tell her to come to the hospital in the morning so she can have the studies done and then go home.

"How much will they cost?" she asks.

"About seventy dollars," I tell her.

"Then why don't you admit me to the hospital, Dr. Nolen? If I'm in the hospital for twenty-four hours my insurance will pay for the X-rays."

Is this cheating? It's awfully close. But a lot of patients make the request and a great many doctors grant it. It's tough to say No.

In Litchfield we have one man who actually earns more money when he's in the hospital than when he's working. He has a job as a watchman that, admittedly, doesn't pay much, but he has three insurance policies, all of which are pretty good. He spends four or five months every year getting hospital treatment for obesity, mild diabetes or minimal arthritis. He loves the hospital.

No wonder insurance rates are so high.

Another group of patients that irritate me are those, like Roger Flynn, who know more than the doctor does. The only reason Roger comes to me is that it's illegal for him to write his own prescription.

Roger came to my office one afternoon on a typical visit. "I've got an ulcer, Doc," he said, "and I need a prescription for some Donnatal. I've already picked up some Gelusil at the drugstore. I've already started on an ulcer diet."

"How do you know you've got an ulcer, Roger?" I asked.

"I've read up on it. And I talked to Ray Vachon—he had one, you know. I've got all the symptoms."

"Don't you want me to examine you and maybe get some X-rays of your stomach?"

"Waste of time and money," Roger said. "All I need is the pills. If I don't get better I'll be back."

Admittedly, Roger is an extreme case, but patients who know, no matter what the doctor says, that they need "a shot of penicillin" are a dime a dozen.

I'll bet at least once a week—twice in the winter—someone will walk into my office and say, "Doc, I've got a hell of a cold. Had it for five days. You'd better give me a shot of penicillin. That always cures me." I examine the patient, agree with his diagnosis and try to explain to him that penicillin won't affect his cold, that aspirin and rest will do as much good as a shot.

It's futile. When I first arrived in Litchfield I'd argue for ten minutes and finally refuse the patient penicillin. He or she would go to another doctor and get the shot—often from one of my own partners.

Now I don't fight as hard. If I can't talk them out of the penicillin in a reasonable length of time, and if I'm sure they aren't allergic to the stuff, I let them have the shot. I know I shouldn't give in, but this type of patient wears a doctor down.

Another group of patients that get under my skin are those who won't follow directions.

For example, when a patient takes an antibiotic it's very important for him to take an adequate dose. When I prescribe an antibiotic for someone with an infection, I prescribe just as many pills as the patient needs—usually enough for five or seven days of treatment. When I give the patient the prescription I always say, "Now, be sure to take these till they're gone, no matter how well you feel."

I'll bet that at least one patient out of every five quits before he's supposed to. As soon as the redness or the pain goes away he stops taking the pill. He has taken enough medicine to suppress the bacteria but not enough to kill it. Unless he's lucky, a few days later the infection flares up again and we have to start all over again.

We see this sort of behavior often: ulcer patients who go back on coffee and cigarettes as soon as their pain goes away; men who rejoin the bowling team as soon as the soreness goes out of the hernia incision; coronary patients who rush back to work as soon as they're out of the hospital. And when the ulcer perforates, the hernia recurs or there is another coronary they blame us.

A third group of patients that drive me to drink are those that don't think they're getting their money's worth unless they take up at least fifteen minutes of my time.

Women are the worst offenders. Sylvia Lazar is typical.

Sylvia came to see me one day on a routine postoperative visit. I had removed a benign breast lump a week earlier. I examined her breast, took out the stitches and was about to leave the room when Sylvia said, "Oh, Dr. Nolen, as long as I'm here would you mind checking my blood pressure?" "Check my blood pressure" is one of the favorite requests of this type of patient.

I did mind checking it, but I didn't have the guts to say so. When I finished checking it—it was normal, of course—and was again about to leave the room, Sylvia grabbed at her shoe. "Before you go, Dr. Nolen," she said, "take a look at this toe of mine. It's giving me a lot of trouble."

Having one's foot examined, I would say, rates second to having one's blood pressure checked as an "extra" the patient can squeeze out of a routine visit. Everyone has some little thing the matter with his feet—a corn, a callus, possibly an ingrown toenail—there's always something for the doctor to examine.

It took Sylvia a minute or two to unhook her stocking and slip it off, after which I gave a cursory examination to a corn she had on her little toe. I recommended a corn plaster, turned and ran, and this time I made it through the door.

One of the reasons it bothers me so much when I have to examine a patient's foot is that I, and most of the doctors I know, aren't really interested in feet. Nor do we know an awful lot about them.

Plantar's warts, for example, those thick painful lumps that people sometimes get on their feet—how should we treat them? There are about ten different ways of going at it—surgery, X-ray, chemicals to apply, special shoes—and, as is usually the case when there are a lot of ways to treat an ailment, none is consistently reliable. Since I don't know how to treat them easily and well, I wince when a patient comes in with one.

Ingrown toenails are another pesky ailment. The treatment is usually surgical—get rid of the ingrown nail—but to prevent a recurrence the patient has to be careful not to wear tight shoes, avoid trimming the nail back too far, watch foot hygiene. Neither the surgery nor the postoperative care is at all interesting, but to get a good result it must be done meticulously. Most doctors don't have any interest in these things and do a rotten job of taking care of them. Which is why podiatrists and chiropodists, who don't have one-tenth of the training that an M.D. has, often do a lot better job on minor foot ailments.

In this "extra time" business, mothers of little kids are the champs. They make an appointment for you to see little Tommy, who may need to have his tonsils out, but they drag little Betty and Billy into the office too. After you've looked at Tommy's throat, they say, "While you're at it would you just take a quick look in Betty's ear; she's been tugging at it a lot lately. And Billy has some swollen glands in his neck that I'd like you to feel." What she wants is three office calls for the price of one. From me, she usually gets them. Anything to get them all out of my office.

When I was in medical school one of my professors used to talk about *le petit papier* disease. This means, I think (I've had four years of French), the "little piece of paper" disease. I see it often. It refers to subspecies of the group of patients who want their money's worth. Again, women have the disease more often than men.

Out of the purse, after the postoperative examination is over, comes a piece of paper that looks like a shopping list. As soon as I see it, I sit down. I know I'm in for a fifteen-minute question-and-answer session. On the list are invariably such questions as, "Why do I get dizzy when I suddenly stand up?" "Why am I always so tired?" "Why does my urine burn?" "What can I take to make my bowels move regularly?" These four almost everyone asks. In addition, there will be a cluster of questions about aches, pains and symptoms specific to the individual patient. "Why do I have this pain right here, low down in my back?" "Why do I get gassy every time I eat cucumbers?" "Why do my ankles swell just before my period?" (this can almost be classified with the universal questions). On, and on, and on it goes, till I think I'll scream.

People with little pieces of paper, you may have gathered, are not among my favorite patients.

Another group of patients who irritate me are those that speak to me through an interpreter. I hate to admit it, but in this area men are the worst offenders.

Typical was a call I got one evening from Doris Lathrop. Her husband, Emil, works at a local bank.

"Dr. Nolen," Doris said, "could you come over and see Emil? He isn't feeling well."

"What's the trouble, Doris?" I asked.

I could hear Doris shouting, "What's the trouble?" to Emil, who was apparently a room or two away. I couldn't catch Emil's reply.

"He says he's got a pain in the stomach," Doris finally got back to me.

"Where in his stomach?" I asked. Again the shouted relayed question and the distant reply.

"High up on the right side. Just under his ribs."

"Has he vomited?"

"Have you vomited, Emil?" I could hear her shout.

"No, but he feels like it."

After about ten minutes of this indirect questioning I decided Emil was probably having gall bladder trouble, and I had him come to the hospital. If I could have talked to him directly I'd have gotten the information in three minutes.

Not infrequently I get the same sort of indirect answer when I allow a wife to come to my office with a husband who is ill. I have a general rule that my office nurse is never to let in a husband and wife simultaneously, but once in a while they sneak by.

I go into the office and say, "Well, Emil, what's bothering you today?"

"He's got a pain in the belly," Doris answers.

"Where is it, Emil?" I ask.

"High up on the right side, under his ribs," Doris replies.

If by any chance I ask a question to which she doesn't know the answer, such as, "Did you move your bowels today, Emil?" Doris will echo my question. "Tell the doctor if you moved your bowels, Emil," as though Emil could hear only her. Then he'll answer Yes or No, as the case may be.

Why men are reluctant to talk directly to a doctor when they're ill I don't know, but I'm certain that in fact they are. Conversations like those I've quoted are not at all rare. They're more a source of laughter than of annoyance, but it is a rather silly way to do things, and a time-waster.

There are some patients with perfectly legitimate complaints who also drive me up the wall. These are the ones whose ailments defy exact diagnosis and treatment. They make me realize how little I really know. Unfortunately, these ailments constitute a large percentage of the average practice.

Bad backs are the perfect example. I shudder whenever a patient comes into my office and says, "Doc, my back is killing me." I'm almost certain that I won't be able to tell the patient, after I'm through examining him, exactly what his problem is.

I start out with the history. "When did you first notice it?" "Is it getting better, worse or staying the same?" "Does it go down your leg?" On and on and on.

Then the physical. "Is this where it hurts?" "Does it bother you when I lift your leg?" "Show me how far you can bend to the side." The history and physical take a full fifteen minutes. When I'm through I know exactly what I knew when Joe walked in the door: he has a sore back.

Next come the X-rays. The odds, again, are at least fifty to one that the X-rays will show nothing of any significance, but they must be taken. The patient with a bad back who doesn't have X-rays feels that he has been cheated.

After I look over the X-rays—which takes about ten seconds —I go back into the examining room, where my patient is putting on his clothes. Without bending, he gingerly hooks one foot into a pants leg, and after struggling for a while, finally asks my help in putting on his socks. When he's dressed we talk.

"Well, Joe," I say, "the X-rays are all O.K. I don't think you've got a disc [every patient with a bad back thinks he has a "slipped disc"] because your straight-leg-raising test is normal. It looks to me as if you've pulled a muscle loose down at the base of your spine [this sounds better than saying, "You've strained your back"]. I want you to use heat on your back for twenty minutes, three times a day; make certain you sleep on a firm mattress; and avoid any heavy lifting or bending. I'm also going to give you some pills to take that should get the inflammation out of your back." (These pills are most important. Not because of their physical action—most of the pills prescribed for back pain are no more than glorified aspirin —but because of the mental effect. Patients with back pain don't feel as if they've really been treated unless they're given some special pill to take, preferably at least three times a day.)

So Joe leaves. He's spent about thirty dollars on the office call and X-rays, and he'll spend another five dollars on his pills. And he's not one bit better off than he would have been if he had stayed home. Anyone ought to know enough to use heat, rest and aspirin for a sore back—and that's all I've prescribed for him.

Remember now—I'm not being objective, I'm being subjective. I'm telling you what sort of patients drive me nuts. When I have a sore back I moan and groan till my wife can't stand me; if I weren't a doctor I'm sure I'd run to one. Bad backs are hell. But from the doctor's point of view they are also one big bore.

In Litchfield we have one group of pesty patients that doctors in bigger cities probably don't have to contend with. These are the farmers, who assume, because they get up at five thirty every morning, that all the rest of us get up then too.

About once a month I'm awakened at five in the morning by some guy like Ernie Washburn. He'll say, "Doc, it's about time for my annual physical again. Think I can get an appointment sometime this week?" When I'm awake enough so I understand what Ernie wants, I mutter something about calling the clinic at half past eight and I crawl back to bed. I don't think Ernie even remotely suspects that he has gotten me out of bed. By five thirty he has finished milking his cows and is ready to settle down to his first breakfast before he tackles his other chores. Farmers work long hours; longer than most doctors.

Patients like Ernie bug me, but at least he's not the calculating type. People who call at six in the evening, on Saturday afternoon or Sunday, often are.

I don't think I've ever heard from Louise Strong except in the evening or on a weekend. Sunday morning, when I'm trying to relax at home, she'll call and say, "Sorry to bother you, Dr. Nolen, but I wonder if I could see you this morning. I've had a cough since Wednesday, but it has gotten much worse today. Could you stop over here or would you like to meet me at your office or the hospital?"

Louise does this deliberately, of course. She could have come in on Thursday, Friday or even Saturday morning, but it might have meant a fifteen-minute wait. This business about the cough suddenly getting worse is so much baloney. She says it only to disarm me. She'd rather be seen on a weekend, when—according to the way she thinks of it—I have "nothing else to do."

When I can I put Louise, and those like her, off till Monday. I can usually tell by talking to them just how sick they are; if in doubt I err on the side of seeing them unnecessarily. But much of the time these night and weekend calls are nothing but a matter of convenience for the patient.

Finally, there's a group well known not only to every doctor but to laymen as well. These are the malingerers.

I shudder whenever a patient walks into my office, neck

held rigidly, staring straight ahead, and tells me his car has just been hit from the rear by some kid. This guy has "whiplash" written all over him, and I know damn well I'm going to be seeing him off and on for months.

My personal approach, after I examine him and find he hasn't actually damaged any nerves, is to be very optimistic. "You've got a little neck sprain there, Charlie, but don't worry, you'll be as good as new in three days." If I get in and make my point early, it sometimes works.

I always take X-rays, even if I know beyond the shadow of a doubt that the films will show a perfectly normal neck. I have to take X-rays because otherwise, as I mentioned in the chapter on malpractice, there's a real possibility that sometime, in the not too distant future, I'll be in the witness stand listening to a lawyer say, "You mean, Dr. Nolen, that you didn't take any X-rays? Even though you knew my client had just sustained a severe neck injury?" I don't ever want to hear those questions.

After I look at the films and find they're normal, I usually say, "Everything looks fine. A little heat and aspirin and you'll be fine in a few days." I'm still using the positive approach.

Sometimes it works, but too often it doesn't. The patient goes directly from my office to his lawyer, who makes a big deal out of the problem. "No diathermy? No pain pills? You be sure to check with your doctor tomorrow if you aren't all better. Now, exactly how did the accident happen?"

Almost invariably the patient winds up coming in for diathermy treatments three times a week. And if the lawyer really thinks he has a solid case the patient starts asking for a collar. There is nothing like a huge neck brace to impress a jury.

All I can say is, Thank heavens I'm not an orthopedist. A friend of mine who is has a little speech he gives to medical groups entitled "The Greenback Poultice," all about how patients throw away their crutches, their neck braces and their canes two days after the jury awards them a pile of dough. Money can do more than surgery, traction or any drug ever discovered, to cure the man who is suing someone.

If this whole chapter sounds like the bitter ravings of a cynical S.O.B., I'm sorry. It's just that we doctors often get almost too good a view of our patients. Under the magnifying glass all the blemishes are obvious.

Most of my patients are nice, cooperative, considerate people, anxious to get well and grateful for whatever I can do to help them. I'm sure fewer than 10 percent would fit into any of the categories I've described here. But that 10 percent, nicely sprinkled throughout the week, can quite efficiently drive me or almost any other doctor wild. Even the nicest patients sometimes bother me. It isn't their fault, it's mine.

30

The Treatment and Mistreatment of the Super-Neurotic Patient

Of all the patients we doctors see, the most difficult and frustrating to treat are the neurotics. I'm not referring to the person who occasionally goes to the doctor, concerned about some minor symptom that proves to be purely emotional in origin. These patients—they constitute about half of any general medical practice—are easily treated. All they need is reassurance that they haven't any serious disease.

Nor am I referring to the hypochondriacs. Hypochondriacs are physically healthy people who sincerely believe they have serious ailments. They are unhappy people, worrying constantly about diseases they don't have. They want to work, enjoy their families, live full lives, but they can't. They can't get their minds off illness.

To differentiate the patients I'm writing about now from the neurotics and hypochondriacs, I'll label them super-neurotics; though doctors almost universally refer to them—admittedly unkindly—as "crocks" or "gomers." These are the patients in excellent physical health who absolutely refuse to be well, patients who enjoy their "ailments."

They're not difficult to recognize. They include people like the woman who loves to phone her friends and describe at great length the horrible "migraine" headaches that plague her constantly; the man who hasn't worked in five years because "my back bothers me if I lift so much as a fork"; the patient who can hardly wait to pack her bags and get back to the hospital for another operation. Enjoying poor health is their hobby, their business, their only interest. They build their entire lives around their symptoms, their trips to the doctor, their stays in the hospital.

These patients—every doctor has several among his clientele—tax the ingenuity, good will and tolerance of any doctor. When you see men and women with disabling, painful, crippling or fatal physical diseases accepting their illnesses gracefully, doing their jobs and living their lives without complaining, it's difficult to retain your composure and not be furious at the super-neurotics.

Now, I don't want to argue with the humanitarian who will say, "But, Doctor, you should be more sympathetic; these patients are ill too. It's just that their problem is psychological rather than organic." I *know* that. I'm perfectly aware that super-neurotics are unhappy people. I do try to be sympathetic to them. It's just that they're such trying patients to treat. They wear us out.

Take Mrs. Jennie Cileo. She's been coming to our clinic for twenty years. She's Steve Charrah's patient, but one Saturday morning a few years ago, he was on vacation when she came in. I wasn't busy, so the girls sent her in to me.

I knew her slightly—Steve had asked me to examine her once when he thought she might have appendicitis—so I didn't have to introduce myself.

"What can I do for you today, Mrs. Cileo?" I asked her.

"Oh, Dr. Nolen," she said, "I'm having one of my migraine headaches. I'm afraid I need a shot."

"Tell me about your headache, Mrs. Cileo." I hadn't treated migraines in a long time, but I remembered enough about them so I could recognize one if the symptoms were characteristic.

Hers weren't. Migraines are usually on one side of the head, often associated with blurred vision or nausea, and very severe. Frequently the patient can tell when he or she is about to get one. There's an odd feeling, a so-called aura, that precedes a migraine. Mrs. Cileo's headache was no migraine at all. It was a simple tension headache.

Since I didn't have much to do, I spent fifteen minutes talking to Mrs. Cileo and looking over her chart. She was fifty-two years old, a teacher in a rural school, married to a salesman who was on the road most of the week. They had one married daughter. According to the record, Mrs. Cileo had been having migraine attacks about three times a month for six years. The attacks always came on Friday night or Saturday morning.

After our brief talk it didn't take a genius to put the picture together. Mrs. Cileo couldn't stand her husband. Things were fine during the week while he was on the road, but when he came home on weekends she tensed up. Her daughter had served as a buffer between the two, but when the daughter married, six years earlier, the weekends became intolerable. That was when the "migraines" had started. For six years she had been coming in every weekend for a shot of Demerol—just enough to cheer her up for a short while and sustain her till her husband left again.

I didn't want to go into all this with Mrs. Cileo—not only because I didn't have the time but because I'm no psychiatrist; but I did suggest to her that maybe we should send her to the White Clinic to see if they could cure her migraines. She was willing to go, so after giving her her shot of Demerol I told her I'd arrange the appointment and call her.

A week later she went to the clinic. I'd written, filling them in on her entire history. After they'd seen her I got a nice note back telling me that my diagnosis had been correct, that the headache was a simple tension problem and that they'd explained it all to Mrs. Cileo. They had assured her that she wouldn't need any more shots; heat applied to her neck and aspirin would be adequate.

Two months later, on a Friday afternoon, I happened to see Mrs. Cileo going into Steve's office. Later that day I dug out her chart. Sure enough, she was right back on her usual week-end shot of Demerol. The diagnosis, as far as both she and Steve were concerned, was still "migraine headache." To hell with the White Clinic.

My reason for mentioning this case isn't to criticize either Steve or Mrs. Cileo. A weekly shot of Demerol isn't hurting Mrs. Cileo any, and it's probably a lot less expensive than either a long-term course of psychotherapy or a divorce. I mention the case just to show how difficult it is to treat super-neurotics. These patients absolutely refuse to get well. It's a waste of time to get too scientific about them: just give them some medicine, reassure them and send them on their way; when they come back, repeat the performance.

But we do have to be careful. As one of my professors used to say, "Remember, neurotics aren't immortal"; it's awfully easy to overlook some real pathology in a patient who has been coming in for years with imaginary illnesses.

Take Helen Ross for example. Helen is sixty years old, forty pounds overweight and a constant complainer. She's been coming to the clinic at least once every two weeks for ten years ("Dr. Nolen, my back is just killing me," "Dr. Nolen, my bowels just won't work," "Dr. Nolen, I'm so awfully weak"). She's had every complaint known to man or woman. I talk with her for a few minutes, examine her briefly and give her a pill, usually a vitamin, a laxative or an aspirin. It always does the trick.

A couple of years ago her complaint was pain in the belly. "Hurts all the time, Dr. Nolen, can't hardly eat. Nothing helps me."

"You shouldn't eat so much anyway, Helen," I said. "You ought to lose fifty pounds."

"Don't I know it?" she said. "But I just can't. Remember when you put me on that diet a few years back? I almost starved to death, and still I gained ten pounds. It must be my metabolism."

"Don't give me that, Helen, I know you. You were drinking malts in between meals. But that's old history. Get up on this table, please; I want to examine your belly."

I found nothing abnormal, as I had anticipated, so I gave her a new laxative and sent her on her way.

Two weeks later she was back. "Damn it, Doc," she said, "those pills aren't doing any good. I've still got that pain. Goes right through into my back."

"O.K., O.K.," I said, "let me look you over."

I checked more thoroughly and still found nothing. I prescribed an antacid and sent her home.

Two days later I got a call from her husband, Tom. "Doc," he said, "can you come over right away? Helen's having an awful attack of pain. She's lying on the bed and she can hardly move."

"Can't she come in?" I asked. "I'm awfully busy." I suspected she was just putting on a good show.

"I really don't think so," Tom said. "She's pale and sweaty. Tell you the truth, Doc, she really don't look good."

"All right," I said, "I'll be over in a few minutes." Cursing to myself I told the girls at the desk I had to go on a house call and I'd be back in twenty minutes.

The Rosses live just two blocks from the hospital, and I got to their home in three minutes. Tom let me in and there was Helen sprawled out on the couch in the living room, moaning and groaning as if she was about to die. She really did look sick, and when I examined her I found her abdomen as rigid as a piece of steel.

"We'd better get you to the hospital, Helen," I said. "Tom and I will help you." With some difficulty we loaded her into the back seat of my car.

When we arrived I got some X-rays of Helen's abdomen and, sure enough, there was free air in her belly. An ulcer had perforated. I took her right up to the operating room and closed the hole. She was sick for a few days, but she recovered.

In retrospect I know I should never have let Helen's ulcer perforate. If I had paid the proper attention to her symptoms, as I would have if I hadn't already labeled her a "crock," I'd have ordered X-rays and made the diagnosis of an ulcer at its early stage. Then I could have treated her with pills and diet and cured her before she got into serious trouble.

I'm the kind of guy who tends to undertreat the super-neurotics, and occasionally, as in Helen's case, it leads to trouble. But there are many other doctors who overtreat these patients, and that can lead to trouble too.

Take Nancy Mann for example. Nancy lives in Minneapolis, where her husband teaches school, but Ray Smith, a local G.P., has always been Nancy's family doctor, and Nancy still drives out to see Ray whenever she's ill. Ray is inclined to be oversympathetic to the super-neurotics. Instead of disparaging Nancy's kooky ailments, as I would, Ray plays up to them.

One of Nancy's repeated complaints over the years has been back pain. "Oh, Dr. Smith," she'll whimper, "my back is so sore I can hardly stand it."

"Where does it hurt, Nancy?" Ray will ask her.

"Right here," and she'll point to some spot low down on her back, just above her buttocks.

About eight years ago Ray found a lipoma, a blob of fat, in the region where Nancy was pointing. These lipomas are common, a lot of people have them, and they almost never cause any trouble. The only reason for removing most lipomas is a cosmetic one. Where a lipoma on the buttock is involved, cosmetic reasons would rarely come into play.

But Ray told Nancy that maybe this lipoma was causing her back trouble, and he removed it in the hospital under general anesthesia. Nancy's back pain went away.

Temporarily. Three months later it was back again, and she was convinced that she must have another lipoma. Ray re-operated on her and took out another blob of fat. More relief.

Over the last eight years Ray has operated on Nancy twenty times. He takes out a bit of perfectly normal fat each time, and each time Nancy gets better.

If Ray could be objective about Nancy's complaints, he'd admit those blobs of fat aren't causing her problems. But he can't be objective. She drives him nuts with her complaints and he talks himself into believing that the next blob of fat he removes will cure her. And the operation does shut her up for the next few months. But sometime she may get into trou-

ble from either the surgery or anesthesia. It's a dangerous way
to treat a super-neurotic.

But it's the easiest way, from the doctor's point of view.
Operate on them, give them a vitamin shot once a week, stick
them in the hospital for a few days. Anything to shut them up.
These are the ways Ray and Steve treat their super-neurotics.
There are certain patients who have been coming to their offices once a week for vitamin shots for years. These vitamin
shots might just as well be water. The patients don't need
them and they serve no useful purpose, except to keep these
anxious people quiet.

Ray has half a dozen patients like Nancy. So does Steve
and so do Dick Hopkins and Jack Nadler. The super-neurotics
gravitate to these doctors like flies to honey because they
pamper them so. When a patient of this sort comes to one of
us doctors who don't give them the time of day, we let them
know that there's nothing the matter with them. They hate us
for it and they don't come back.

I don't claim my attitude toward these neurotic patients is
the proper one. It's just that—my temperament being what it
is—this is the way I react to patients who are healthy and
want to play sick.

But I don't think Steve and Ray are doing them any favors
either. Playing up to their illnesses is at least as bad as disparaging them. I, at least, occasionally shame some super-neurotic
out of his moaning and groaning. I occasionally convince one
he's well. Steve and Ray never do.

Most of the super-neurotics I see are referred to me by other
doctors. They get worn out treating these people week after
week, month after month, year after year. Finally, after they've
tried every possible pill and potion, they send the patient to
me. They're hoping I'll find some organ I can remove that will
cure the patient once and for all.

I have to be very careful not to get trapped on these cases.
Not only does the referring doctor want me to operate but so
does the patient. They are both desperate for a cure. They
want me to pick up a knife and solve everyone's problem.

Sometimes I can make the diagnosis just by looking at the

abdomen. If it looks like a road map, if the appendix, gall bladder and uterus are missing, and if the patient has had one or two operations for "adhesions," then I'm very wary. Anyone who has had four or five operations, particularly if the operations were done to relieve vague pains, probably doesn't have a physical problem. I stay out of those abdomens unless there is an indisputably clear reason for operating—like a tumor I can see or feel.

Often these super-neurotics are referred to one of the white-tower clinics or hospitals. The hometown doctor sends them away just to get them off his back.

When this happens the super-neurotic often winds up undergoing an unnecessary operation. One patient with vague abdominal pains, who I and every other doctor in town knew was simply neurotic, underwent a complicated blood-vessel operation to improve circulation in her intestine; another, whose current complaint was "tingling" in her hands, had her wrists operated on to relieve pressure on the nerves. Six months after their operations both patients were back in their family doctors' offices with new nebulous complaints. The operations hadn't helped them at all.

I wouldn't have operated on either of these patients. I've known them for years and could have predicted that time, all by itself, would have eventually cured them. But the white-tower surgeons, seeing them for the first time, believed all that these patients said and insisted on finding a physical explanation for their symptoms. Another example of why it's safer, often, to get your medical care from someone who really knows you.

One of the rationalizations I have to avoid is to say, "Well, since everything else has been done, since every conceivable X-ray and blood test has been taken without finding the cause of the pain, the only thing left to do is look inside. It's just possible we might find an explanation." Possible, yes; but so unlikely that ninety-nine times out of a hundred it is not justifiable to operate. Yet every surgeon—and I'm no exception—has succumbed to the temptation at one time or another. We open the abdomen, look around and close. Hopefully we don't do the patient any harm; definitely we don't do him any good.

I suppose the best treatment for these neurotics would be in-depth psychoanalysis. Get to the root of the problem, find out what emotional problem is producing this physical symptom. But who in the world is going to do this? All the psychiatrists in the world, working twenty-four hours a day, couldn't cure all the super-neurotics that are around. The G.P.'s, even if they have the psychiatric knowledge and the interest, don't have the time to spend with these people.

It's easier to do as I do, brush them off; or as Ray and Steve do, overtreat them just to get them off their backs. That's the way doctors treat super-neurotics now and I'm afraid that's how they'll continue to treat them in the future. It isn't "right," but at the moment there's no obvious alternative.

31

Unjustifiable Surgery

Occasionally, as in managing the super-neurotics, a surgeon performs an operation not because he thinks he's going to cure the patient but because he feels that the operation has to be done to rule in or out certain diseases.

Patients with vague abdominal symptoms, for example, may have tumors of the pancreas. If all possible X-rays and blood tests have been done, and no other explanation for the symptoms can be found, I'll occasionally operate on a patient on the remote chance that the pancreas is diseased. (There's no way to X-ray a pancreas.) Usually the pancreas is normal, so in a sense the operation was unnecessary. Still, it had to be done so that we wouldn't miss a potentially curable disease. The surgery was unnecessary but not unjustifiable.

More common, but in the same category, are the appendectomies which are done in which a normal appendix is found and removed. If a child has the signs and symptoms of appendicitis, if I think the child has appendicitis, I have an obligation to operate. If I don't and he has appendicitis, the appendix may rupture. A child can die of a ruptured appendix. So if I remove a normal appendix and if the child's symptoms were caused by indigestion, I've done an unnecessary operation, but not an unjustifiable one. In fact, since the diagnosis of appendicitis can only be made with probability, not certainty, if a surgeon isn't removing one normal appendix in every ten cases he's probably not doing enough appendectomies. He's trying to be too certain, and probably letting some appendices go on to rupture.

Having now differentiated between unnecessary and unjustifiable surgery, let me admit that there are, unfortunately, some surgeons who perform operations that are not only unnecessary but unjustifiable as well. But not nearly as often as the layman would think, from reports he reads in the press.

Whether a tonsillectomy or hysterectomy is justifiable, in any particular case, is often a matter of opinion. Even if the pathologist, after examining the tissue, reports "normal tonsils" or "normal uterus," it does not necessarily mean the operation was unjustifiable. "Normal tonsils" can cause breathing problems and a uterus which looks normal under the microscope might have caused uncontrollable hemorrhage. The publicized statistics on unjustifiable surgery based on pathology reports are inflated and unreliable.

The unjustifiable surgery that's done can hardly ever be proved unjustifiable. Most of what is done is caused by ignorance. Some, admittedly, is caused by greed.

In the first category I'd put some of the operations done by Tom Brogan.

Take the operation I helped Tom perform on Randy Gustafson. Randy came to Tom complaining of pain in the groin, which he noticed right after a high school football game. Tom examined Randy, decided he had a hernia and scheduled the case. He asked me to assist him.

I didn't examine Randy before the operation—Tom didn't ask me to, and I have to assume that a guy who has been practicing medicine for fifteen years can diagnose a hernia —but when we operated on Randy, after we'd cut down to the area where hernias lie, there was absolutely no evidence of a hernia.

But hernias are sometimes vague things—just weak areas in the muscular wall of the abdomen—and it's always possible to put a few stitches in the muscle to tighten up a weakness, even if the weakness exists only in the mind of the surgeon.

Tom did just that. He pretended there was a weakness, a hernia, and he sewed it up. Randy recovered nicely.

Now, I know Tom Brogan well enough so that I think he operated out of ignorance. The surgery was unjustifiable because he should have been able to tell preoperatively that there was no hernia, but it was an honest mistake.

On the other hand, Noel Rysdale will occasionally schedule a hernia repair on some patient whom I've examined very recently, and who I know does not have a hernia. I know this is a basically healthy man who would do quite nicely without the operation.

But how do you prove it? If 30 percent of the appendices a doctor removes prove to be normal when examined by the pathologist, you've got something to hang your hat on. But when you repair a hernia you may not have to remove any tissue, and if you do it, it has no diagnostic value. Doctors joke about "acute remunerative appendicitis"; I suspect that acute remunerative hernia is a much more common disease.

Most of the unjustifiable surgery that's done is relatively minor in nature—removal of blobs of fat from beneath the skin, D and C's (dilatation and curettage of the uterus), hemorrhoidectomies. The risk to the patient is negligible, and there's no chance of being caught. Everyone has hemorrhoidal veins—they're a normal part of the anatomy—and the ones that didn't need to come out look the same under the microscope as the ones that bled. So a doctor is relatively safe when he's very liberal in advising these operations.

When the layman reads about hospitals where, we'll say, the number of operations per unit of population done is 50 percent higher than the national average, he can't understand how the surgeons get away with it. I can. The surgeons in that hospital don't have enough legitimate work to keep them busy, so they loosen up on their standards. They start removing gall bladders that aren't diseased, on the off chance that doing it may get rid of the patient's indigestion. They take out a uterus because it may, possibly, relieve a backache. They open up the spine and look around, because "maybe there's a slipped disc, even if the X-rays don't show it." They lie to their patients and to themselves. They're operating for the money but won't admit it.

How often this is done I can't say. There are statistics which show that among subscribers to prepaid medical-care plans the incidence of hysterectomies is about 50 percent lower than in the population treated by fee-for-service doctors. This suggests that one-third of all hysterectomies are done strictly for money. The figure seems awfully high to me, but I have no way of refuting it.

From my own experience I can say this: I can't imagine decent, informed, experienced men—and I think most surgeons fall into this category—performing unjustifiable operations, even minor operations, for the sake of a few bucks. I know it happens, I've seen it, but I can't understand it. If there's one thing you learn by experience it's that in surgery disaster can strike at any time. I find it difficult to believe that many men are willing to operate unnecessarily and run the risk of living the rest of their lives knowing that because of their greed they were responsible for the death of even a single patient. I don't know how they can get to sleep at night.

But there is one group of patients who I know are sometimes unfairly and unjustifiably subjected to surgery. These are the patients with terminal diseases. As a surgeon, I can easily see how it happens.

George Engel called me to the hospital one afternoon to see a patient of his, Leo Barrett, a man of eighty-nine. I had operated on Leo one year earlier and had removed a malignant tumor of the intestine, but at the time of that operation the cancer had already spread to the liver and to several spots on the peritoneum, the inner lining of the abdomen. We couldn't get all the cancer out. George and I knew after the operation that Leo probably wouldn't live very long. I was surprised to learn he had lived six months.

When I got to the hospital George said, "Take a look at him, will you, Bill? He's been at home, vomiting for three days. His son finally brought him in. See if there's anything you can do."

So I examined Leo. Pressing on his abdomen I could feel hard lumps of tumor. I ordered an X-ray and it showed that the tumor had blocked his intestine. What was there to do? The right answer was, "Nothing"; give Leo enough morphine to keep him comfortable and let him die peacefully. Operating on him would be a hopeless venture. I knew I couldn't give him even an extra three days of comfort.

But "Nothing" was a difficult answer to give. George Engel wanted me to do something, Leo's son wanted me to do something, Leo himself wanted me to do something. If I had said, "I don't think we can help, but let's operate and see," everyone would have been pleased. I could have taken Leo to the operating room and poked around in his abdomen for an hour, trying unsuccessfully to unblock his intestine. No one would have criticized me; the family would have said, "We know you did the best you could," and Medicare would have paid me three hundred dollars.

I didn't do it. I let Leo die in comfort. But I can understand, though I don't condone, surgeons giving in to the temptations to undertake obviously hopeless operations. Unfortunately, this is happening with increasing frequency, now that Medicare will pay for operations on the elderly. Knife-happy surgeons are operating on people with extensive cancers, serious lung diseases and heart ailments that can't possibly be remedied; their rationalization is that "If I don't operate he's certainly going to die—so I may as well operate even if there's only a one-in-a-million chance we can save him." We surgeons often think in terms of odds when trying to decide whether or not to operate—it's reasonable to do so—but there's a time to admit defeat and let the patient die quietly, peacefully and unoperated on. Lately we've started to deny some of them this right.

32

Never Take Surgery Lightly

I feel about surgery the way I feel about flying. I don't worry about anyone else going up in a plane—not even my wife or children. I know they're as safe up in the sky as I am on the ground. Probably even safer. But I'm terrified when I'm the one who has to get on a plane. There just isn't a plane in the world, or a pilot either, to whom I'm willing to entrust my life.

About surgery I feel almost the same way. If one of my kids or my wife needed an appendectomy I can think of several surgeons and anesthetists to whom I'd entrust their care with a reasonably easy mind; but, personally, I'd be scared to death to let anyone operate on me.

I've seen too much trouble: cardiac arrests occurring when someone's in for "minor" surgery; testicles deprived of their blood supply by a surgeon fixing a "simple" hernia; hemorrhage from a stress ulcer of the stomach after a "routine" appendectomy. These things scare the daylights out of me. If and when I ever need surgery they'll have to drag me screaming to the O.R.

The first case I did after moving to Litchfield was enough to cure me, early in my career, of ever taking any surgery lightly.

The patient was a man named Hugh Parrot, a farmer, sixty years old, big and husky. Tom Brogan had called me in to see him at nine o'clock on Monday, my first day of work. As I sat on the side of the bed examining him, it quickly became apparent that Hugh had a hot gall bladder.

If I so much as touched his belly up under the ribs on the right side, he groaned. "That hurts like hell, Doc," he said. I began to question him.

"Ever had yellow eyeballs, Hugh?" I asked.

"Nope."

"Has your urine ever been dark, like Coca-Cola?"

"Not that I can remember."

"No one ever told you you had jaundice?"

"No."

As I talked I pushed lightly on his belly—always the same old groan when I hit the gall bladder region. I was convinced.

"Hugh," I said, "your gall bladder is inflamed. Dr. Brogan and I have talked it over and we think we'd better operate on you. Your blood count is high—three times normal—and you're not getting any better on the antibiotics. Your gall bladder will have to come out."

"Suits me," Hugh said. "Anything to get over this goddam bellyache."

"We'll operate in about half an hour. The nurse will be in with a hypo in a few minutes." Tom and I left the room.

Out in the corridor, as we walked toward the operating room, I said to Tom, "I wish we didn't have to do him now. He's so big it may be a tough one to get at. But I'm afraid to sit on him. He's awfully tender and the damn thing might rupture."

"Don't worry too much about Hugh," Tom said. "He's a tough old Swede. He works hard and he drinks hard. It would take a lot to kill Hugh."

There was really no good reason for me to worry so much about this case. I'd done my share of gall bladders and plenty of other surgery in the bargain. I certainly ought to be able to handle this one. It might be tough, but not that tough.

Still, it was my first private case, the first patient I'd handled outside the protective halls of the teaching hospital where I had trained, and, naturally, I wanted things to go well. After all, I was the new big daddy of the hospital, the surgeon

brought in from the East to save lives, and great things were
expected of me. I had to be good.

Tom and I got into our scrub suits and walked out to the
sink. "Who else is going to scrub?" I asked.

"What do you mean?" Tom said.

"Aren't we going to have three doctors in the O.R.?"

"Hell, no," said Tom, "are you kidding? Everyone else is
busy. We never have more than two guys in on a case. I'll
take that back. Maybe on something real big, like a lung, we
might have three of us, but not on anything like a gall
bladder."

"O.K.," I said. "Just asking." At Bellevue we'd always had
three men on a gall bladder—the operator plus two assistants.
But this was private practice, where time meant money and
you didn't tie up three men when two could do the job.

Hugh was on the table now. "Who's the anesthetist?" I
asked. Tom looked into the O.R. "That's Jim Sommers," he
said. "He's from Saint Paul. He fills in sometimes when Sam
is on vacation." Sam Longworth was the regular anesthetist,
a male nurse. I'd met him a day earlier.

As I scrubbed I watched Dr. Sommers working on our
patient. He had shot the Pentothal into him and he was asleep.
Now Sommers had the laryngoscope in his mouth and was
trying to get the endotracheal tube in his trachea so he could
give him oxygen.

It didn't look to me as if things were going well. Hugh was
a bull-necked guy and Sommers was obviously having trouble
bending his neck so that he could see between the vocal
cords. He pushed on the tube trying to slide it in blindly, but it
wasn't going into his windpipe. He looked flustered to me as
he pulled the tube back out and slapped the mask on Hugh's
face. He started squeezing the bag trying to force air into
his lungs.

I was beginning to get nervous. "Tom," I said, "take a look
in the O.R. It seems to me Dr. Sommers is having trouble."
Tom looked in.

"Yeah," he said, "Hugh doesn't look too good."

I dropped my scrub brush and I stepped into the O.R.

"Excuse me," I said, "but have you got a problem?" Hugh's face was blue and well on its way to being purple. Sommers was squeezing the bag like crazy but the air was leaking back out at the corners of Hugh's mouth.

"I'm afraid he's in laryngospasm," he said. "I can't seem to get any oxygen into him."

I grabbed a stethoscope and listened. Not a sound in his lungs. I slapped the scope over his heart. I could just barely hear a beat—damn slow. Hugh was suffocating and pretty near dead.

"Give me a knife—quick," I said.

The scrub nurse put it in my bare hand; there was no time for sterile technique.

"Drop his head back," I yelled at Sommers. He did.

Quickly I made a gash in Hugh's neck over his windpipe. In the meantime the circulating nurse, who was obviously on the ball, opened a tracheotomy set. I cut straight down till I could see the trachea, grabbed it with a towel clip, cut through the cartilage, and as the air blew blood all over my face I jammed in the tracheotomy tube. I was soaked with blood and perspiration.

Within seconds Hugh began to look better. His purple face was back to blue and getting lighter all the time. His heartbeat was loud and steady. The whole episode hadn't taken more than two minutes.

Sommers had hooked the oxygen into the tracheotomy tube and was pumping oxygen into Hugh's lungs. The crisis was over, but it had been a close thing.

"If it's all the same to you, Tom," I said, "I'm going to cancel this case. We'll take a chance on Hugh's gall bladder. He's had enough for one day."

And that was my first private-practice case: I took the patient to the O.R. to take out his gall bladder and sent him back to his room with a hole in his neck and his gall bladder still in his belly.

Surprisingly, it didn't upset Hugh a bit. When he woke up I explained to him what had happened and he accepted the news quite calmly. I treated his gall bladder with antibiotics and warm wet pads applied to the abdomen, and he got over the attack. Six months later I brought him back to the hospital and took out his gall bladder.

A surgeon friend of mine, Bob Ranovitch, had a patient whose course demonstrates the hell that can break loose when a patient comes in for "simple" surgery. This patient, Ross Lofgren, also had gall-bladder disease. He was fifty-two years old, in excellent general health, and his gallstones were not much of a problem. He'd had one mild attack after eating an anchovy pizza a few months earlier. After examining him Bob assured him that he should be out of the hospital in a week, ten days at the most, and back to work in eight weeks.

It didn't, to put it mildly, work out like that. When Bob got into the abdomen he found that one of the gallstones had passed from the gall bladder into the common duct, the channel along which bile runs from the gall bladder to the duodenum, the first part of the small intestine. Bob had to open up the duct to fish out the stone, usually not too difficult a job.

But this stone was stuck at the lower end of the duct and Bob couldn't budge it. After working for an hour and a half he finally had to open up the duodenum and take out the stone from below.

Postoperatively Mr. Lofgren ran a stormy course. The suture line in the duodenum broke down four days after the surgery and Bob had to reopen the abdomen and drain the bowel.

Ten days later the patient developed intestinal obstruction from adhesions, and Bob had to go back in and untwist the bowel.

Two weeks after that, this unfortunate patient began bleeding vigorously from an ulcer, and Bob had to remove part of his stomach. Finally, six months after he had entered the hospital for a "simple" cholecystectomy, Mr. Lofgren went home —thirty pounds and $30,000 lighter than when he entered.

Fortunately, he was a wealthy man. After his discharge he went to Florida to recuperate. When he came back he stopped in at Bob's office for a final postoperative check. Bob asked him how he'd enjoyed his vacation.

"Fine," he said. "I had one humorous experience. I was lying on the beach one day with my poor scarred-up belly out in the breeze, and a guy struck up a conversation with me. His eyes kept wandering to my stomach and he finally said, 'I hope you don't mind but I can't help asking—what happened to you?' When I told him I had had my gall bladder out, he just looked at me for a second, to see if I was kidding. When he saw I wasn't he finally smiled and said, 'Did you do it yourself?'"

Bob and Mr. Lofgren both had a good laugh.

One dandy way to get into trouble is to let a patient talk you into doing something against your better judgment. It happens every now and then to any surgeon. After it's over, you kick yourself for giving in to the patient, you swear you'll never do it again and, of course, a few months later you fall into the same trap.

One case I remember particularly well was that of Roland Laplante, a forty-two-year-old man who works at a local bank. Roland came into my office one day and said, "Bill, I'm almost embarrassed to bother you with this thing—I know you do a lot of major surgery—but it hurts me." He held out his hand and showed me a big wart at the base of his thumb. "I've had this thing removed twice before but it always comes back. I want to get rid of it for good."

I examined the wart. Its base was circular and about three-quarters of an inch in diameter. "I think I can freeze this with a little Novocaine and get it off completely," I said. "It may take a little tugging but I'm sure you'll be able to stand that."

"Don't be too sure, Bill," Roland said. "I'm a darn poor patient when it comes to pain. When I was a kid I was in the hospital for over a year after a car accident. They must have operated on my back twenty times. It turned me into a sissy." He took off his shirt and I could see scars of his many previous operations.

I thought about it for a minute and then said, "Maybe you're right, Roland. We want to get it off completely this time and that means a fairly wide incision. It could be painful. I hate to put you to sleep for such a minor problem, but you're in good health and you should take it fine. Come to the hospital without breakfast next Tuesday about seven thirty in the morning and we'll get it off. You can go home the next day."

On the morning of surgery I checked Roland over completely and everything seemed fine—heart normal, lungs clear, no problems other than his wart. We wheeled him into the operating room, put him to sleep, and I went to work.

The case went well. I cut out the wart, and by undercutting and loosening the skin of the palm, was able to close the incision without too much tension. I could have done the job under local anesthesia, but it would have taken more time and effort on my part and would probably have caused Roland some discomfort.

Roland went back to the recovery room. It was almost noon, so I went home, changed my clothes and headed for the tennis court.

Half an hour later, in the midst of the first set, Joan drove up to the court. "Bill," she shouted, "the hospital called—they want you right away. They're afraid Roland Laplante has died."

I raced off to the hospital. In the three minutes it took me to get there I cursed myself a thousand times. Why, oh why, didn't I do the case under local? What would I say to Nancy Laplante, left alone with three little kids? Why, to avoid a little discomfort and save a few minutes' time, did I take even the small extra risk that general anesthesia inevitably adds to a case? God, how I wished I had that case to do over!

I raced upstairs, sweating in my tennis shorts and shirt. One quick look at Roland and I breathed a sigh of relief. He didn't look good, his skin was bluish, from lack of oxygen; but he obviously wasn't dead. Sam Longworth, our anesthetist, was at the head of his bed, pumping oxygen into him.

"What happened?" I asked the nurse.

"I don't know," she said. "He seemed O.K. one minute, the next he was blue and gasping. I couldn't hear his heart sounds. I sent for you and Mr. Longworth."

"I think he vomited coming out of anesthesia," Sam said. "When I got here he was gurgling and very dark. He was almost gone. I sucked a lot of junk out of his windpipe. I bet he ate something this morning. He's beginning to look better now."

And he was. His color was improving and he was trying to push the mask away. Within the next five minutes he was breathing comfortably, not yet wide-awake, but obviously out of danger. I drove home grateful for both Roland's escape and mine. When I talked to him later, it turned out that he had indeed had a piece of toast that morning. He had gotten away with it before, when he was a child, and thought we doctors were overcautious. Now he knew better. I'd learned a lesson too; I swore I'd never again let a patient talk me into doing something against my better judgment. But, of course, I have.

Surprisingly, a G.P. who does occasional surgery or a young surgeon just out of training is much more likely to take surgery lightly than a more experienced surgeon would. Now that I fall into the latter category I frequently find myself bailing out of trouble doctors who have bitten off considerably more than they could chew.

A while back I was called to the operating room by Dick Ryan. He had a patient asleep on the table and he was operating on the man's foot. I stuck my head in the door of the O.R. and said, "What's up, Dick?"

Dick turned around and I could see that he was perspiring profusely, a certain sign of tension. "Bill," he said, "this is Mr. Lewis. He stepped on a needle a week ago and a piece broke off in his foot. I've been trying to get it out but I can't seem to find it. Do you want to give it a try?" Mr. Lewis looked over at me. Dick was operating on Mr. Lewis under local anesthesia.

"Sure," I said, "I'll change and be right in."

Dick had X-rays of the foot up on the view box in the O.R.; I studied them, and after putting in more local anesthesia, I tripled the length of Dick's incision in the foot. He had been trying to get at this needle through an incision less than an inch long. After about ten minutes of dissection I found the needle. Dick had been operating for an hour and a half.

This is a perfect example of the sort of trap inexperienced operators get into. What could be simpler than making a small incision, reaching in and taking out a needle or a bullet, or a piece of glass? To the inexperienced operator it looks like a cinch.

It never is. Sure, an operator can be lucky and come right down on a foreign body, but nine times out of ten, little pieces of metal or glass are extremely difficult to find. You have to be burned once or twice, as I have, before you learn (1) not to do them under local anesthesia and (2) never, never to do these cases in the office. The operating room certainly, and general anesthesia usually, are necessary to do these "simple" cases.

I suppose it's easier for me to admit defeat than it is for some of the G.P.'s I know. After all, I'm the guy who gets called in to see the difficult surgical cases; that's a boost for my ego. The G.P. is the guy who has to take care of all sorts of ailments —some boring, some challenging—but he's never called in as an expert. So sometimes he gets a little sick of eating crow, and refuses to do so even when he should.

One night, a seventy-two-year-old man, Pete Jacoby, came to see Lou Rosetti, a G.P.; he complained of pain in his abdomen. "It hurts right here, Doc," Pete said, pointing to the area of the appendix. Lou examined him, decided that appendicitis was indeed the diagnosis, and took Pete to the O.R. He asked Brian O'Connor to help him.

When Lou opened up Pete's belly he found to his dismay that instead of appendicitis Pete had a cancer of the large intestine. This happens once in a while, particularly in the elderly. Cancer in the cecum (the portion of the large bowel to which the appendix is attached) may not give any symptoms till it starts to leak, and the symptoms of a leak are the same as those of appendicitis.

Lou was chagrined. He hated to admit that he had made the wrong diagnosis. He hated even more to admit that he was up against a surgical problem which was more than he could handle. So instead of calling me in to do the case he decided to go ahead and remove the cancer himself.

Lou took four hours to do the job. I could have done it in an hour, an hour and a half at most. The chances of a complication developing after an operation are always greater after a lengthy procedure than after a short one, and old Pete had several complications. He developed pneumonia, his wound broke down—he almost didn't make it. All because Lou was too proud to ask for my help.

There's an adage, promulgated with exceptional vigor by the American College of Surgeons: "There is no such thing as minor surgery, only minor surgeons."

I don't subscribe completely to this theory. Sewing up lacerations, removing small skin growths, fixing an uncomplicated hernia—all these operations are relatively minor and can be performed by any doctor who wants to spend the bit of time it takes to master the fundamentals of surgery. The mistake that some part-time, inexperienced surgeons—usually G.P.'s—make is in not being able to differentiate between a simple case and one which requires a lot of surgical knowledge, experience and proficiency.

Some of the worst and most inexpert surgery that I've seen done has been on the hand and wrist. The G.P.'s who live in farm areas, such as Litchfield, see a lot of mutilated hands, the result of accidents involving farm machinery, so they quickly learn respect for the difficulties of hand surgery, but G.P.'s elsewhere who wouldn't even consider taking out a gall bladder will sit down to repair a badly cut wrist without giving it a second thought. There are two reasons for their fearlessness. First, the surgery is in a superficial part of the body; second, hardly anyone ever dies of a wrist injury. Even if the poor guy cuts through the radial artery (the big artery in the wrist), the vessel will generally go into spasm and shut down before the patient bleeds out.

Somebody may come in who has rammed his car into a telephone pole; he has a pain in his belly and it looks like a ruptured spleen; they call a surgeon in for consultation right away. Most G.P.'s wouldn't think of going after a ruptured spleen, even though removing a spleen is a relatively simple procedure. But let the same guy shove his hand through a window and cut all the tendons and nerves to the wrist, and what happens? The G.P. takes the patient to the O.R. and does the job himself. Only, he sews the wrong tendon ends together and he fails to find the median nerve at all. The patient winds up with a crippled hand. There are few things more disabling than a hand that doesn't work properly.

My personal fear of surgery isn't unique. I know a lot of surgeons who are wandering around living with problems for which they'd recommend an immediate operation to their patients. One guy has huge varicose veins, but instead of having them out he wears elastic stockings. Another has a hernia, and I know for a fact that he uses a truss, which any surgeon knows isn't worth a damn. I know one plastic surgeon who does nose jobs galore and whose own beak is as crooked as a ram's horn. I asked him once why he didn't have it straightened and he said, "Like hell. I'm not planning any trips to Hollywood. Anytime someone puts the knife to me it's going to be a matter of life or death."

And that, of course, is what surgery is all about.

33

Iatrogenic Disease

The doctor who does unjustifiable surgery may take a well patient and make him ill. The doctor who carelessly dispenses pills or advice can do the same thing.

One afternoon, when two of my partners were on vacation and the clinic was loaded with patients, I was asked if I'd see a few general medical patients. I agreed.

The first patient shown into my office, a Mrs. Taylor, was complaining of "dizziness." "Dizziness" ranks with low back pain and that "all-tired-out feeling" in the top level of complaints that doctors hate to treat. Almost never do you find any physical, treatable cause for the symptom. Generally you wind up spending ten minutes trying to persuade the patient that she'll be better soon even if you don't give her any medicine. Often the doctor offers some half-baked, half-true physiological explanation—"It's neuritis," or "You've strained a muscle," or "Your blood is a little low"—hoping the patient will accept the explanation, go away and leave him alone.

I sat at my desk for a minute trying to decide what I'd offer this seventy-year-old woman as an explanation for her dizziness—I'd examined her and could find nothing wrong—and as I pondered I thumbed through her past record. Suddenly my eyes lit on the discharge summary from the hospitalization for pneumonia six months earlier; here, under "treatment," was a list of fourteen different medications that Mrs. Taylor was given by the doctor who had hospitalized her. She had pills to get rid of fluid, pills for her blood, pills for her nerves, three different pills for her circulation, a pill for her blood pressure, two different pills for "dizziness," several different vitamin tablets. Fourteen different medicines! I couldn't believe it.

I went back into the examining room. "Mrs. Taylor," I said, "it says here that when you left the hospital six months ago you were taking fourteen different kinds of pills, some three or four times a day. Is that correct?"

"Yes, it is, Dr. Nolen," she said. "In fact, I've brought my medicines with me so you could look them over and see if I need any more." With this she opened up her purse and took out fourteen bottles containing pills and capsules of all sizes, shapes and colors. Mrs. Taylor was a walking pharmacy.

"Mrs. Taylor," I asked, "how can you keep track of all these medicines? Don't you sometimes get confused about which to take and when?"

"Oh, no," she said, "I have it down to a system. I keep all the four-a-day medicines on one shelf, three-a-days on another, and once-daily on a third. I never get confused."

"Well," I said, "I don't think I'll add any more pills to your pile. In fact, I think that possibly you should stop taking some of these pills now. They've served their purpose. It may even be that one of them may be causing your problem."

I discontinued twelve of her medications—I let her keep her blood pressure pills and a vitamin—and in three days her dizziness was gone. It had resulted, as many symptoms do, from too much medication.

One reason doctors prescribe unnecessary pills is that it's such an easy way to treat patients, far easier than treating them for what's really bothering them.

Consider Judy Moriarity. Judy came in complaining of low back pain. I examined her and couldn't find anything except some slight tenderness over the spine, so I gave her a prescription for a painkiller, a muscle-relaxing drug, and told her to come to the clinic for diathermy. She came to the office every day for a week but her back didn't improve much.

Then, at dinner one evening, Joan said to me, "Did you hear

that Paul Moriarity has started drinking again? He's been back at it for the last two weeks."

No, I hadn't heard that; and, of course, it was Paul's drinking and not any problem with her spine that was causing Judy's backache. If I had sat down and talked to Judy I could have made that diagnosis earlier and saved her the cost of two weeks of unnecessary therapy. But I didn't take the time.

The women who tell us, "I'm all tired out," are often simply bored with their lives. We treat them with liver, iron, vitamins or some other unnecessary medication when what they actually need is someone who will listen to them and help them see their real problems. It's a job we doctors should do, but often we don't.

I've mentioned several times that only about 50 percent of the patients who go to a doctor's office are physically ill. It's the doctor's job to cure these patients. The other 50 percent, those who have nothing physically wrong with them, should not be treated with pills or surgery; it's the doctor's job, after talking to these patients and examining them, to convince them that they're in good health. They can then leave the doctor's office happy in the knowledge that they're healthy.

Unfortunately, when some patients leave a doctor's office they're sicker than when they entered. Sometimes the ailment is physical, often it's emotional. Whichever it is, the doctor is the cause of it. *Iatros* is the Greek word for "physician"; *genic* means "caused by." Iatrogenic diseases are diseases caused by physicians. Unfortunately, they aren't uncommon.

Cases like Mrs. Taylor's, where symptoms have been produced by medications, are hardly rare. When I see the quantities of medicine that some doctors pour into their patients, I'm amazed that more patients don't suffer ill effects from them. What saves us from ourselves, I guess, is that at least some of the medicines are harmless—worthless, perhaps, but harmless as well. Hardly anyone gets into trouble from taking too many vitamins.

But other medicines aren't so innocuous.

Take the case of Mrs. Blondings. She went to see Dr. Brogan for a routine follow-up examination six weeks after he had removed a lump from her thyroid gland. The scar was well healed and she seemed to be in good health.

"I feel just fine, Dr. Brogan," she said, "except for my sinuses. They're draining again. Do you suppose while I'm here I could get a shot of penicillin? That always clears me right up."

Dr. Brogan saw no real reason for giving her penicillin. She didn't have any fever and there was no evidence of any infection in her sinuses. But looking back on her record he saw that she'd had penicillin shots a dozen times before for "sinusitis," and he thought, Oh, why not? He had a roomful of patients to see and he couldn't be bothered taking the time to talk her out of it. He told his office nurse to give Mrs. Blondings a million units of penicillin and went on to his next patient.

Two days later Mrs. Blondings was back in his office. Her skin was blotchy red and peeling, her eyes were puffy; she was a very sick woman. She had one of the worst allergic reactions to penicillin Tom Brogan had ever seen. He had to put her in the hospital for two weeks before she finally recovered —from a bad case of iatrogenic disease.

Every drug we doctors administer has some potentially dangerous side effects. The cortisone we give to a patient with arthritis may cause an ulcer of the stomach; the antibiotic we use to treat an earache can be responsible for severe diarrhea; the insulin we order to control diabetes can put the patient into a state of shock. All these things happen, once in a great while, even when we're very judicious about prescribing medicines. When they occur we accept them as unavoidable complications, not really our fault. But when complications occur because we've used drugs promiscuously, without good, solid reasons for using them, then it must be said that we're to blame.

The physical diseases caused by physicians are not rare, but neither are they anywhere near as common as the psychiatric ailments, the neuroses, that are physician-induced.

The doctors who exaggerate the seriousness of diseases, who tell patients with a cold that they're "on the verge of pneumonia," who tell people with small blobs of fat under the skin

that "that lump may very well be a cancer," who tell apprehen-
sive patients with nervous headaches, "Though I don't think
it's serious, and I can't find any explanation for it, the possibility of a brain tumor can't be ruled out"—these doctors (and
every doctor in practice knows one or two of these alarmists)
cause a lot of unnecessary anguish. They cause more trouble,
I'm certain, than the pill-dispensers.

Dick Ryan, for example, is responsible for a lot of iatrogenic
disease, some of it extremely debilitating.

Take the case of Ron Whitcomb. Ron is thirty-seven. He's
in the insurance business. He's a hard-driving, hustling guy.
Ron's father died of a heart attack at the age of fifty-eight.

Ron went to see Dick a couple of years ago, complaining of
chest pain. "I get these twinges," he said. "Real sharp pains.
Right here." And he pointed to the left side of his chest.

Most men, at one time or another, experience vague chest
pains. Ninety-nine times out of a hundred the pain has nothing to do with the heart. It's caused by a sore muscle or neuritis or some elusive thing that never can be tracked down.
The chest pain is of no importance and will go away by itself
in a few days.

The patient doesn't know this. Like Ron, he worries that
every pain on the left side of the chest means heart disease.
If there's a history of heart disease in the family, as there is
in Ron's, then any mild twinge becomes even more terrifying.
These men run to the doctor expecting the worst, hoping for
the best.

Dick listened to Ron's heart, took a chest X-ray and got an
electrocardiogram. Everything was normal. Not a trace of
heart disease.

So what did Dick tell Ron? Dick said, "All our tests are normal, Ron. I can't find any definite evidence of heart disease.
However, it's possible, of course, to have heart disease, even
a heart attack, without anything showing up on the electrocardiogram or on any of our other tests. I think I'd better put
you in the hospital and keep you under observation for a few
days, just to make sure."

So Dick stuck Ron in the hospital and watched him for a

few days. No new signs or symptoms developed. When he discharged Ron, he said, "Though I can't find a thing now, it's possible that you might have a coronary tomorrow. Be sure to check with me if you have any more chest pain." How reassuring can you be?

Over the next year and a half Ron was in and out of the hospital about every two months. Dick would admit him for observation. He'd take electrocardiograms and blood tests, and listen to his heart three times a day. Dick never found anything, but he had Ron convinced that he had heart disease. Ron stopped playing golf, asked for a smaller territory to cover in his insurance business, and lived an almost completely sedentary existence. He was physically healthy, but he was crippled by iatrogenic heart disease, caused by Dick Ryan.

Fortunately for Ron, after a year and a half of misery he had an attack of chest pain when Dick was out of town. He called Carlo Germain and Carlo examined him, looked at all the electrocardiograms at the hospital and reviewed his history. When he was done he said, "Ron, there's not a thing the matter with you. Your heart is perfectly healthy. All these vague chest pains you've been having are nothing but minor muscle strains. You've been so worried about your ticker you've magnified those little aches way out of proportion. My advice to you is to stop worrying about your health. Get back on that golf course and live a little."

"But gee, Carlo, Dr. Ryan warned me I might have a coronary any time. Was he wrong?" This was a touchy question.

"No, he wasn't wrong. Sure, anyone can have a heart attack any time. But Dick is a worrier. You're as healthy as a horse. If it makes sense for you to sit around waiting for a coronary, then Dick and I and every other person in the world should be sitting around worrying too. Forget about it. Enjoy your good health. Go out and have a good time."

Happily, Ron took Carlo's advice. Dick had caused Ron's heart disease by inaction. Dick is one of those doctors who are afraid to be positive and reassuring; he's frightened that something will go wrong and he'll be blamed. He doesn't have the courage to take a stand—a sad defect in a physician.

One of the oddest cases of iatrogenic disease was one I caused, with the cooperation of a radiologist.

A sixty-eight-year-old farmer, Bernie Rogers, came in to see me one morning, walking with his neck as stiff as a piece of steel. "What's the matter, Bernie?" I asked.

"Fell off the goddam tractor," he said. "Landed right on the back of my neck. Hurts like hell whenever I move it."

I examined Bernie and couldn't find any nerve disorders, but in view of the rigid way he held his neck I thought I'd better get some X-rays. I did, and the radiologist reported that Bernie had a fracture of the odontoid, a piece of bone at the top of the spine.

A fracture of the odontoid can be very serious. If it becomes displaced it may sever the spinal cord. To keep it from sliding I put old Bernie in a plaster cast that ran from the top of his head to his hips.

Bernie hated it, as anyone would. He needed help to get out of bed, and he walked like the tin man from *The Wizard of Oz* before his joints were oiled. Every morning when I'd come in to see him he'd say, "Doc, when are you going to get me out of this goddam thing? My neck don't hurt any more."

I planned to keep Bernie in the cast for six weeks, but after ten days I got an X-ray. I didn't expect it to show anything, but patients in casts feel neglected if they aren't X-rayed once in a while. I thought the film might keep Bernie from bugging me.

An hour after I ordered the film I got a call from X-ray and went down to see the radiologist—not the one who had read the original films.

"Bill," he said, "I just looked at the film on your patient Rogers, and I've reviewed his old one. I'm sure he hasn't got a fracture. When Louis read the film two weeks ago there was an artifact [a blemish on the film itself] that looked like a crack. It's not there today."

"Great," I said. "You mean poor Bernie has been walking

around for two weeks in a plaster cast from head to butt for nothing? How am I going to break that news to him?"

I needn't have worried. He was so happy to get out of the cast that he never once complained because I'd misdiagnosed a fracture. He had had the most extensive treatment for a neck sprain available anywhere, and he was happy it was over.

Iatrogenic disease, whether it arises from insecurity, ignorance or carelessness on the part of the doctor, is always sad. One of the key lines in the Hippocratic oath says, in essence, Do no harm. Once in a while, unfortunately, we do.

34

Venereal Disease

Iatrogenic disease is usually caused by overtreatment. Undertreatment of illness can be almost as bad. In private practice we often fall into the trap of inadequately treating the social, as well as physical, complications of venereal infections.

One evening, about half past seven, I got a call from Sam Smith. "Bill," he said, "would you mind coming over to take a look at June? I just got back from a three-day trip to Duluth, and I found her in bed with a bellyache. She's been sick for two days. She thinks it's just indigestion, but I wonder if it might be appendicitis."

"It would probably save time if you brought her to the hospital, Sam," I said. "I may need to get a blood count. I'll call and tell them you're coming and I'll see you over there."

Fifteen minutes later I examined June in the hospital emergency room. She was tender in the lower abdomen, mostly on the right, and her white blood count was elevated, evidence that she had infection somewhere. I asked the usual questions—appetite O.K.? Bowels working? Any burning when you pass your urine?—and her answers all fitted the diagnosis of appendicitis. I wasn't completely satisfied because her tenderness wasn't as well localized as it usually is in cases of appendicitis, but it still seemed like a good bet. I told Sam and June I'd have to operate; they agreed; and an hour later, with Carlo Germain assisting me, I opened June's abdomen.

There are two incisions commonly used to get at an appendix. One is a straight up-and-down incision just to the right of the midline; the other is a McBurney incision, which crosses over McBurney's point, the point on the abdomen under which the appendix lies which was first described by—you guessed it—Dr. McBurney. When the diagnosis is almost absolute, as is often the case with children, surgeons are apt to use the McBurney incision because it heals strongly and quickly. But if there's any doubt about the diagnosis the up-and-down incision is safer. The McBurney incision affords only a view of the area where the appendix lies; through an up-and-down incision a surgeon can explore the entire abdomen.

I make it a policy never to use a McBurney incision on women. There's always a chance that there'll be something the matter with their pelvic organs.

With the abdomen opened, I pulled the appendix up where I could see it. "Looks O.K. to me," Carlo said.

"Yeah," I said, looking it over. "No swelling, no redness, no nothing. That's not giving her a bellyache." I dropped the appendix back into the abdomen. "Let's take a look at her tubes and ovaries."

Carlo pulled the intestine out of the way, the nurse readjusted the operating-room light, I looked down into June's pelvis, and there was the explanation for her pain. Both tubes were swollen, red and dripping pus.

"Dammit," I said to Carlo, "she's got P.I.D. [pelvic inflammatory disease]." Carlo looked in. "She sure has. A real case of Broadway appendicitis." (Carlo had interned in New York, where pelvic inflammatory disease, gonorrhea of the uterine tubes, is known as Broadway appendicitis.)

I took a sample of the pus so that it could be examined by the bacteriologist, but there was no doubt it was gonorrhea. Then I took out the appendix* and closed the wound. Carlo

---

* It's common practice to remove a normal appendix under these circumstances. Otherwise it's possible that sometime in the future June would develop pain in the abdomen, and the doctor examining her might assume, from the scar, that the appendix was out and miss the diagnosis of appendicitis. Removing the appendix, once the abdomen has been entered, adds no significant risk to the operation.

and I didn't discuss the problem any more while we finished operating. The fewer people to know that June had gonorrhea, the better.

Back in the doctor's dressing room Carlo and I sat, had a cup of coffee and discussed the case.

"What are you going to tell Sam?" he asked me.

"I don't know. Did June pick it up from someone else, or did Sam bring it home? I'd bet Sam picked it up on one of his trips. What do you think?"

"I'm with you. I don't think June plays around—certainly not with anyone who'd give her the clap. On the other hand, Sam surprises me. Not that I didn't think he might get a little something now and then when he's out of town, but that he'd sleep with someone who might give him a dose. He must have been bombed."

"Probably. Anyway, I'm going to assume it was Sam. He's the best bet. I'll talk to him."

I met Sam out in the visitor's lounge, took him aside, and stumbling a little, told him what I'd found.

"June's appendix was O.K., Sam," I said. "She had something else—infection of the uterine tubes. In all probability it's gonorrhea."

"God," Sam said, "how in the world could that happen?"

"Only one way," I answered. "June didn't pick this up off a toilet seat. She got infected during intercourse. It's best if you level with me, Sam. I'm not going to talk about it to anyone else, but I have to know. Have you had a discharge from your penis lately?"

Sam sat down. "Damn it, Bill," he said, "I hate to admit it but the answer is yes. About two weeks ago. I went to a doctor in Minneapolis and he gave me a shot of penicillin and some penicillin tablets. I got treated as soon as I noticed it and I stayed away from June for a week. I don't see how I could have infected her."

"It must have been just before you noticed the drip. Is that possible?"

"I suppose so," Sam said. "Yeah—I'm sure it's possible. I'd been home for three days before the discharge began. Goddamn it, I feel like a crumb, doing this to June. Do you have to tell her, Bill?"

"No," I said, "at least not specifically. I'm going to tell her the truth—I have to do that—but I won't elaborate. I'll tell her that her appendix was normal, that her pain came from infection in her tubes. I'll tell her I'm going to treat the infection with antibiotics and that she should get better quickly. I don't think she'll ask me if it's gonorrhea. I imagine that's the last thing she'd think of.

"I'm going to have to treat you too, Sam. You've been treated once but you gave it to June and she probably gave it back to you. And we'll have to get blood tests on both you and June to make certain you haven't got syphilis.

"Two other things. I don't like to ask these questions but I have to, and you've got to answer them honestly. First, from whom did you get the infection? Second, could you possibly have passed it on to someone besides June? I'm not suggesting that you're running all over town—but I have to know for certain. If you have had any other contacts it's only fair to notify them so that they can get treated."

"Not another soul, Bill, I swear. As for where I got it, I got loaded one night in Denver, picked up a hustler in a bar and I suppose it was her. I don't even know her name. God, what an idiot I've been."

I believed Sam, though there are very few men who will admit that they've had other contacts.

I went in and spoke to June. As I had anticipated, she asked no difficult questions. She made an uneventful recovery and, fortunately, blood tests on both Sam and June showed no evidence of syphilis. I think Sam learned a lesson. I hope so.

Syphilis is less common than gonorrhea. Still, we do a blood test on every gonorrhea patient looking for it, because it's such a dangerous disease. If it isn't properly treated with heavy doses of penicillin or some other antibiotic it can go on undetected for many years, eating away at the liver, the blood vessels, the brain. And once the spirochetes, the little corkscrew-shaped organisms that cause syphilis, have done their damage, it can't be undone.

The only evidence of primary, or early, syphilis is the chancre, a little, hard, painless wart. It lasts a week or two, then goes away, even without treatment. The disease has by that time gotten into the bloodstream and begun to spread to other organs. Men will usually see the chancre on the glans of the penis, but in a woman the chancre may be on the inside of her genitalia, where it will go unnoticed.

That's why the blood tests are so important.

One major reason why venereal disease is on the increase, even though it's an infection that can be treated very effectively, is the reluctance of patients to admit that they've got the disease. And even if they get scared enough to see a doctor themselves, they'll swear up and down that they haven't had any other "contacts." They're ashamed to admit they've been promiscuous.

The majority of the patients that I, and most other doctors, treat for V.D. are not our regular patients. Whenever I find that my office nurse has brought me a new male patient from out of town, I begin to wonder about V.D. even before I see him. And if, when my nurse asks him, "What can we do for you today?" he answers, "I'd rather discuss it with the doctor," the possibility of V.D. becomes a probability.

Frankly, I can understand why patients go out of town to see a doctor they don't know if they think they have venereal disease. I'd do the same thing. Even though I'm certain that Carlo Germain would keep his mouth shut if I came to him because I had gonorrhea, I still wouldn't go to him. I wouldn't want even him to know what I'd been up to. So we rarely see our own patients when they contract V.D.

The men, that is. With women it's different. Their symptoms aren't so obvious—often just a slight discharge—or, as in June's case, pain in the belly. Besides, most of them have no reason to suspect they might have V.D. It's usually a little gift from hubby, a memento of some trip out of town, on "business," so to speak.

There is a danger in not telling a woman that she has venereal disease; if she has had other "contacts" they aren't going to be warned. Assume, for example, that Sam came back from Denver, infected June and then left on another business trip. While Sam is gone June spends an afternoon in a motel with Leo Williamson, "a good friend." June hasn't any symptoms yet, but she is contagious. So Leo gets infected.

The next day June comes down with abdominal pain. I operate and tell her she has an infection. Leo hears about the operation and figures it was appendicitis—he'd never suspect that June might have gonorrhea—and he, in the meantime, has infected his wife, Helen. And who's to say what Helen might be up to?

So it is dangerous, and not really good medical practice, not to tell a woman she has a venereal disease. Nor is it fair to the woman; she has a right to know what disease she has. But the policy of keeping silent is one that many doctors—I'm among them—sometimes follow. We may possibly be contributing to an epidemic of venereal disease by not giving specific information unless the patient asks us; but if we volunteer the information we'd certainly be working havoc on the marriage. Unless I'm reasonably suspicious that the woman may have other contacts, I take a gamble on the epidemic. I shouldn't, but I do. And I know I'm not alone. I don't think I've made a misjudgment yet, but I'll admit that if I had I'd probably never have heard of it. Some doctor in another town probably treats my V.D. patients, just as I treat—or mistreat—his.

35

House Calls

Doctors undertreat venereal disease, epidemics spread, and no one complains. But let one doctor turn down a house call, and patients are up in arms. House calls are an emotional subject with the public.

Patients love house calls. Most doctors hate them. I'm with the doctors.

When I first moved to Litchfield I used to go on house calls two or three times a week. Now I average about one house call a month. I've learned to avoid them like the plague. Usually they're a waste of time.

One night I got a call from Leroy Sunquist, an elderly farmer who lives five miles out of town. "Doc," he said, "you'd better come out and see Ma. She slipped on the bathroom floor and hurt her hip. I'm afraid she may have broken something."

I was new in town and reluctant to say no to any call for help. I wrote down the directions, got dressed and drove out to Leroy's farm. By the time I arrived Leroy had called in his son, who ran a neighboring farm, and they had lifted Ma onto the bed. With Leroy and his boy standing by, I proceeded to examine her.

This was no easy job. Under her dress, Ma had on an old-fashioned corset with more straps and buckles than a strait jacket. Every time I turned her, trying to get her out of the darn thing, she moaned with pain. It took me ten minutes just to get a glimpse of her hip.

The skin was black-and-blue, which only meant yes, she had hurt her hip. Moving her hip joint caused her pain. All I could say, after struggling through this examination, was, "It's possible that you've broken your hip, Mrs. Sunquist. We'd better get some X-rays." I called the ambulance, and an hour later at the hospital I saw the films. She had a broken hip.

I went on that call about nine years ago. Now when patients call me about possible fractures, I refuse to go to their homes. We'll certainly need an X-ray to satisfy them and me, and it's a waste of time, mine and theirs, to bother with a house call. I can't take an X-ray machine to their home. I send the ambulance for them.

Much as I hate them, however, I still go on some house calls. For example, when I'm on call on a weekend I sometimes take care of minor nonsurgical problems. One night, about 2 A.M., I received a call from a young housewife, Linda Backus. "Dr. Nolen," she said, "I hate to bother you at such an awful hour but Debbie, my three-year-old, just woke up. She's holding her ear and crying. She feels awfully hot."

"What's her temperature?" I asked.

"I don't know," Linda said, "our thermometer is broken." (I have learned, over the years, that in almost every home, ours included, the thermometer is broken.)

"O.K.," I said, it sounds like an earache [I'm a great diagnostician]. I'll be right over."

Much as I hated to, I got dressed, picked up my bag and drove off in the February snow to the Backuses' home. Debbie had a red eardrum, I gave her a shot of penicillin, and she was all better within twenty-four hours.

Unlike a hip fracture, this sort of ailment is the kind that can be easily and adequately treated in the home. Much as I hate to get dressed and go out, I think it's better for me to go to a child's home than to make the parents bundle up a half-awake little kid with a high temperature and drive her to my office or the hospital. Fair is fair.

In between these two clear-cut situations there are many

others where the desirability or practicality of a house call is a matter of judgment and taste.

One night, about ten, I got a call from Helen King, the wife of one of our local insurance men. "Dr. Nolen," Helen said, "would you come over and look at Ralphie? I kept him home from school today with a stomach ache, and I'm wondering if it might be appendicitis."

This is the sort of call that really irritates me. This kid has been sick all day with a stomach ache, and now, at ten o'clock at night, his mother wants me to come over and see him.

"To tell you the truth, Helen," I said, "I think it would be better if you brought Ralphie to the hospital. I'll examine him in the emergency room and then if we need a blood count we can get it. I'll call and tell them you're coming."

I could have gone to the Kings' house. It would have been inconvenient for me, but I might have been able to tell simply by examining Ralphie that he didn't have appendicitis. In that case we wouldn't have needed the blood count. But it was easier for me to see him at the hospital, and since they had waited till ten at night to call me, I was damned if I was going to make things difficult for myself. As it turned out, Ralphie didn't have appendicitis. All he needed was an enema.

Sometimes it's actually dangerous to make a house call. One night Mona Robertson called me at my home. "Dr. Nolen," she said, "would you come over and see Lee? We've just finished dinner and he's complaining of pain in his chest. He's lying on the couch, soaked with sweat."

Lee was about forty-eight at the time, a big, heavy man, a salesman of farm equipment. The Robertsons' home is on the edge of town.

It sounded to me as if Lee might be having a heart attack. "I think it would be better if I sent the ambulance, Mona," I said. "I'll get them over there right away and I'll meet Lee at the hospital."

Since I don't take care of patients with heart problems unless no one else is around, I called Carlo Germain and asked him to meet the Robertsons at the hospital. I went over there, too, just so they would know I wasn't neglecting them.

Less than five minutes after Lee arrived he had a cardiac arrest—his heart stopped—but by that time Carlo had him in the coronary care unit. He grabbed the electrodes, shocked him and got his heart re-started. Lee survived his heart attack, took off thirty pounds, and is back working regularly. If I had wasted fifteen minutes on a house call, Lee would have had his cardiac arrest before he got to the hospital. He wouldn't have made it.

Among the calls I dread most are those that come from the sheriff's office. "Doc," the desk man will shout into the phone, "hurry. There's been a bad accident about ten miles out of town at the junction of old Highway 15 and the gravel road that runs out past Diamond Lake. They want you out there right away."

Much as I hate to go, I don't have the courage to refuse. I jot down the directions, jump in the car and go.

Invariably, about eight miles out of town, I meet the ambulance, siren screaming, racing back from the accident. I turn around and drive back to the hospital, but by the time I arrive some other doctor is taking care of the patients. It never fails.

The reason for these mixups is a simple one: Whenever there's an accident everyone panics—the sheriff, the civil defense man and all those who are anywhere near the accident when it occurs; they call every doctor, ambulance and hospital in the area. We wind up with everyone running every which way, just like a Keystone Kops comedy—though the results of the accidents are anything but funny.

I don't dare refuse these calls to the scene of an accident. Nor do I dare say no when the nursing supervisor calls and says, "Dr. Nolen, the ambulance just called and they're on their way in with three badly injured patients. They want you here when they arrive." I know only too well that most of the time these patients won't have serious injuries, that the ambulance driver or the police officer is overestimating the damage, but I curse and go anyway. If one time in ten the injury is serious, I'd better be there. A few minor lacerations can make a bloody mess and scare the layman, but it's not his fault that he suspects the worst. So I may waste a few minutes sitting around waiting to sew up a superficial cut. I can spare that much time.

Not everyone has my philosophy on house calls. Old-timers, such as Paul Hauser who have been in practice for years, hardly ever refuse to make a house call. When he first started practice, patients rarely went to the hospital. He's used to caring for them in their homes. He does a good job and he doesn't mind doing it. And his patients, mostly elderly people now, are used to his visits and expect them. They like him so much that if they come to the clinic to see him and find he's going to be gone for a month, they go home and wait for him to come back. Unless it's a dire emergency they won't see anyone else.

Carlo Germain, on the other hand, will almost never go on a house call. He feels it's a waste of his time and energy, and that the patient has more of both to waste than he does. Sometimes patients get angry with him, but there's nothing they can do. He's a good doctor in every other way, so they learn to live with the fact that he won't make house calls.

I think the middle course, which I try to follow, is the reasonable one. I've found, and it certainly isn't an original discovery, that one of the big reasons why people resent doctors is their refusal to make house calls. If all of us would give just a little and make an occasional house call when it seems reasonable to do so, we could eliminate some of the public's griping about doctors.

We certainly need some relief.

36

You Can't Afford to Be Sick

Doctors need relief from griping patients; patients need relief from one of the major causes of their gripes—gigantic medical bills. When I see the bills my patients are expected to pay after going through an illness, I can't understand how they can do it. Medical care is unbelievably expensive.

In 1971 we spent seventy-five billion dollars on health care in the United States. That's a lot of money, but it doesn't mean anything to the average doctor or patient. Billions are beyond our comprehension. It's the specific case, the sickness that costs us hundreds or thousands, that really frightens us. Those are the expenses we understand.

Take, for example, the case of Charlie Granger, an eighty-six-year-old farmer who used to live ten miles south of Litchfield. Charlie had had a stomach ulcer for years but never wanted any surgery done. Every time his ulcer flared up he'd take medicine, go on a diet and in a few weeks he'd be better.

In 1964, however, on an October afternoon when Charlie came in to see me, I could tell he was in serious trouble. His skin was pale, his pulse rapid, and when I checked his blood level in my office I found it was very low. "Charlie," I said, "I'm going to have to send you to the hospital. I think you're bleeding from that ulcer of yours."

"O.K., Doc," he said, "I'll go. I have to admit I don't feel too good."

Now, at the risk of sounding mercenary I'm going to list Charlie's expenses as we go along, so I'll mention that at this initial visit I charged $5 for an office call and $2 for the blood test. Charlie left my office owing me $7.

And again, because this chapter is concerned with money, I'm going to review briefly Charlie's course in the hospital, emphasizing expenses.

As soon as he got to the hospital I went over and put a rubber tube through his nose into his stomach ($2) so that we could suck out the old blood ($2 a day for suction) and could tell if he stopped bleeding. Then we started transfusing him ($16.25 for the first pint and $13.50 for each subsequent unit). We did a lot of other things too: put a catheter into his bladder ($7), ordered special blood studies of his electrolytes ($10 each time), gave him medicines designed to help his blood clot. Then we waited.

He stopped bleeding. When his blood was back to a decent level we took him down to the X-ray department and got some films of his stomach ($45). We wanted an exact diagnosis in case he should bleed again.

And he did, just three days later while he was still recuperating from his first episode. He bled heavily.

As a general rule, any patient who rebleeds while under treatment for an ulcer should be operated upon promptly. Usually they'll die without surgery. I didn't follow the rule this time—after all, Charlie was eighty-six—and fortunately he quit bleeding again quite promptly. I patted myself on the back for showing such excellent judgment. Prematurely.

Two days later, his tenth day in the hospital, this elderly man cut loose again, and this time I did what I should have done earlier. I took him to the operating room and got rid of his ulcer.

As you might imagine, he was shaky for several post-operative days. We gave him blood, antibiotics and close supervision. It paid off. Six weeks after he entered the hospital he went home, as healthy as an eighty-six-year-old man can be.

Here's what this intensive surgical care, everything he needed but no frills, cost him:

Hospital Costs

37 hospital days at $45 a day	$1,665.00
Special nurses around the clock for ten days	960.00
Transfusions—ten pints	137.75
Medication, laboratory studies, tubes, intravenous medication, gastric suction, catheters, electrocardiograms, oxygen, etc.	1,229.20
	$3,991.95

I charged $500 for the care I'd given Charlie in the hospital, and Tom Brogan, whom I'd asked to check on Charlie's heart all through the case, charged $100. So Charlie's total charges came to $4,590.95. In 1964; they'd be almost twice that in 1972.

That's an awfully big bill for anyone. Charlie was alive, well and grateful to be. He didn't complain about the bill, he knew it was justified, but he simply didn't have the money to pay it; this was before Medicare. Charlie had been just getting by on his farm, barely earning enough to keep his wife and himself comfortably. He didn't have an extra $5,000. Few people do.

Tom Brogan and I both told Charlie to forget about our bills, but the hospital couldn't, legally, cancel its charges. Charlie swallowed his pride and went to the welfare people to see if they could help him. They turned him down. As long as he owned a farm and a car he wasn't eligible for any aid. Once he was completely broke and destitute they could step in, but until then he was on his own.

Much as he hated to do it, Charlie mortgaged his farm to get the money and pay his bill. For the rest of his life—he died four years later of heart disease—he continued to pay for that one trip to the hospital. After his operation the poor guy never again had a dollar to spend on little extras for himself or his wife.

Surgical problems tend to be expensive—there are always charges for the use of the operating room, the anesthesia, intravenous fluids—but medical ailments can run into big money too.

Consider what it cost Burt Raske when he had his heart attack. He was in the hospital thirty-eight days and these are the charges that accumulated in that time.

Hospital Costs

Coronary care unit, 5 days at $90 a day	$ 450
33 days at $45 a day	1,485
Medication, X-rays, electrocardiograms, laboratory studies, intravenous fluids, oxygen	1,985
	$3,920

Doctor's charges

$25 a day for 5 days	$ 125
10 a day for 5 days	50
5 a day for 28 days	140
	$ 315
TOTAL	$4,235

Like Charlie, Burt was lucky to have survived at all. Without the coronary care unit and the new medicines and machines that have been produced in the last ten years, Burt probably would have died of his heart attack. He knows he's a fortunate man.

But at the age of forty, with four kids to educate, Burt had a huge bill to pay. He had no insurance—rheumatic fever as a child had given him a heart murmur that ruled him out of any program—and his job as an appliance salesman didn't pay very well. What Burt's illness meant was that his daughter, who had been accepted at a private college she wanted very much to attend, had to cancel her application and go instead to a school near Litchfield so she could live at home. His boy, when he graduates from high school, will have to do the same thing. Burt will spend years recovering from the financial drain of his heart attack. If he has another, and he well may, he'll never be solvent again.

All illnesses which require hospitalization are expensive; $100 a day is about average, and in some cities you have to pay even more.

The reasons for the rising cost of hospital care are complex, but one reason is very obvious—it takes more people to run a hospital now than it did a few years ago.

When we put in our coronary care unit in 1968 we had to hire four extra nurses to keep it staffed. That meant more money for hospital salaries. And these girls had special training and deserved decent pay for what they did. Our hospital room rates had to be increased to pay for this new service.

For years hospital workers were notoriously underpaid. When I was at Bellevue Hospital in 1953 there was hardly a job in New York that paid less than that of orderly in a city hospital. Hospital workers still aren't paid princely sums, but since unionization their salaries have improved and deservedly so. Increased salaries, plus the fact that because of new advances in medicine, hospitals now require almost twice as many employees per patient than they did ten years ago, account for a lot of the mounting cost of health care.

Even if you don't have to go to the hospital medical care can be expensive. We charge $5 for an office call in Litchfield. On a national basis we're low, near the bottom. Doctors elsewhere may charge anywhere from $7 to $15 per call.

When it comes to office care, however, the philosophy of the doctor and/or his greed can make a big difference in how much the patient spends.

Most of Carlo Germain's patients get by for $5 a visit; the patients who see Warren Johnson, another G.P., almost never spend less than $7, and probably average closer to $10. Warren likes money and in office practice the doctor who is out to make a bundle can really go to town.

Patients have to accept the doctor's word when he tells them they must have their blood checked and their urine examined or that they need an X-ray of their chest or an electrocardiogram. These tests don't hurt the patient. It's easy for the doctor to justify them to himself by rationalizing that he's "just being thorough." And every one of these tests is a big moneymaker for the doctor. The markup is often as much as 200 percent. The doctor who orders a lot of unnecessary examinations can really clean up on office calls.

He can also make a killing by dispensing unnecessary but harmless medication. Liver shots, vitamin shots and iron shots for "low blood" are favorites. They all pay very well.

The real beauty of the "shot" routine is that the patient can be kept coming back to the office indefinitely, once or twice a week. The doctor doesn't even need to see the patient; his nurse can give the injection. Once a month the doctor checks the blood level and chats for a few minutes with his victim. Then back the patient goes to his once-a-week routine.

I'd say that unnecessary shots must rank very high as a medical money-waster. Compared with the cost of hospitalization for a heart attack it's peanuts; but $5 or $10 a week for hundreds of patients, year in and year out, adds up fast. By ordering unnecessary tests and shots some doctors add an "extra" ten or fifteen thousand dollars to their income every year. Unfair? Of course. But it happens.

If anyone can devise a system that will guarantee quality medical care for everyone without bankrupting either the individual or our country, I'm for it. Because as things now stand, with taxes the way they are and six children to support, I could hardly afford to have an ingrown toenail removed if I couldn't do it myself or rely on the professional courtesy of another doctor. If I weren't a doctor, I'd have to work myself sick just to keep well.

Which is asinine, of course.

But then, so is the cost of medical care.

37

Medical Costs— How to Reduce Them

What are we going to do about it? How can we cut back on medical costs? I won't pretend I have an answer; I don't. I realize it's a very complex problem to which a great many men are currently devoting much time and energy. But from my vantage point as a practicing surgeon I can see a few possible solutions and problems that those who are more removed from the front lines of medical-care delivery might not see or see differently.

First, we've got to get rid of the waste. We doctors can do more work in our offices and out-patient departments, and even—I hate to admit this—in the home than we do now. There's really no sound medical reason for admitting patients to the hospital for X-rays of the stomach, removal of skin cysts, treatment of colds. If I can cut back one hundred hospital days a year, and I'm sure I can, I'll reduce medical costs by about ten thousand dollars. If every doctor in the country did it, we'd save about two hundred million dollars. That buys a lot of groceries.

This isn't a one-sided affair. We doctors have to have the cooperation of our patients. When they ask us to admit them, their child or their elderly parent to the hospital for care when there is no real need for hospitalization, they put us on the spot. Patients have to realize that just because their insurance will pay for hospitalization, it isn't free; that their premiums go up every time they're hospitalized unnecessarily. They have to take the long view of the money problem.

Insurance companies have to cooperate by writing sensible policies. As it is now, many of them won't pay for anything but hospital care. What's done in the doctor's office, the patient's home or even the hospital out-patient department is paid for out of the patient's pocket. Under these conditions it's easy to understand why the patient who is paying big premiums says, "Admit me to the hospital so my insurance will pay for the X-rays." Policies have to be written to cover out-of-the-hospital care.

Too expensive, the underwriters answer. Frankly, I doubt it. I think that the money they now pay out for unnecessary hospitalization would more than pay for home and office treatment. Financially they'd be ahead.

The building of hospitals has to be planned on at least a regional basis. All over this country there are hospitals running at far less than full capacity. But if you've got a 300-bed hospital, you have to keep on the payroll a staff large enough to take care of three hundred patients, even if you have only two hundred patients in the hospital. So hospital care for those two hundred patients becomes much more expensive than it ought to be; the two hundred sick people are paying for the care of a hundred nonexistent patients.

Doctors and hospital administrators are very jealous of their prerogatives. They resent it when some authority says, "Look, you're only delivering two hundred babies a year in the Plainsville Hospital obstetrical department; close down your obstetrical department and have your obstetricians do their deliveries at Mercy Hospital. You'll save a lot of money for your other patients." It's a logical step, but try to find the doctor or administrator who will take it—unless a gun is pointed at his back. They want their hospital to be a complete unit (cobalt radiation, heart-lung machine, the whole works); let someone else economize.

Let me add that patients are no different; the pregnant

woman from Plainsville wants to be delivered at the Plainsville Hospital. She doesn't want to go three miles to Mercy.

So much for hospital costs; what can we do about doctors'
fees? They constitute only about 19 percent of the total cost
of medical care—still, that was fourteen billion dollars in 1971.

Some things have been done. In 1972 we doctors are caught
in the price freeze just like everyone else. We can't go up more
than 2.5 percent a year on our charges. So it's difficult to gouge
our patients even if we wanted to.

Many of the visits patients pay to doctors are unnecessary.
Patients give millions of dollars every year to their doctors for
treatment of colds, flu, backaches, minor bruises and sprains.
They go to the doctor because they don't feel safe treating
themselves.

Education could solve all this. There isn't any reason why a
course in the recognition and self-treatment of minor illnesses
couldn't be offered in high school and adult education classes.
No one needs eight years of medical education to safely
manage minor medical problems. If doctors would cooperate
by teaching the general public, over the years men and
women could save themselves thousands of dollars they're
now wasting.

In Litchfield, during a flu epidemic, we made one brief
foray into this field. Our offices were swamped with patients
who had the fever and muscle aches typical of the epidemic.
Each paid us five dollars for an office call, during which we
told them to rest, take aspirin and wait—that their symptoms
would disappear in three or four days. We realized these patients were wasting their money and our time, so we put no-
tices in the local newspaper and over the radio telling them
how to recognize and treat the flu. We substantially reduced the flow of patients and saved them a lot of money.

As I said earlier, we've also been forced to employ what's
called peer review in our hospitals. Every month hospital
charts are reviewed by a committee to try and make certain
that doctors aren't keeping patients in the hospital unnecessarily, aren't performing needless operations, aren't ordering
unnecessary tests. It isn't a perfect system—we're reluctant to

blow the whistle on our confreres—but with improvements it could work reasonably well. When I know that other doctors and laymen are going to be checking up on what I do, I'll have to keep my standards high. To keep my hospital privileges, if for no other reason.

We doctors fought these review policies—organized medicine usually fights this sort of thing—but we've lost, and it's probably just as well. I hate committees, am probably the worst committee member in the world, but I have to concede that peer review is a good idea. It has already started to reduce the length of hospital stays, and it will undoubtedly keep quality of care from slipping.

Medical-assistant programs can do a great deal to reduce expenses. Doctors waste a lot of time doing jobs that someone with a lot less training could do at least as well.

George Engel, for example, always gives his patients their shots—penicillin, liver extract or whatever it is they need. A nurse or a nurses' aide could give the shot just as well as George and give him a few extra minutes to spend on a more demanding job. But he'd never think of delegating this work.

Carlo Germain always cuts the plaster casts off his patients. This means, if the patient had a broken leg, at least twenty minutes spent working with a vibrating saw and scissors, doing a job that a high school kid could do after an hour of instruction and practice. While he's whittling away, patients pile up in the waiting room.

I waste time removing stitches. I go in to see Mrs. Stevens seven days after I've removed her gall bladder. I look at her incision and decide it's time to remove the stitches. Then I have to walk back to the treatment room, get the scissors and a clamp, come back and cut eight or ten pieces of silk. I waste five or ten minutes doing a job that anyone—and I mean anyone—could do as well.

If I feel that way about the matter, then why don't I just write "Remove stitches" on Mrs. Stevens' chart and leave the job for a nurse to do in her spare time? I can't. The nurse won't do it.

The nurses have their jobs, the nurses' aides have their jobs, the technicians have their jobs, and we doctors have our jobs. It's nearly impossible to get people to do jobs that aren't "theirs." Nurses don't take out stitches, nurses' aides don't give shots, and that's that. No one wants to take on any "extra" work—unless, I suppose, they get more pay.

This, admittedly, is one of the problems. Suppose a patient has a cut sutured in another town and a week later stops by my office to have the stitches removed. I charge him five dollars, the price of an office call, for removing the stitches. If the nurse in the hospital removes the stitches at my request, she doesn't get anything extra for doing it, so she'd just as soon not have the job.

So money is one factor that must be seriously considered when we talk about using people with less training to do some of the simple jobs doctors now do. If the doctor doesn't do the job, is he going to be paid for supervising? How much? And how much are we going to pay the doctor's helper? We should be able to reduce costs by using doctors' assistants, but we've got to be careful or we'll wind up paying twice for the same service.

Even if we solve the problem of who gets paid and for what, we've got other hurdles to clear before we can use the doctor's assistant to extend medical care and reduce medical expenses. One of these hurdles is the proprietary attitude of doctors.

Doctors are zealous defenders of their special provinces. The gynecologist gets furious if the general surgeon takes out a uterus, the internist doesn't like it very well when a G.P. reads his own electrocardiograms, the orthopedist raises hell if a doctor who isn't an orthopedist sets a simple fracture; the chest surgeons keep such a tight rein on their domain that the diaphragm, which separates the chest from the abdomen, is known in surgical circles as "the iron curtain." The professed reason for the rigid restrictions on "who can do what and to whom" is protection of the patient. Only the expert, the super-duper specialist, can do these special jobs properly. Which is only partly true. An "occasional surgeon" shouldn't be doing complicated operations on the spine, but no one needs five years of orthopedic training to set a wrist properly.

One strong reason for the restriction is economic. If there are a lot of orthopedists around, it just won't do to have the G.P.'s setting fractures; the orthopedists can't spare the cases. So the hospital rules committees divide up the patient and award one segment to one specialist, a different segment to another. And woe to the specialist who infringes on another man's territory; his referrals from the other members of the specialty clubs will dwindle down to nothing.

The surgeon's grip on the operating room is virtually a strangle hold. The College of Surgeons makes appropriate hospital rules to discourage M.D.'s who haven't had five years of formal surgical training from doing operations of any sort. They want all the surgery for the fully trained surgeons.

But here in Litchfield I've seen excellent surgery done by G.P.'s with no formal surgical training at all. Sure, I've seen them get in over their heads, but not the G.P.'s with common sense. A jackass with five years of surgical training can get in over his head too. It's no prerogative of the G.P.

If he has the interest, any G.P. who can tie his shoes can learn to do vein strippings, hernias, hemorrhoidectomies and appendectomies if some surgeon will teach him. I know, because I've taught G.P.'s to do these things, and they do them well. It's utter nonsense to say, as the College of Surgeons does, that there's no such thing as minor surgery.

But if surgeons won't let their fellow M.D.'s get into their act, do you think they'll ever allow a layman to sew up a wound? Not on your life. Even though any woman who can knit a sweater could sew up most lacerations and do a beautiful job.

Doctors aren't going to turn over the routine physicals, the application and removal of casts, the suturing jobs or even stitch removal to "helpers" if it means the money they get for these things is going to be turned over to them too. Not without one hell of a fight.

There's another point to be considered.

If we doctors should be persuaded, or forced, to turn some

of our jobs over to lesser trained personnel, how are the patients going to react?

George Engel's patients love him because he, and not his nurse, gives the shots. My patients don't like it when I have my nurse take their blood pressure instead of doing it myself. Patients are going to have to develop confidence in doctors' assistants so that they'll be willing to accept the help from them that they now get from the doctor. At the moment I don't know anyone who thinks he is seriously ill who would happily accept diagnosis and treatment from anyone but a fully accredited M.D. Patients are reluctant to let interns, fresh from four years of medical school, treat them. Much less will they accept a "medical assistant."

The fact remains, there are many steps that can be taken to reduce medical costs. Whether they will be taken is another matter; everyone—the government, doctors, insurance companies, hospital administrators, nurses, aides and, most important, patients—has to cooperate if we're going to get the job done.

If we don't voluntarily make an effort to reduce medical costs, another approach may be employed; the government may perform radical surgery on the system of health-care delivery in the United States and totally amputate the profit motive.

This doesn't mean simply eliminating the fee-for-service system, though this would undoubtedly be part of the package; to be effective the modifications would have to include restrictions on profit-making by the drug manufacturers, effective controls on hospital utilization and a complete revision of our system for providing health insurance. It would, of necessity, involve government financing, government supervision, government control. In essence, it would be a shift from medicine as practiced in our free enterprise system to—a nasty term—socialized medicine; though, to avoid the outrage that label evokes from organized medicine, the plan would be called by some euphemism such as National Health Service.

Such a radical change wouldn't be as lovely and as satisfactory as the public might hope it would be; there are, as I've tried to point out, some real advantages to the patient in the fee-for-service system.

But we're going to have unscrupulous people looking for unreasonable profits while selling health care as long as a doctor can earn money by administering unnecessary treatment; as long as drug companies thrive on the sale of drugs, necessary or not; as long as private insurance companies profit from hospitalization. These problems are not only built into our medical system, they're part of our entire economic system.

Whenever the fee-for-service system coexists with a national health program, as it does in England, many of those who can afford to do so get their medical care from doctors working under the former system. Those who can't afford to pay by the fee utilize the national health program. The same, I suspect, will apply to any program instituted in the United States. From the patient's point of view, if he has a lot of money, there's no system that will assure him better medical care than the fee-for-service system; the difficulty is that many patients can't afford it.

A radical switch from private to public medicine will require something tantamount to a medical revolution. It may occur, but certainly not tomorrow, probably not for years, perhaps never.

Meanwhile there is much that can be done to reduce medical costs within the framework of our present system. As a practicing physician, I can see that it's possible, and after looking over my patients' bills I'm convinced it's necessary. The only question is, Will we do it?

A Final Note

I like being a surgeon. I enjoy the challenge of my work, the gratitude of my patients, the satisfaction I get from doing my job well. I wouldn't trade my profession for any other.

I think most doctors feel as I do; otherwise they'd be doing something else. Because, though the practice of medicine is rewarding, it isn't easy. When the phone rings at two in the morning and you climb out of bed, dress and drive to the hospital to deliver a baby, treat a coronary or remove an appendix, you're tested. You ask yourself, Isn't there some easier way to make a living? and the answer is, of course, yes. But you don't switch, you don't desert, you don't give up your profession for something else, because you can't. Once you've practiced as a physician, you're hooked; no other way of life is as fulfilling.

But though doctors are, generally speaking, dedicated men, they are not saints, and no one—doctor or layman—should regard them as such. They can't live up to the image. No one could. Doctors have all the faults and frailties that membership in the human race implies. The sooner all of us realize this, the sooner we can get on with the job of improving ourselves and our profession.

We're doing our job pretty well now; we can certainly do it better.

About the Author

WILLIAM A. NOLEN, M.D., was born in Holyoke, Massachusetts, and graduated from the College of the Holy Cross and Tufts Medical School. His five-year surgical internship at Bellevue was the basis for his first book, *The Making of a Surgeon.* After completing his surgical training, he settled in Litchfield, Minnesota, where he is currently in practice at the Litchfield Clinic. Dr. Nolen is a Fellow of the American College of Surgeons and is Chief of Surgery at the Meeker County Hospital. He was formerly an attending surgeon at the Hennepin General Hospital in Minneapolis, a teaching hospital associated with the University of Minnesota. He is on the board of editors of the Minnesota state medical journal. His articles have appeared in both medical journals and leading American magazines; his column, "A Doctor's World," appears monthly in *McCall's* magazine. Dr. Nolen and his wife, Joan, have three sons and three daughters, ranging in age from nine to seventeen.